Conceptual Frameworks in Geogr

General Editor: W.E. Marsden

Human Impact on the Ecosystem

Joy Tivy, B.A., B.Sc., Ph.D., F.R.S.G.S.

Professor, Department of Geography, University of Glasgow

Greg O'Hare, B.Sc., Ph.D.

Senior Lecturer in Geography, Derby Lonsdale College of Higher Education

Maps and diagrams drawn by Ann Rooke and Andy Skinner, cartographers at Derby Lonsdale College of Higher Education

Oliver & Boyd

Edinburgh and New York

To Edith, Alice and Harry

Acknowledgements

The authors and publishers wish to thank all those who gave their permission for us to reproduce copyright material in this book. Information regarding sources is given in the captions.

Oliver & Boyd
Longman House
Burnt Mill
Harlow
Essex CM20 2JE
England

A Division of Longman Group UK Limited

Library of Congress Cataloguing in publication number: 81-11199

British Library Cataloguing in publication data

Tivy, Joy
  Human impact on the ecosystem.–(Conceptual
  frameworks in geography)
  1. Man —Influence on nature
  I. Title   II. O'Hare, Greg   III. Series
  574.5'223   GF75

ISBN 0 05 003203 8

Distributed in the United States by Longman Inc., New York
First published 1981
Eleventh impression 1993

Produced by Longman Singapore Publishers Pte Ltd

Printed in Singapore

The publisher's policy is to use paper manufactured from
sustainable forests.

Contents

Editor's Note

An encouraging feature in geographical education in recent years has been the convergence taking place of curriculum thinking and thinking at the academic frontiers of the subject. In both, stress has been laid on the necessity for conceptual approaches and the use of information as a means to an end rather than as an end in itself.

The central purpose of this series is to bear witness to this convergence. In each text the *key ideas* are identified, chapter by chapter. These ideas are in the form of propositions which, with their component concepts and the interrelations between them, make up the conceptual frameworks of the subject. The key ideas provide criteria for selecting content for the tutor or teacher, and in cognitive terms help the student to retain what is important in each unit. Most of the key ideas are linked with assignments, designed to elicit evidence of achievement of basic understanding and ability to apply this understanding in new circumstances through engaging in problem-solving exercises. Evaluation of such abilities is vital at all stages of education.

This text is intended for use in geography, environmental science and applied biology courses in colleges of education, polytechnics and universities, and also in equivalent 'A' level courses. This particular subject area is relatively new to geography courses at this level. Its increasing importance is indicated by the recent appearance of environmental science syllabuses. In both of these the study of the human impact on the ecosystem is a vital concern. This text therefore covers both the academic requirements at 'A' level standard and above, and the increasing demand for environmental education at both secondary and tertiary levels.

As this text overlaps the fields of geography and biology, and also secondary and tertiary levels of education, it is clear that certain sections will present more technical difficulties for some students than others. A glossary is included clarifying terms not defined in the text. In addition, conversion tables have been provided for standardisation purposes. A larger selection of assignments and readings has been provided than could be used by any particular individual or group. It is hoped that many of the assignments and additional activities will be used by students for self-assessment. Where this is not appropriate, the teacher or tutor is clearly the best person to choose those which most nearly fit the students' needs.

W.E. Marsden
University of Liverpool

June 1980

Preface

"Let no man say that I have said nothing new; the arrangement of the material is new: just as the same words differently arranged form different thoughts." *Pascal*

This book was prompted by the rapid development that has taken place in academic biogeography during the past decade. It has two closely related objectives. The first is to illustrate the importance of the ecosystem as the core concept in biogeography. The second is to demonstrate the potential integrative role of biogeography within geography. The means to these ends is the theme of human impact on the ecosystem which is central to our thesis; it is hoped that it will be of interest to, and will stimulate thinking among, both geographers and biologists — indeed all those intrepid students who work in the hazardous but exciting border area between the natural and social sciences.

The material presented has been gleaned from a very wide variety of sources. Many of the ideas, however, are a product of what proved to be the mutually stimulating and rewarding task of co-operative authorship. In the process of writing we had occasion to question many of our own and each other's firmly entrenched assumptions. As a result, we achieved new insight into classic concepts while learning much from recent developments in biology and ecology. The end product is an original interpretation of both traditional and modern ideas and approaches to the subject. As such, it is inevitably controversial and we hope that in reaching our conclusions we have not been guilty of any inadvertent misinterpretation, or misrepresentation of the work of others in this field. We would like to thank all those who helped us pursue what may be regarded as a pedagogically unorthodox path.

Joy Tivy
Greg O'Hare

June 1980

1 Introduction: The Systems Approach

A. Human and Physical Geography

Geography, in common with many other disciplines, covers a very wide and extremely complex field of study. Its basic aim is to understand the spatial distribution of phenomena on the earth's surface. However, in order to cope with this mind-boggling task, the geographer (like other scientists) has had to subdivide the subject into more manageable sub-fields according either to types of phenomena or types of processes. The division into *physical* and *human* geography is a long-standing one, and within each of these an ever increasing number of sub-fields has been identified for the purpose of even more detailed studies.

However, just as essential to the geographer's aim is a clearer understanding of the ways in which phenomena and processes interact within and between the major fields of physical and human geography. The relationships between these two main branches of the subject have varied considerably over time. The traditional study of how physical factors affected or influenced human actions has, however, long since been rejected as too simplistic and deterministic. As a result, there followed a change of emphasis from human 'response to' to human 'control of' the physical environment with, particularly in the teaching of systematic geography, an almost complete separation of physical and human geography. Latterly, concern about resource misuse and depletion, about the consequences of environmental pollution, and about the necessity for resource and environmental conservation has helped to revitalise studies in the border area between physical and human geography. Related to this trend has been the recent rapid growth of the *environmental sciences*. The systems approach has been of particular relevance and has played an important part in these developments.

B. The Systems Concept

The word system is commonly used for a large number of familiar everyday phenomena, some of which are natural, some man-made. River and reproductive systems are examples of the former; transport and postal systems of the latter. In each case, the word *system* implies an *organisation* of 'things' that are *linked* together. Very simply a system can be defined as a collection of components, parts or events which are linked together in such a way as to form a working unit or unified whole. As a result any change in one part of the system will react on, and be reflected in changes in, all the other parts.

1. Man-made systems

The concept of the system as used in geography and other environmental sciences today is that derived from engineering systems, with the classic example or model being the thermostatically controlled central heating system (see Figure 1.1a/b). Nearly all such types of mechanical system are open. This means that in order to function, they must take in matter and materials (*inputs*), process and change them in the system, and give off waste by-products (*outputs*). The most important input is *energy* in a concentrated form (coal, oil, electricity); the most important output is energy in a dispersed form (heat).

Such systems are also capable, up to a point, of regulating themselves by what are called *feedback mechanisms*. These occur when an output from the system modifies the surrounding environment in such a way as to influence future inputs to the system. For instance, in the case of central heating systems, if the outside temperature increases or decreases and the system gives off more or less heat than is required to maintain the room or building at a constant temperature, the change in heat output will trigger off a mechanism which automatically cuts down or increases the input of energy to the system. This is an example of a *negative feedback* mechanism. It enables the system to maintain itself in what is called a state of *dynamic equilibrium* (i.e. near the *set point* or *ideal state*), in spite of variations in the surrounding environment and hence of inputs to the system. If the central heating system were not thermostatically controlled and the supply of energy did not change, the temperature of the room would vary with outside conditions. If the supply of energy remained constant and there were no ventilation, the room would become progressively warmer. This is an example of a *positive feedback* or '*run away*' mechanism. Indeed, the same sort of feedback mechanism can operate in an overcrowded, badly ventilated classroom. In this case, the heat from people's bodies plus the CO_2 level builds up, consequently mental activity and concentration decreases; students begin to yawn and feel drowsy.

2. Natural systems

Natural systems function in ways that are analogous to those of man-made systems. An individual organism, be it a plant, animal or human being, can be thought of as a system. For instance, a warm blooded animal, such as a rabbit or a human being, can be compared to a self-regulating, homeostati-

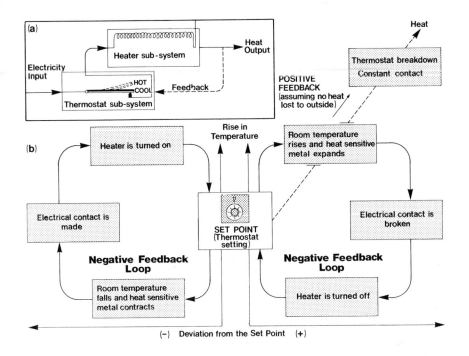

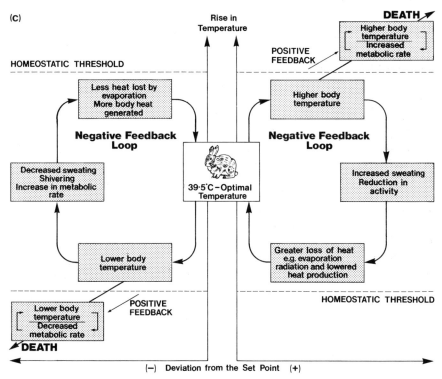

Figure 1.1   Thermostat-heater system (a). Regulatory (homeostatic) controls showing negative and positive feedbacks in (b) a thermostat-heater system and (c) a rabbit

cally controlled system. It is capable, within limits, of maintaining its body at a constant temperature, even though that of the surrounding environment may vary considerably. Figure 1.1c shows that when the atmospheric temperature increases the body loses heat by increased sweating; when it falls, heat is generated by shivering, and conserved by the contraction of blood vessels and decreased sweating. This ability of a system to regulate itself has been called homeostasis. All self-regulating systems have homeostatic limits within which they can operate. These limits determine the degree to which the condition of the system can vary from the equilibrium (ideal or set point) without an irreversible change or complete disruption of the system occurring. Negative feedback mechanisms tend to check, slow down and eventually halt any tendency of the system to fluctuate too widely from the ideal state.

However, as often happens, an input from the environment into the system may vary in such a way as to exceed or fall below its homeostatic limits; that is to say, the fluctuation with which the system has to cope may be too great. There will, as a result, be a continually increasing departure from the system's ideal state or set point and its equilibrium will be permanently disrupted. As can be seen in Figure 1.1c, if a rabbit is exposed to temperatures above its homeostatic limits of tolerance, internal temperatures will continue increasing until it eventually dies of heatstroke; conversely, if outside temperatures drop below these limits, the rabbit will die of hypothermia.

C. Classification of Systems

While all systems share common basic features, they vary according to the nature of their components and according to the processes which link these components together. Apart from mechanical systems, we can recognise three principal types of natural systems on the basis of their main components: physical (inorganic), biological (organic) and social (human) systems. Each of these can be further subdivided into smaller and smaller systems. However, no system, as far as we know, can exist as a completely independent unit. All systems are open; that is to say, the outputs from one can become the inputs to another. For example, gaseous materials given off by a factory can become part of the circulatory system of the atmosphere and can also be incorporated in the bodies of living organisms.

As a general rule, it is true to say that any system is always made up of smaller sub-systems and is itself part of a larger super-system. The world (or 'earth system' as it has been termed), which is part of the solar super-system, is composed of the three main natural, interacting systems, each of which can be broken down into groups of smaller (simpler) systems.

D. The Systems Approach in Geography

It should now be obvious that the systems concept is particularly relevant to all types of geographical study. It provides the geographer with a means of organising and analysing — i.e. of thinking about — the extremely complex set of interrelationships and interactions that exist between the components of the earth's surface and, more particularly perhaps, between humans and their environment. The main advantages of the systems approach in geography are: (a) that it provides a conceptual framework or model by which the component parts of the earth's surface, and the links between them, can more easily be studied; (b) that the mutual interaction of components throughout a particular system can be more easily illustrated and analysed; (c) that humans can be studied as integral components of any system, be it physical or human; (d) that interactions can be studied at any scale.

E. The Aims of This Book

One of the long-established sub-fields of physical geography is that of biogeography which focusses on biological systems, their distribution and their interaction with other systems. The principal unit of study — the most important type of system from the biogeographer's viewpoint — is the *ecological system* or *ecosystem*. This can be simply defined as a group of interacting organisms and their physical environment (or habitat). The majority of recent biogeographical textbooks are concerned, primarily, with analysing the form, function and the distribution of former or existing natural or semi-natural ecosystems at varying scales. The emphasis is also on those which can be distinguished either by the nature of their vegetation component (wood, grassland, etc.) or the characteristics of their physical habitat (limestone, arctic/alpine, etc.). The importance of humans as components of all ecosystems has also received increasing attention and emphasis.

The main aim of this book is to analyse the role of humans as ecological factors more closely and from a somewhat different viewpoint to that in previous biogeographical texts. The theme is that of humans as ecologically disturbing and disrupting beings. The objective throughout is to illustrate the effect of *human impact* on the main ecosystem components and functions. To this end the chapters follow a logical sequence. Chapters 2 and 3 are analytical, in that Chapter 2 deals with the characteristics common to all ecosystems, and Chapter 3 deals with the ecologically significant ways in which humans differ from other animals. Chapters 4, 5 and 6 consider human impact on the main components (organic and inorganic) of the ecosystem and on the two principal links (biological cycling and energy flow) within it. Chapter 7 assesses ecosystem stability, fragility and resilience in relation to different types and magnitudes of human impact. Chapters 8 and 9 analyse the nature of the ecosystem resource values and the problem of their conservation in the face of increasing exploitation and disturbance. The final chapter considers ecosystem measurement and monitoring, prerequisites to both an understanding of human impact and to sound ecosystem management and conservation. It should, however, be noted that while the concepts are dealt with in a logical sequence, aspects of the same ecosystems are often used to illustrate different concepts and hence may be referred to in more than one chapter.

As in other books in this series, we have identified the *key ideas* in each chapter. It is intended that, as well as providing aide-memoires, these should help the reader to identify the basic concepts which, with the aid of the suggested Additional Activities and Reading, can be explored at greater depth. The authors would like to emphasise the importance of fieldwork, for both geographers and biologists, for an understanding not only of the phenomena but also of the complex interactions between the physical, biological and social systems involved in this study.

Key Ideas

A. Human and physical geography
1. The subdivision of geography into human and physical sub-fields is long-standing.
2. Relations between physical and human geography have changed in approach and emphasis through time.
3. Latterly the systems concept has helped to forge a new approach to the relationship between human and physical geography.

B. The systems concept
1. A system can be defined simply as a collection of components linked in such a way as to form a working unit.
2. The classic example of a system as used in geographical studies is the central heating system.
3. Such mechanical systems are open and capable of regulating themselves within defined limits.
4. Natural systems function in ways that can be compared with man-made systems.

C. Classification of systems
1. Systems vary according to the nature of their components.
2. No system is a completely independent unit.
3. Any system is part of a more complex system and can be subdivided into simpler systems.

D. The systems approach in geography
1. The systems approach provides the geographer with a particularly valuable conceptual framework
2. It facilitates study of interactions within and between systems.
3. It can be applied at any scale.

E. The aims of this book
1. The basic unit of study in biogeography is the biological system or ecosystem.
2. The main objective is to illustrate the effect of human impact on the principal ecosystem components and functions.

2 The Ecosystem Concept

A. Structural Components of Ecosystems

1. Definition

An ecological system, or *ecosystem*, is a set of interacting, interdependent living (organic or biotic) and non-living (inorganic or abiotic) components or sub-systems. It is a neat, concise term originally coined to convey the idea of a group of organisms and the place or *habitat* (i.e. home) they occupy, and the way the two are linked together to form a working or functioning unit.

Obviously, the biosphere can be regarded as an ecosystem, and is sometimes referred to as the *ecosphere* (*Scientific American*, 1971). This, however, is rather too large and complex to be a useful or manageable unit of study. At the other extreme, a single cell is probably too small a sub-system, too simple a level of explanation to be of any real assistance in understanding the relationships and interactions between organisms and their environment. Hence we tend to use the word ecosystem for a set or group of organisms and their habitat which are at a scale that we can comprehend, and for which we have the necessary analytical techniques. Figure 2.1 illustrates the relationship between the range of systems, or levels of organisation, in the

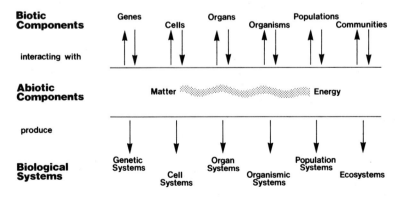

Figure 2.1   The biological spectrum (After E.P. Odum, 1971)

13

biosphere. It shows how the biological world can be thought of as a type of spectrum composed of many levels of organisation varying from units so small that they cannot be seen with the naked eye to large complex groups composed of different kinds of organisms. Ecologists and geographers are concerned primarily with the two 'higher' levels of organisation — populations and communities.

2. Biomass

The biosphere comprises a tremendous number of different species of plants (one million) and animals (two million). The number of individuals or *population size* in each species varies considerably. Some are rare, others abundant. The collection of species populations living together in a particular habitat form what is called a *biotic community*.

The total amount of all organisms in a given ecosystem can be expressed in terms of its *biomass* (or *standing crop*), i.e. the volume or weight of total living material. The amount present in any particular place will be related to

Table 2.1   Distribution of biomass in land, freshwater and marine ecosystems (After (1) H. Leith, 1975 and (2) S.R. Eyre, 1978)

Land and Freshwater Ecosystems	Biomass 10^9 tonnes (1)	% Biomass below ground (2)
Tropical rain forest	47.4	20
Rain green forest	13.2	30–40
Tropical grassland	12.0	20
Cultivated land (cereals)	9.1	(15)
Boreal forest	7.8	21–25
Temperate grassland	7.2	65–90
Cool temperate deciduous forest	7.0	15–33
Warm temperate mixed forest	5.0	20
Woodland	4.2	n.a.
Freshwater swamp and marsh	4.0	—
Desert and scrub	1.3	40–90
Tundra and alpine	1.3	70–85
Mediterranean forest	1.2	20
Lakes and streams	1.0	—
Total	121.7	
Marine Ecosystem		
Open ocean	41.5	—
Continental shelf	9.2	—
Estuaries	2.5	—
Algal beds and reefs	1.2	—
Upwelling zones	0.2	—
Total	55.0	
Grand Total	176.7	

n.a. = not available

a variety of factors, among which the most important are: (a) the type of organisms; (b) the nature of the surrounding environment (climate and soil in particular); (c) the season of the year; (d) the stage of ecosystem development and, of course, (e) the nature of human activities.

As Table 2.1 shows, the distribution of biomass can vary vertically as well as horizontally. The ratio of that above to that below ground is closely related to plant forms. For instance, it is greater in woody vegetation than in grasslands and deserts. The below ground ratio in both cold and hot deserts can be surprisingly high. However, it must be remembered that the seasonal variations, particularly in above ground biomass, are greater and more obvious in herbaceous than in forest, woodland and scrub ecosystems.

The biomass also varies in composition and structure. In some ecosystems it is composed of plant and animal populations belonging to only a relatively small number of species (i.e. it is species poor), in others to a very great number (i.e. it is species rich). Biomass structure refers to the spatial organisation of the organisms within an ecosystem. The most obvious structural characteristic is the stratification or layering of plants, according to height above and rooting depth below the ground surface. As is shown in Figure 2.2, the greater complexity of structure occurs where, as in the woodland community, groups of plants of differing height potential can grow together; the simpler structure occurs where there is only one group of individuals of uniform height and size.

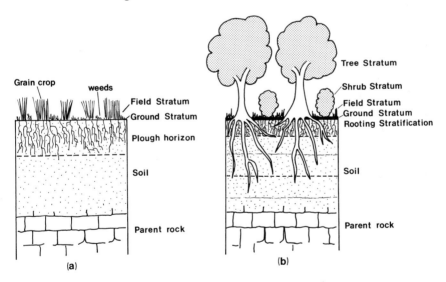

Figure 2.2   Vertical stratification of: (a) grain crop and (b) woodland ecosystems

3. Dead organic matter

Obviously the amount, type and distribution of animal biomass will be affected by that of plants. The more complex and species rich the plant

15

Table 2.2   Stages in ecosystem development and associated increase in bird populations (After D.B. Sutton and N.P. Harmon, 1973)

Ecosystem Development	Grassland	Shrubs	Low Trees	High Trees
Years	1–10	10–25	25–100	100+
Number of different species of birds	2	8	15	16
Density (pairs/40 ha)	27	123	113	233

Table 2.3   Biomass and dead organic matter (DOM) in 1970 in a 50 year old. standing second-growth deciduous woodland in New Hampshire (After J.R. Gosz et al., 1978)

Organic component	MJ/m^2
Above ground biomass	249.5
Below ground biomass (roots)	49.0
Litter	143.5
Dead organic matter to a depth of 36 cm	368.4

biomass, the greater the number of different animal species it can accommodate. Table 2.2 illustrates this point with reference to bird populations.

However, the distribution of animal biomass is not always directly related to that of plant biomass. In all terrestrial ecosystems a very high proportion of the above and below ground living plant material is not eaten by grazing animals. A large proportion either dies and falls to the ground surface as litter or, in the case of roots and other underground organs, exists in the soil. Together with the carcases of animals, these form the material described as *dead organic matter* (DOM). The ratio of dead to living organic matter can be surprisingly high; even in a forest ecosystem the former can be nearly twice that of the latter (see Table 2.3).

The detrital material, or DOM, on and beneath the surface of the ground provides a source of food energy for a very large population of organisms. These include worms, millipedes, springtails, together with fungi and bacteria. All are involved in the vital process of decomposition. The amount and species composition of the soil animal biomass are dependent on that of the DOM. Nutrient-rich organic matter will obviously support a larger and more varied soil fauna than nutrient-deficient material.

4. Classification of ecosystems

The characteristics used to identify ecosystems are usually dependent on the

Plate 2.1 Salts Hole, Holkham National Nature Reserve on the north Norfolk coast (Grid Ref. TF/893440). A primary hydrosere with a zonal succession from emergent reed beds (*Phragmites australis*), scrubby evergreen oak trees (*Quercus ilex*) to Corsican pines (*Pinus nigra*). (*Nature Conservancy Council*)

interests and objectives of the particular investigator. The two most common features by which ecosystems are classified are, on the one hand, the form and species composition of the *vegetation cover*; on the other, one or more characteristics of the *physical environment*.

For instance, one of the most fundamental distinctions in the biosphere is that between marine and terrestrial ecosystems. Sub-systems of the former may be defined on the basis of such physical characteristics of the water as variations in depth, salinity, nutrient content and temperature. Sub-systems of the latter have, traditionally, been categorised on the basis of variations in the appearance and/or composition of the vegetation cover. This is because the plant cover is often the largest and most obvious component. This is particularly well illustrated in Plate 2.1 where at least three ecosystems can be identified on the basis of form (height) and composition of the vegetation. Because of their interest in the possible relationships between climate, vegetation and soil, biogeographers early tended to concentrate on types of vegetation at global, continental or regional scales. Ecologists, in their attempt to understand how the ecosystem works, have tended to study much smaller, more discrete, and hence more manageable units, such as islands, coral reefs, lakes and ponds.

Ecosystems can be studied at any *scale*—from an ephemeral drop of water on a pavement or a crack in a wall, to the whole of the tropical rain forest. The spatial limits or *boundaries* of ecosystems are often difficult to establish because variation in the physical environment tends to be gradual and continuous, though the rate of change (i.e. the steepness of the environmental gradient) is greater in some cases than in others. Groups of organisms or communities merge one into the other across zones of transition or *ecotones* of varying width. But even where clear-cut boundaries can be identified, as between different types of rock or of vegetation, these may not coincide with other possible ecosystem boundaries. The boundary of an ecosystem defined by the feeding or nesting range of bird species is much less easy to identify and may well transgress those determined by the form of the vegetation cover. Also, both organic and inorganic components can move or be moved from one ecosystem to another. One of the most obviously discrete, well-defined ecosystems is the freshwater pond which, because of its scale and relatively clearly delimited boundaries, is a popular field laboratory for ecologists.

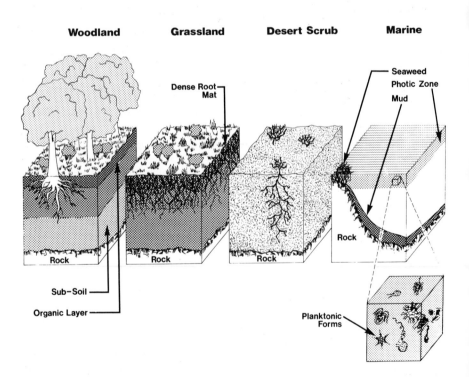

Figure 2.3   Types of ecosystem indentified on the basis of vegetation; note that the marine ecosystem is drawn at a scale c. 4X that of the others.

Look at Figure 2.3. Analyse the differences in (1) amount; (2) vertical distribution; and (3) composition of organic matter in the four types of ecosystem shown.

B. Functional Characteristics of Ecosystems

Despite the diversity of their components, however, all ecosystems *function* in the same way. They are all open systems in that they take in energy in one form or another in order to convert it into organic material and give off waste products. As a result, there are two basic types of links or flows between the component parts of all ecosystems, namely *energy flow* and *biological cycling*. In addition, all ecosystems are self-regulating systems and have the ability, up to a point, to modify the condition of their internal energy and materials. It is now proposed to examine in greater detail how ecosystems function.

1. Energy flow

(a) Photosynthesis

Energy can be defined simply as the ability to do work, and all organisms need a source of energy to live. The organic components of the ecosystem are very intimately linked one to the other by a mutual interdependence on food energy. The initial source of all but a minute fraction of this energy is the sun — the incoming solar radiation (i.e. insolation) which flows continually from the solar to the earth system. Light energy is the means whereby plant materials which have chlorophyll (green pigment) in their cells can build up complex organic substances, such as carbohydrates, from simpler inorganic substances such as carbon, oxygen and hydrogen. This process is known as photosynthesis, carbon assimilation, or primary biological productivity, and can be briefly summarised in the following equation:

$$6CO_2 + 6H_2O + \text{light energy (2.8MJ)} = C_6H_{12}O_6 \text{ (sugar)} + 6O_2$$

$\longleftrightarrow$
(low chemical
 energy)

$\longleftrightarrow$
(high chemical
 energy)

(b) Primary and secondary productivity

All plants, irrespective of their size or form, have a particular role or *niche* in the ecosystem as primary producers.

The total amount of chemical energy fixed by an ecosystem per unit area per unit of time is referred to as the *gross primary productivity* (GPP). Green plants in synthesising organic material must perform metabolic work, and the energy for this is derived from the oxidation or breakdown of their own organic substances. This process is known as *respiration* (R) and is chemically the reverse of photosynthesis:

$$C_6H_{12}O_6 + 6O_2 = 6H_2O + 6CO_2 + heat\ (2.8MJ)$$

(high chemical energy)   (low chemical energy)

Gross primary production less that used in respiration is called *net primary productivity* (NPP). Because energy flow within the ecosystem obeys the First Law of Thermodynamics, which states that 'energy is neither created nor destroyed but may be transformed from one form into another', we can express the relationship as follows:

GPP = NPP + R

The energy of net primary productivity is 'stored' in new living plant tissue or plant biomass which may be either directly consumed by animals or may die and accumulate as dead organic matter (DOM) or detritus. The NPP, expressed in terms of volume or weight, provides the food base for all *secondary biological productivity* of animals.

(c) Photosynthetic efficiency

The ratio between the chemical energy fixed by plants in photosynthesis and the amount of solar energy involved in the process (i.e. the photosynthetically active radiation, or FAR) is called *photosynthetic efficiency*. Recent work under the auspices of the International Biological Programme (IBP) suggests that the *average* efficiency for the biosphere is as low as 0.2 per cent; maximum efficiencies, such as are found in fast growing tropical crops (Napier grass for forage), rarely exceed 5 per cent.

The total amount of living plant and animal material present in an area at any one point in time is usually expressed in units of dry weight or energy equivalent per unit area. Figure 2.4 shows characteristic trends for plant

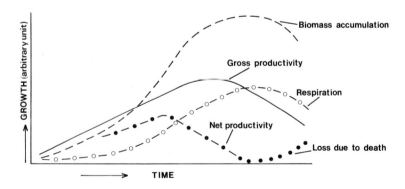

Figure 2.4   Trends in gross primary productivity, net primary productivity and biomass in a herbaceous plant (After Open University Press, 1974)

20

productivity, respiration and plant biomass accumulation. From this it should be carefully noted that a large biomass does not necessarily mean that the rate of either gross or net productivity will be correspondingly high. Normally after a certain age plant productivity (gross and net) declines although the biomass may continue to increase.

(d) Food chains and webs

Energy fixed in net primary productivity is consumed by animals unable to manufacture their own food — first by herbivores (primary consumers) then by carnivores (secondary consumers) and eventually by predatory or top carnivores (tertiary consumers). The remains of plant and animal tissue are eventually consumed by decomposing organisms (e.g. bacteria and fungi). Figure 2.5a illustrates how the transfer of food from one reasonably distinct group of organisms, with generally similar feeding habits (or niches), to another forms a sequence called a *food chain*. The stage or position occupied by an organism in the food chain is called the *trophic* or *feeding level*, denoted (Tn) in Figure 2.5a.

There are two distinctive types of food chain in most ecosystems. One is the *grazing* food chain by which plant material passes from one group of consumers to another. The other is the *detrital* food chain whereby dead and decaying plant and animal material is broken down by a parallel series of decomposing organisms. As Figure 2.5b shows, a food chain can be thought of as a sub-system of a much more complex macro-system in which a great number of chains form an interlocking *food web*.

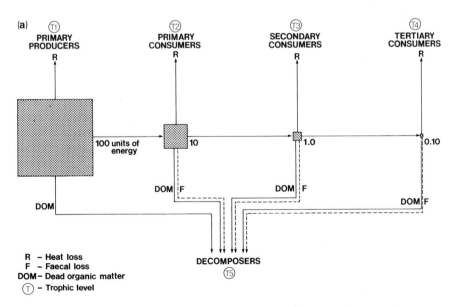

Figure 2.5a Simple food chain showing average energy conversion ratios

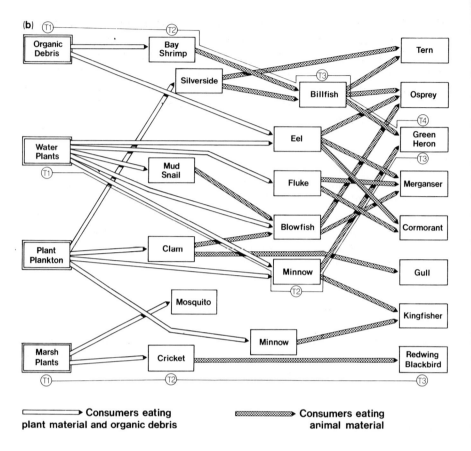

Consumers eating plant material and organic debris
Consumers eating animal material

Figure 2.5b   Energy flows within a freshwater marsh foodweb (After G.M. Woodwell, 1967)

In the process of eating and being eaten, energy flows through the ecosystem, passing from one trophic level to the next. However, food webs do not normally have more than five or six levels. This is because the process of energy transfer is not very efficient. As shown in Figure 2.5a, on average about 90 per cent is lost as heat (R) and discarded as faeces (F) to the surrounding environment at each trophic exchange. In other words, only about 10 per cent of the energy at one trophic level is subsequently fixed in the tissues of the succeeding level. Hence the amount of animal biomass that can be supported at each succeeding trophic level decreases at a geometric rate.

Because energy flows through the system and is eventually dissipated as heat, the ecosystem is dependent on a continuing input of solar radiation. The ecosystem conforms to the Second Law of Thermodynamics because, in its passage, energy is transformed from a highly organised and concentrated form (food) to a less organised and dispersed form (heat).

From the point of view of energy flow, the earth is an open ecosystem which can only exist because of a continuous input of solar radiation. At the same time, large amounts of heat energy leave the earth system and pass into the 'energy sink' of space. The steady state of the earth's ecosystem in terms of the relatively constant temperature of the earth's surface is a result of a balance that is maintained between the input of light energy and the output of heat energy.

ASSIGNMENTS

1. *Look at the equations of photosynthesis and respiration; do these processes always occur at the same time?*
2. *Photosynthesis, from the given equation, requires water, carbon dioxide and light energy; but what other requirements are necessary for plant growth to take place?*
3. *How many different types of food chain can be identified from Figure 2.5b?*

2. Biological cycling

The second major link between the component parts of the ecosystem is biological cycling. This process is dependent on and driven by the flow of energy through the ecosystem.

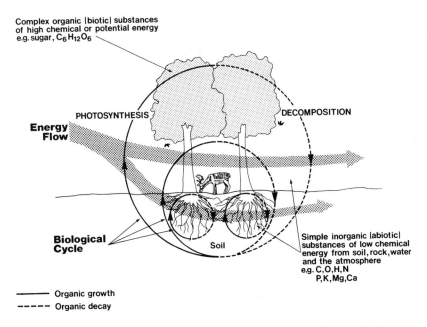

Figure 2.6   The biological cycle showing interaction between photosynthesis (growth) and decomposition (decay)

(a) Biogeochemical cycling

Figure 2.6 shows just how closely the organic (or biotic) and the inorganic (or abiotic) components of the ecosystem interact. Both are linked by the continuous alternation of the processes of growth and decay, of synthesis and breakdown, of biological productivity and degradation. In primary biological productivity, the simple inorganic elements and compounds of carbon, oxygen, hydrogen, nitrogen, phosphorus and potassium, together with those of other essential minerals, are converted into complex organic substances. These comprise plant and animal tissues which eventually die and undergo bacterial decay and decomposition. In this process of biological degradation, the inorganic elements are eventually released and can be re-used by the living plants. As a result, there is continuous circulation of elements from an inorganic (geo) to an organic (bio) form, and back again. The process is succinctly expressed by the term *biogeochemical cycling*. In nature, the geo-phase and the bio-phase are parts of a continuum in which matter exists in every form between the two and in which it is often very difficult, if not impossible, to identify where one phase begins and the other ends.

(b) Nutrient pools

Figure 2.7 demonstrates how the earth's ecosystems draw on three main *nutrient reserves* or *pools* — the atmosphere, the lithosphere and the hydro-

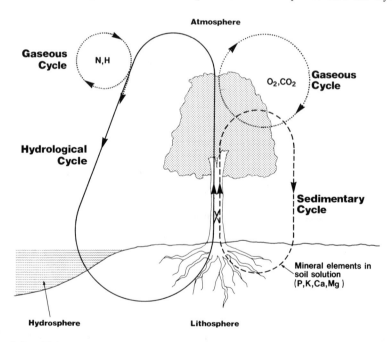

Figure 2.7   Global nutrient reservoirs (or pools) and related types of biological cycle

sphere — in the process of biogeochemical cycling. Some elements, such as carbon dioxide and oxygen, enter and leave the cycle in a gaseous form and follow a simple route from the atmosphere to the organism and back. Others, such as hydrogen, nitrogen, phosphorus, potassium and calcium, are absorbed in solution from the soil; their circulation is, therefore, dependent on the hydrological cycle by which water is circulated from the atmosphere to the land and/or water and evaporated back to the atmosphere again. Nearly 45 per cent of the insolation reaching the earth's surface is expended in evaporating water from land and plant surfaces (evapotranspiration). In addition, energy is used by plants to 'pump' solutions from the soil, and by the bacteria which effect biological degradation.

(c) Recycling period

The length of time materials are held in the nutrient pools, and hence the rate at which they are locally and globally recycled, varies. Atmospheric carbon dioxide and oxygen circulate rapidly between organisms and the environment in the basic processes of respiration and photosynthesis. It has been estimated, as shown in Figure 2.8, that atmospheric carbon dioxide and atmospheric oxygen may be completely recycled by the biosphere in as little as three hundred and two thousand years respectively. Water and nitrogen have more complex local routes from the atmosphere via the soil to plants, and their global circulation times are somewhat more protracted.

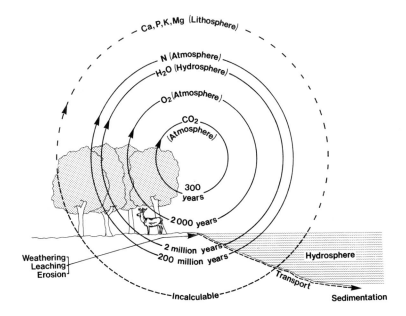

Figure 2.8   Total biospheric turnover time of atmospheric oxygen, atmospheric carbon dioxide, the global water supply and elements of the lithosphere (Modified from P. Cloud and A. Gibor, 1970)

Mineral or sedimentary elements, in contrast, are released relatively slowly from rocks in the process of weathering and soil formation. Moreover, unlike the elements of the gaseous cycle, mineral elements follow an essentially 'one-way' global flow from land surface to ocean basin (see Figure 2.8). Mineral elements have thus the potential to be 'lost' to the biological cycle, and the time taken for these elements to be completely recycled by biological processes is inestimably long. Finally, the actual length of time minerals are stored in organic form depends not only on the lifespan of the organisms, which may vary from a few hours to hundreds of years, but also on the rate and character of decomposition. Minerals may be locally stored in undecomposed organic matter (peat) for thousands, and in coal deposits, for millions of years.

(d) Material transfer between ecosystems

The earth ecosystem (or *ecosphere*) is to a great extent a closed system with regard to matter and, unlike energy, there is not seemingly an infinite external supply. However, although there is a continuous circulation of materials within individual ecosystems, they rarely act as closed systems. There can be a transfer of both inorganic and organic material into and from other systems. As in the case of energy flow, if a system is to maintain a steady state, or what is often described as a dynamic equilibrium, between organic and inorganic components, losses must be counteracted by gains.

ASSIGNMENTS

1. *Using Table 2.4, analyse the relationships between living organisms and the chemical composition of the earth's atmosphere, hydrosphere and lithosphere.*
2. *Refer back to Figure 2.8. What do this figure and Table 2.4 tell us about the differences between gaseous and sedimentary cycles? Comment on the implications of these differences in terms of human use of the biosphere.*

3. Eco-regulation

All ecosystems display certain common processes and features which result from the fact that they are also, within given limits, self-regulating systems. An ecosystem can regulate itself in two ways — as a result either of the interactions between one system and another, or of the interactions within a system. In the latter case, one of the most important results of interactions between the organic (biotic) and inorganic (abiotic) components is to modify the system in such a way as to produce physical (abiotic) conditions which did not exist prior to the biological occupation of a particular site. The main instruments of change are plants, because of their much greater bulk or mass in proportion to that of animals and also because of their relative immobility.

Table 2.4   Relative amounts by *volume* of elements in the biosphere, the atmosphere, the hydrosphere and the lithosphere (After E S Deevey, 1970)

	Biosphere	Atmosphere	Hydrosphere	Lithosphere
Hydrogen (H)	49.8		66.4	2.92
Oxygen (O)	24.9	21.0	33.0	60.4
Carbon (C)	24.9	0.03	0.0014	0.16
Nitrogen (N)	0.27	78.3		
Calcium (Ca)	0.073		0.006	1.88
Potassium (K)	0.046		0.006	1.37
Silicon (Si)	0.033			20.5
Magnesium (Mg)	0.031		0.034	1.77
Phosphorus (P)	0.030			0.08
Sulphur (S)	0.017		0.017	0.04
Aluminium (Al)	0.016			6.2
Sodium (Na)			0.28	2.49
Iron (Fe)				1.90
Titanium (Ti)				0.27
Chlorine (Cl)			0.33	
Boron (B)			0.0002	
Argon (Ar)		0.93		
Neon (Ne)		0.0018		

(a) Environmental modification

As a result of the shade and shelter plants provide, they modify the layer of the atmosphere they occupy in such a way as to produce a *microclimate* (i.e. the climate near the ground), substantially different from that of the free atmosphere. Also, through the addition of living roots, stems and dead plant litter, they make the major contribution to the biologically active layer called the *soil*. Consequent on microclimatic modifications and soil formation, plant, and to a lesser extent animal, components can give rise to physical conditions more favourable for other groups of organisms and less favourable for themselves.

(b) Ecological succession

Plants improve the physical site in such a way as to allow more demanding and usually larger plants to establish themselves. These plants are better able to compete for the available resources, and to shade or crowd out all previous occupants other than those which can tolerate the new internal environment.

This process, whereby one group of organisms or one type of ecosystem replaces another in the same place through time, is called *ecological succession* or ecosystem development (see Plates 2.1 and 2.2).

(*i*) *Climax and seral stage* The theoretical endpoint of succession is that stage at which the ecosystem shows little tendency towards further change in a particular direction. At this stage the system will have attained a steady

Plate 2.2 Fetcham Downs, Surrey (Grid Ref. TQ/155540). Secondary vegetation succession of former chalk grassland by hawthorn scrub. (*Nature Conservancy Council*)

state; this has traditionally been described, particularly in relation to vegetation, as the *mature* or *climax* stage.

The whole progression or development towards a steady state or climax ecosystem is called a *sere*, the development stages of which are *seral stages*. The type of sere and number of seral stages, in terms of both biotic and abiotic components, can vary considerably depending on the physical conditions of the initial site and the availability of organic material. Because of an excess of biological productivity over decay, which acts as a positive feedback mechanism, all such seral stages are inherently unstable. Thus, *net community* or *ecosystem productivity*, in terms of amount of organic matter (e.g. biomass + DOM) produced per unit area per unit time, is high. In contrast, the climax or steady state ecosystem is relatively stable. As Figure 2.9 indicates, it is characterised by (a) a balance between input and output (i.e. production (GPP) = decay (R)); (b) maintenance of the maximum biomass possible under prevailing environmental conditions; (c) a very low

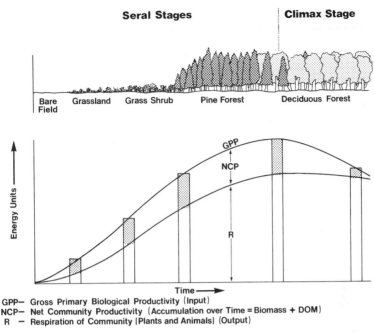

Figure 2.9   Energy relationships during biological succession

to zero net community productivity; and (d) the most diverse and complex combination of plants and animals that can make the optimum use of the available energy and material resources.

At this stage, the structure and function of the ecosystem will remain relatively constant, with fluctuations reflecting short-term external and internal variations. It is also the stage at which homeostasis is most highly developed in the ecosystem. Provided fluctuations are not so great as to exceed the limits of tolerance of the ecosystem, negative feedback mechanisms will operate to maintain it in a state of relative equilibrium.

(ii) Steady state: fact or fiction? It is, however, highly unlikely that any ecosystem can, in the long term, perpetuate itself. There is sufficient evidence to indicate that gradual environmental changes have occurred in the past which have brought about continuing ecosystem changes. Catastrophic events, such as lightning-set fires, hurricanes or epidemic disease can, locally and very rapidly, completely disrupt a system. Also, organic evolution in general is a process which will tend to produce long-term ecosystem change. The climax, steady state, therefore, is largely a theoretical and relative concept.

Furthermore, there are few ecosystems existing today which have not been subjected either directly or indirectly to the impact of human activity. Humans are an integral part of the biosphere and it would be unrealistic to consider any ecosystem without regard for them as one of its essential components. Their role in, and hence effect on, the ecosystem is, however, very different from that of the other organisms. The purpose of the next chapter is to analyse the ways in which humans differ from other organisms, and the ecological significance of these differences.

ASSIGNMENT

Consider the following environmental factors: soil moisture content; soil temperature range; light intensity; wind speed; atmospheric humidity; air temperature; soil nutrient content. How do they alter in the course of plant succession?

Key Ideas

A. Structural components of ecosystems
1. An ecosystem is a set of interacting, interdependent living and non-living components.
2. The total volume of living material can be expressed in terms of its biomass.
3. The amount, distribution and composition of biomass varies with type of organisms, physical environment, stage of ecosystem development and human activities.
4. A large proportion of the organic component in most ecosystems is composed of dead organic matter (DOM), of which the largest proportion is composed of plant material.
5. Ecosystems can be of any scale.
6. Ecosystems can be classified in terms of either their living or non-living components.
7. Ecosystems rarely have well-defined boundaries.

B. Functional characteristics of ecosystems
1. All ecosystems function in the same way.
2. The common functional characteristics of all ecosystems are energy flow, biological cycling and eco-regulation.
3. Energy flow refers to the initial fixation of energy in the ecosystem by photosynthesis, its transfer through the system along a food web, and its final dissipation by respiration.
4. Biological cycling refers to the continuous circulation of elements from an inorganic (geo) to an organic (bio) form and back again.
5. Self-regulating mechanisms within the ecosystem result in ecological succession, the process by which one community replaces another in a given site.
6. Self-regulating processes also enable the ecosystem to achieve, at least in theory, a final steady state known as the ecological climax.

Additional Activities

1. Examine Table 2.2, Figure 2.9 and Plates 2.1 and 2.2.
   (a) What other changes not illustrated occur during biological succession?
   (b) Would you expect the change in number of plant species to follow the same trend as that of birds? Explain your answer.
   (c) Study Plates 2.1 and 2.2. What are the similarities and differences in the zonation of vegetation? Suggest reasons for the differences.
2. Analyse the main differences between marine and terrestrial ecosystems under the following headings: nature of physical environment; primary producers; food chains; biological cycling. (See *Biogeography* by Joy Tivy, 1977).

3 The Role of Humans in the Ecosystem

There are few ecosystems in the world today in which humans do not have either a direct or indirect effect, and there are many which in part or in whole they have created. Humans are now the most important organisms, or living components, in the biosphere — the biologically inhabited part of the atmosphere above, and the land and water on the earth's surface. The aim of this chapter, therefore, is to explain, why humans are so important; to analyse the ways in which they are similar to or different from other organisms; and, in particular, to illustrate the ecological significance of the differences.

A. Humans as the Ecological Dominants

1. The concept of ecological dominance

Humans are important because they are the ecologically *dominant species*. When a particular type of organism, be it plant or animal, is described as ecologically dominant it generally means that: (a) it can compete more successfully than other organisms for the essentials of life (particularly nutrition) in the same habitat or physical environment; and/or (b) it can exert a greater influence on the habitat in which it lives and, hence, on the other associated living components.

Ecological dominance is more usually applied to, and is easier to demonstrate in relation to, plant than to animal communities. In the former, the dominant type (grass, shrub, tree) or species of plant is that which either because of the number and/or size of the individuals comprises the greatest proportion of the plant biomass. For example, in a wood or forest the trees, though not necessarily the most numerous type of plant, form the bulk of the biomass. Because of their size, they can compete more successfully for light, water and nutrients than smaller plants. Also, trees modify the atmospheric conditions of light, temperature and humidity within the wood, as well as the physical and chemical nature of the soil. Only those plants tolerant of the woodland environment will be capable of growing in the same habitat. In contrast to plants, animals can attain ecological dominance not only by reason of their size and/or numbers, but also because of their mobility, aggressiveness, lack of predators and intelligence.

2. Human ecological dominance

Human ecological dominance is dependent on a combination of attributes, among which the most important are *anatomical and mental characteristics* which have allowed humans to compete more successfully for what they want, and in doing so to exert a greater effect on the environment than any other organism in the ecosystem. Humans are a distinct species of animal (i.e. *Homo sapiens*); they can interbreed, but do not crossbreed with any other species; they share a great many anatomical and physiological features in common with all other animals, and more particularly, with the other primate mammals (e.g. monkeys and chimpanzees). However, as Figure 3.1 demonstrates, they possess certain ecologically significant features which, to a greater or lesser extent, distinguish them from the other primates.

ASSIGNMENT

Study Figure 3.1 carefully. Make a list of all the differences you detect between the human and the ape. Now read on.

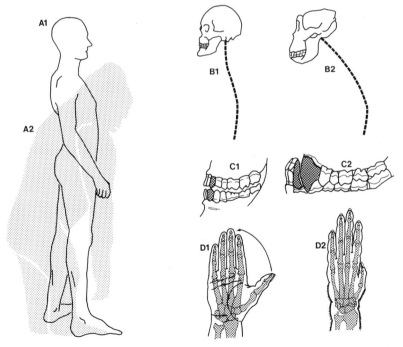

Figure 3.1   Anatomical characteristics of a human (1) compared with those of an ape (2): A = posture; B = cranium and spine; C = teeth; D = hands (Modified from M. Bates, 1964)

33

First, the human has a completely upright posture combined with a bipedal locomotion. Second, the hands have large, particularly well-developed thumbs which can be brought into easy contact with any of the four fingers. The human is therefore much more prehensile (i.e. capable of grasping, clinging, holding, of generally using the hands) than any other primate mammal. Third, humans are peculiar among other carnivorous animals in being both predatory and herbivorous. Their omnivorous habit is reflected in a combination, but less specialisation, of the pointed canine teeth of the carnivore and the broad molars of the herbivore. Fourth, and very important, the human brain is exceptionally large in proportion to the size of the body; and that part of the brain known as the cerebrum, the frontal lobe which commands thinking, is larger and more complex than in any other animal.

Numerically, humans are the most abundant single species of large mammal. The only other species with comparable or larger populations are small animals like fish (e.g. sardines) or such insects as the ubiquitous housefly (Bates, 1964).

They occupy the *highest trophic level* (see page 21) in the ecosystem and have no predators. However, unlike other animals they can and do exploit all other trophic levels, indeed the whole ecosystem, for their nutritive and other requirements.

ASSIGNMENT

What particular features might account for the ecological success of the following: elephants; locusts; sharks; eagles; zebra?

B. Humans as Tool Making Animals

1. Why tools?

Humans cannot move so rapidly as many other large mammals; their sense of hearing and of smell is less well-developed; they lack a protective covering, for which reason they have been nicknamed 'The Naked Ape'; and their young are dependent on them for a much longer period than in the case of any other mammal species. These disadvantages, in terms of human ability to survive and compete successfully in the animal world, are more than compensated for by three-dimensional vision, greater powers of reasoning and by the fact that humans are the only animals that use and make tools. Some other animals use natural objects as rudimentary tools; for instance, it is known that chimps can trim and shorten twigs or straws. However, humans are the only animals that use tools to make tools. Humans and their tools evolved together, and crude stone artefacts have been discovered which date back some two million years.

The distinctive trait of humans as tool making animals is closely related to their upright position, which leaves their hands free to work; to their good vision combined with their manipulative dexterity; to their reasoning power and the high degree of inventiveness which are the result of a brain superior in these respects to that of any other animal. The development of human ecological dominance in the ecosystem, therefore, has gone hand-in-hand with the development of tools designed, initially, for the basic processes of (a) killing animals for food; (b) digging for and cultivating plants; (c) making clothing and shelter; and (d) locomotion. The three most important initial technical advances were the discovery and use of fire and of digging implements, and the invention of the wheel.

2. Humans as fire makers

Fire is not a tool in the strict sense of the word. Natural fires can be started by volcanic eruptions and lightning strikes. It has, however, been described as the first tool used by humans which made a major impact on the ecosystem in which it occurred. Before the discovery of fire, the number of humans was probably too small and their tools too crude to give them a competitive advantage over other animals or to have a marked or lasting effect on their environment. However, humans early used fire for other than purely domestic purposes (i.e. warmth/cooking). They used it to clear woodland and forest; to flush and drive wild animals out of hiding; and, eventually, as a means of removing dead and decaying surface vegetation, to stimulate the regrowth of new fresh herbage for the grazing animals they initially hunted and eventually domesticated. Fire is still the dominant tool in pastoral farming in areas as far apart as the upland moors of Britain and the savanna grasslands of inter-tropical South America and Africa. There is also considerable evidence to suggest that the absence of trees and the dominance of grassland vegetation in prairie, steppe and savanna ecosystems are a result of fire and grazing rather than physical conditions. The use of fire allowed humans to extend their influence over an area that was very extensive in proportion to their numbers. In other words it gave them a degree of ecological dominance independent of, and out of proportion to, their numbers at the time.

3. Humans as cultivators

With the exception of a few specialised insects, humans are the only animal species that cultivate their own food plants. Termites are known to cultivate a species of mushroom in their mounds, and ants domesticate greenfly for their sweet sap. The transition from gathering and collecting of food, as in the case of other animals, to the deliberate planting, propagation and harvesting of crops was a major technical achievement of far-reaching ecological significance. It saw the introduction of tools of a different kind. Cultivation required the clearing of surface vegetation and the breaking and up-turning of the soil. The primitive digging stick, still used to scratch the surface of soils in certain inter-tropical areas, was the first agricultural tool and the precursor of the modern plough. It allowed the disturbance of the natural ecosystem in a way and on a scale greater than ever before. It was the second major step in the widespread creation of new human-initiated or human-created habitats. The resultant larger and more reliable food supply contributed to an increase of population and hence to an even greater and more widespread impact on the environment.

ASSIGNMENT

See if you can find illustrations of a digging stick, a primitive hoe and a modern plough. How do they operate? Make a list of other items of modern agricultural machinery used to cultivate the soil.

C. Humans as Robber Animals

1. Why a robber species?

Human ecological dominance has grown and spread with the invention of ever more sophisticated tools which have allowed the exploitation of the whole ecosystem with increasing effectiveness. Humans are characterised by being the most exploitive of all animals; in fact, they have been called a robber species. They make greater use of both terrestrial and aquatic ecosystems than any other species. This is only partly because of their omnivorous habit and a diet which is more varied than that of any other animal. It is also because their 'needs' or 'demands' are more diverse. At a relatively early stage in their development, humans were exploiting their natural environment not only for food but also for non-food products. Primitive humans are known to have used plant fibres and poisons for catching fish. Since then their use of organic materials for such purposes as medicines, beverages, skins and furs, timber and paper, and industrial fibres, to mention but a few, has grown in type and volume.

As well as cultivators of food, humans also became herders of a small number of large herbivorous mammals (goats, sheep, cattle, horses) which they selected and gathered together for particular purposes, either as draught animals or for animal food products. Eventually, in order to produce increasing amounts of animal food, they had to cultivate fodder crops with which to feed and fatten their domesticated animals.

2. Humans and food chains

In all ecosystems, as has been noted in Chapter 2B, the component organisms are linked by a complex of interconnecting food chains (or a food web). Within such food webs in any particular ecosystem, many different types of organisms may share the same food supply. In this respect, humans differ from other animals in that they endeavour to reduce or eliminate completely those plants or animals (the weeds and pests) which compete for, and re-duce, the particular food supply they have selected to produce. In their agri-cultural ecosystems, therefore, they tend to reduce the number of links in the food chain between the food and/or fodder crop and themselves.

3. Overcropping and overgrazing

The human method of plant cropping and animal grazing differs radically from that of nearly all other animals. In terrestrial ecosystems, at least, animals do not normally completely exhaust their own food supply. The animal biomass, in any trophic level, is usually less than the maximum which the food supply could support at a given moment. Also, a high proportion of the nutrients which pass along the grazing food chains is eventually recycled in the process of decomposition (in the detrital food chains) in the soil.

Humans, however, tend to overcrop and overgraze. In the first respect, when they harvest a particular crop they remove most of the above ground, and sometimes all of the above and below ground biomass, from the ecosys-tem. The nutrients incorporated in the crop are lost and this must be made good by the addition of organic or inorganic fertilisers if crop yields are to be maintained. Similarly, by their methods of animal husbandry, humans increase the numbers of a particular type of domestic herbivore and initiate overgrazing. This operates in several ways. As in the case of arable crops, removal (cropping) of animals from the ecosystem constitutes a drain on the soil nutrients incorporated in the forage plants; selective and intensive graz-ing tends to deplete the more nutritive at the expense of poorer, less nutritive plant species, and the feeding value of the pasture, unless rectified, will decrease. Finally, the density of selective grazing animals may be such that they crop the forage plants at a rate greater than they can grow, and they can be so overgrazed as to be eaten out completely.

4. Humans and non-consumptive uses of the ecosystem

Humans differ from other animals in that they exploit the ecosystem for what might be called non-consumptive uses, i.e. for uses other than for nutrition and purely domestic purposes. These uses can be cultural, parti-cularly when associated with peoples' beliefs in the supernatural power or significance of plants and animals. The early deification and worship of nat-ural phenomena reflected human dependence on and control by nature. Plants and animals were imbued with magical powers to cure or to kill. Animals were sacrificed to propitiate the gods, while others were deemed too sacred to kill. Animals also acquired a social use in being an expression of a person's wealth and hence power, and the number of domesticated animals acquired was more important than their food value.

From time immemorial, humans have used plants and animals for their pleasure and satisfaction. The dog, the most ubiquitous of pets was probably the first animal to be domesticated (initially to be eaten!). Plants have long been used for purely decorative and ornamental purposes. Today the use of organic resources for aesthetic satisfaction is reflected in the considerable areas devoted to the cultivation of gardens, and to the use of extensive tracts of land for either the pursuit of outdoor recreational activities or the conservation of natural beauty.

ASSIGNMENTS

1. *Refer back to Figure 2.5a. Construct annotated diagrams to illustrate three types of human food chains.*
2. *Construct two diagrams based on Figure 2.6, one to illustrate the effect of overgrazing, the other of overcropping on the biological cycle. What are the similarities and what are the differences?*

D. Humans as Agents of Evolution

With their increasing technical skills and knowledge humans have emerged not only as the ecologically dominant species but also as the most powerful agent in the process of organic evolution today. Natural evolution is a relatively slow process. As a result of the accidental and, later, deliberate disturbance of the ecosystem, the rate of organic evolution has been accelerated to a degree probably previously unknown in the history of the earth. Many species of both plants and animals have either had their population numbers reduced to a critical level or have become extinct as a result of their activities. Others, in contrast, have increased in numbers while many new varieties, sub-species or species have emerged in consequence of direct or indirect human intervention. Humans have directed the course and speeded up the rate of organic evolution in three principal ways.

1. Domestication

Through the process of domestication (meaning, literally, 'bringing into the home'), plants and animals have been produced which are dependent, to a greater or lesser degree, on humans for their continued survival. These are the so-called *cultigens* or *cultivars*. It is surprising that, in the course of the past ten thousand years or so, so few plants and animals have been chosen for domestication. The process started early in human history, and evidence to date suggests that animal domestication preceded that of plants. The result has been to produce species of plants and animals which are so completely dependent on humans for their propagation that they cannot survive in the wild and, in a few cases, have no known wild relatives. Domesticated races of wheat, maize, rice and potatoes, indeed of most other important food crops, as well as domesticated animals, would eventually disappear without human aid. Sheep and goats would have little chance of survival in the wild unless protected from predators.

Domestication of plants and animals probably started with the selection of certain wild species for particular and intensive uses, and the selection of those individuals in which the required properties were noticeably well-developed. In the case of food plants, large seeds or tubers were obviously desirable. In other cases, the absence or reduction of spines, hairs or other features which would reduce palatability in plants would have been advantageous. These plants were then cultivated and the process of selection continued each time seed plants were gathered for propagation. Later, with increasing scientific knowledge, the controlled breeding of plants with the desired qualities has speeded up this process of domestication. Figure 3.2 is a particularly good example of the process of domestication in one species of the cabbage (*Brassica oleracea*) family. From one original species six different types of vegetable have been produced by the process of selecting and propagating strains which, in each case, have increasingly well-developed leaves, flowers and stems.

The domestication of animals is no different in principle and may have been initiated by selective hunting and/or herd management. In the process,

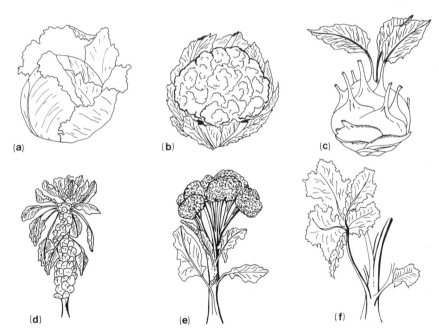

Figure 3.2   Six separate vegetables which have been produced by selection from a single species (*Brassica oleracea*) of the cabbage family (After J. Harlan, 1976).
    a) cabbage — large terminal bud
    b) cauliflower — flower
    c) kohlrabi — stem
    d) Brussels sprouts — lateral buds
    e) broccoli — stem and flowers
    f) kale — leaves; kale most closely resembles the wild plant

wild animals are tamed. Individuals may originally have been selected for docility, and in cattle and pigs this led to the evolution of smaller animals that were easier to handle. However, it must be remembered that, because the process is evolutionary, the degree of domestication can vary widely from species to species, and all the intermediate stages can be found in the same species.

2. Man-made habitats

Domestication implies the selection of species best adapted to human needs and also to the human home or habitat. The second way in which the nature and rate of organic evolution has been affected is through the creation of disturbed, highly modified or new man-made habitats. These have multiplied over time. The first disturbed sites were probably confined to footpaths and to those areas around human dwellings where the vegetation had been cleared or was disrupted by physical impact or where middens (rubbish dumps) provided new habitats for plant and animal colonisation. These were initially very limited areas and probably less important than the home itself, which provided a habitat for a great number of associated species of now common house animals such as flies, cockroaches, mice and scorpions.

More extensive open habitats created by humans are cultivated fields, parks and gardens; those along major routeways, be they road or rail; waste or derelict land once used and now abandoned; canals, drainage ditches and reservoirs; and even the concrete jungles of the urban habitat. These have been described as *hybrid* habitats resulting from the interaction of humans and their physical environment. Their role in evolution has been to give a foothold to plants and associated animals uncommon, or previously unknown, in formerly closed ecosystems. The organisms which can take advantage of open, exposed sites are the opportunist weeds and pests, many of them hybrids which, once established, can grow with considerable vigour, can take over and fill vacated niches and can compete very successfully with other species.

Not only do opportunist hybrid species tend to become established on disturbed habitats, but species (particularly of plants) which formerly would not have been associated come into close contact, and new opportunities for crossbreeding are provided. The evolution of important food crops such as wheat and maize are now known to have occurred as a result of crossbreeding with associated grassy weeds of cultivation; while oats and barley probably originated as weeds of cultivation. Existing varieties of wheats (see Figure 3.3) fall into three groups according to their chromosome numbers: first, the einkorns (7) are the most primitive form of cultivated wheat (A); the second group (14), of which Persian wheat is an example, is thought to have evolved as the result of natural hybridisation between an einkorn and an unknown wild grass (B); and third, the modern common bread wheats (21) which emerged most recently as a result of natural crossing between a known wild grass (D) and Persian wheat (AB).

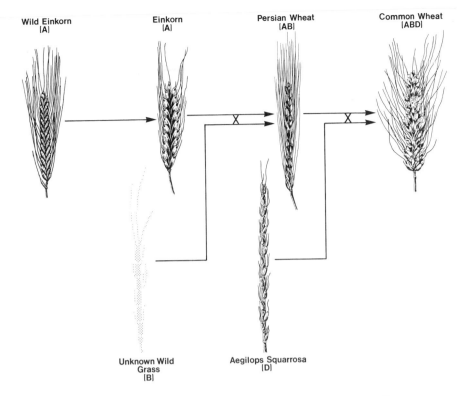

Figure 3.3 The evolution of common wheat (After P. Manglesdorf, 1953)

3. Effects on distribution

Finally, humans have contributed to the process of evolution as increasingly important agents of plant and animal distribution. They have deliberately and accidentally transported species from one part of the world to another. The rate and areal extent of plant and animal distribution has increased with the development of varying and faster modes of transport. As a result of extended plant and animal distribution, species have been brought into contact that formerly were isolated and separated by physical barriers (oceans, mountains and deserts) too extensive to be crossed by natural means of dispersal. Intermingling of species in combination with the availability of the man-made habitats facilitated the evolution of new, fertile, vigorous hybrids which, in some instances, have all but displaced their parent stock. The hybrid larch (European × Japanese) in Scotland, and rice grass (American × British) in southern England are cases in point.

The process of domestication continues as new varieties of the long-used plants and animals are bred for particular purposes, and adapted to climate, soil, methods of cultivation and even to machinery. Interdependence between humans and their food crops has become ever greater and the area occupied by these has expanded at the expense of wild species, which have been reduced in both area and population.

1. *For each of the following cultivated plants, identify the part or organ used by humans: rice; maize; celery; coffee; potato; tobacco; cotton; sugar cane.*
2. *On outline maps of the world, indicate the general area of origin and present area(s) of cultivation for three crops originally native to the New World and three to the Old World.*

E. Humans as Dirty Animals

Humans differ from all other animals in being a particularly dirty species. Others, in comparison, have clean habits; their waste material consists essentially of the remains of uneaten food, droppings (faeces) and dead carcases. All is composed of organic material that can be broken down and disposed of by the biological process of decomposition; hence it is called *biodegradable* material. It can be recycled because the elements into which it is broken down can be used again by both living plants and animals. The habitats where animal waste accumulates in any appreciable amount are coastal areas where exceptionally high concentrations of sea-birds result in the progressive build up of phosphate-rich droppings, such as guano off the coast of Peru.

In contrast to other animals, humans are the only animals that 'foul their own nests' and pollute their environment. In addition to the faeces produced by all animals, humans create additional organic waste, as well as other substances normally present in the environment but in significantly greater amounts, and distributed and concentrated across a wide variety of habitats. In contrast to animals, however, they also produce synthetic waste materials that are either non-biodegradable or which can only decompose very slowly. Finally, they produce toxic waste material in greater and more concentrated amounts than natural plant or animal toxins.

The main sources of human waste material are from the home, farm, place of work, transport and increasingly, in the modern world, from leisure activities. The variety of pollutants and their effects, however, is such that it is easier and more sensible to categorise them according to the form in which they occur and hence the way they are distributed in the environment. In this respect three main types of pollutant can be recognised:

1. Solid waste

Materials such as litter, trash and garbage are being produced in ever increasing amounts. Some, particularly waste food, is easily biodegradable; some materials including paper, metal, glass and plastics, are less easily decomposed or are non-biodegradable (see Plate 3.1). All could be recycled but, except in the case of larger amounts of scrap metal, it is generally considered uneconomic to do so. Accumulation and disposal of all kinds of

Plate 3.1 Motor vehicle dump or 'car cemetry', Whetstone, Leicestershire (Grid Ref. SP/557975). (*Aerofilms Ltd*)

garbage is a major environmental problem, and the increase in the use of packaging in cans, paper, cardboard and plastic containers has contributed to a phenomenal post-war rise in the per capita production of garbage in, particularly, the more affluent, developed countries of the world.

2. Gaseous waste

Among the most common pollutants are those emitted in a gaseous form or as minute particles of dust into the air. Most are substances naturally present in the environment but which are being released in additional and increasing amounts. These include compounds of carbon (CO, CO_2, hydrocarbons), sulphur-dioxide, and oxides of nitrogen. Most are the by-products of combustion or other chemical processes associated with domestic heating, garbage burning, such industries as iron and steel, oil-refining and associated petro- and chemical industries, and motor vehicle manufacture (the internal combustion engine). While air pollution, particularly over large urban/industrial regions, has become a problem only within the last two hundred years, the balance in source and type of pollutants has changed radically

Plate 3.2 Northern Outfall Sewage Works, River Lea, Essex (Grid Ref. TQ/396860) showing expansion of anaerobic and aerobic tanks to meet London's ever-growing need for sewage treatment and disposal facilities. (*Aerofilms Ltd*)

since the beginning of this century. Carbon compounds and particulate matter from domestic and industrial coal-burning has decreased with alternative sources of heating and new cleaner industrial techniques. The by-products of the chemical industries and, more particularly, of the automobile (hydro-carbons and nitrogen-oxides) have increased, and the latter have become the main sources of pollutants in large cities. The particulate yellow smog formerly more common in the older industrial areas has been replaced by the blue photo-chemical smog produced by a reaction between sunlight and automobile exhaust gases.

3. Effluent

The third type of waste is that produced and dispersed in a liquid or semi-liquid form. One of the main sources of water pollution is human sewage (see Plate 3.2). Although highly biodegradable and still, in various parts of the world, used as organic fertiliser (or night soil), the concentration of populations in towns and cities has created problems of sewage disposal. Effluent sewage is drained into rivers and into coastal waters. Unless treated (i.e. wholly or partially decomposed before disposal), the water becomes overloaded, oxygen is used up in decomposition at a rate greater than it can be replenished, and natural water purification cannot operate. The water hence becomes polluted with partially decomposed sewage, anaerobic bacteria, excess carbon-dioxide, ammonia, suspended solids and other substances which make it inimical to other types of life and unsafe for human consumption.

Figure 3.4. shows the effects of organic effluent on a river at the outfall and downstream. The biological oxygen demand (BOD) is high and the oxygen content of the water is low near the outfall, where large numbers of bacteria consume oxygen in the process of organic (sewage) decomposition. Variations in the levels of oxygen have, in particular, a direct effect on populations of different types of fauna; plants (algae, *Cladophora*) on the

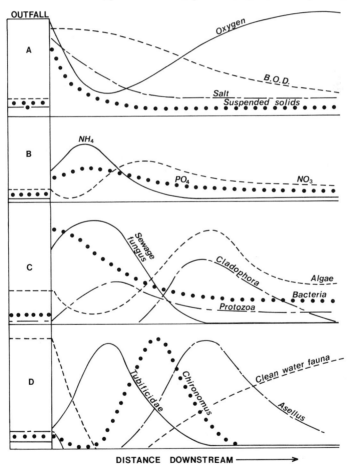

Figure 3.4   The effects of organic effluent upon a river at the outfall and downstream: A and B are physical and chemical changes; C micro-organisms; and D larger fauna; NH_4 = ammonium; NO_3 = nitrate; PO_4 = phosphate (After K. Mellanby, 1972)

other hand, are much less directly affected by oxygen levels and respond more to the availability of light and a suitable nutrient supply, such as phosphate (PO_4) or nitrate (NO_3).

Fauna include: (i) Sewage fungus, a tiny plant/animal organism which lives in sewage itself; (ii) Protozoa, microscopic single-celled animals moderately tolerant of low oxygen levels; (iii) Bacteria, very rudimentary microscopic organisms able to live in and to decompose sewage by consuming oxygen; several species are able to exist in anaerobic (oxygen deficient) conditions; (iv) *Tubificidae* (sludge worm), a small red worm tolerant of very low levels of oxygen; (v) *Chironomus* (red midge larvae), tolerant of low oxygen levels; (vi) *Asellus* (water louse (crustacean)), tolerant of moderately low oxygen levels, feeds on rotting plant life. Plants include: (i) *Cladophora*, branching, filamentous green algae attached to substrate; (ii) Algae, floating blue-green single-celled algae.

Manufacturing industries use vast quantities of water for processing, and are another important source of water pollution. The composition of industrial effluent varies with the type of processes involved. Among the dirtiest are those such as pulp and paper manufacturing, which use large quantities of detergents; among the commonest of these are organic compounds of phosphorus and chlorine. In addition, the increasing use of nitrogen-fertiliser, and of pesticides and herbicides in agriculture, have contributed to the load of chemical effluent entering the hydrological system. Some of these substances break down easily and rapidly, others do so more slowly. Others, particularly phosphates and nitrates (in domestic, agricultural and industrial effluents) are valuable nutrients. However, if the water becomes overloaded with nutrients, then growth of algal water plants can be accelerated to such an extent as to cut out sources of oxygen and light for the other organisms. Finally, there are some minerals, such as heavy metals like mercury, lead and arsenic, which are highly toxic to aquatic organisms and to humans who drink polluted water.

In polluting the environment, therefore, humans tend to create an environment not only less favourable for other organisms but also for themselves. Unlike other animals, they have created the problem of how to cope with, how to adapt to and survive in, their own environment.

F. Humans as Animals with a Sustained Rate of Population Growth

1. Human and animal population growth

Humans differ from other animals not only in being the most abundant single species of large land animal but in having a rapid and sustained rate of population growth. Within a relatively short evolutionary history of one or two million years, the total world population has, as far as can be ascertained, attained nearly four billions and, as Figure 3.5 illustrates, most of this increase has occurred within the last eight to ten thousand years.

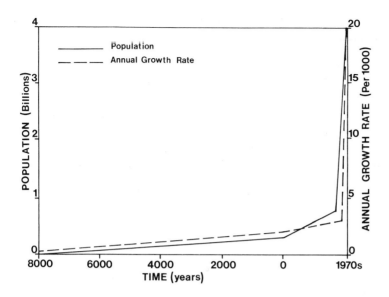

Figure 3.5   World population 8000 BC — 1970; size of population (continuous line); rate of increase (dashed line) (After A.J. Coale, 1974)

In common with all other animals, increase in population is dependent on the difference between crude birth rates and crude death rates and is characterised by what is called an *exponential growth*. This means that a population increases by a fixed percentage (e.g. rate) over any given time period. For example, at the recent rate of growth (1960–1970) of two per cent per annum, the world population would double every 35 years. The exponential growth rate can vary, but in animals other than humans it is not sustained.

In some, the rate of growth slows down and becomes relatively stable, fluctuating around a mean, at a certain limit determined by the *carrying capacity* of the environment. The graphical expression, shown in Figure 3.6, of this type of growth (which is also the most common in all biological processes) is the 'S' or sigmoid curve. With this type of development, growth

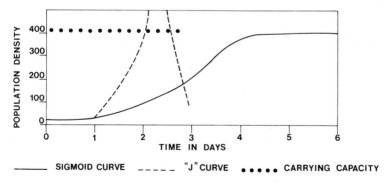

Figure 3.6   Sigmoid and 'J' population curves (After R.H. Whittaker, 1975)

starts slowly during the early stages, attains its maximum, exponential rate during the middle, mature phase, and then slows down to a constant or even declining rate during the stage of old age. However, as can also be seen, there are other animals which have a rapid and increasing exponential rate of population growth that continues until carrying capacity is exceeded, after which numbers decline very rapidly to low levels. They are, in particular, small organisms, such as insects, with a short life cycle which breed prolifically. Their growth is characterised by what is known as a 'J' curve with widely fluctuating and relatively unstable populations. Although some animal populations are more stable than others, all have upper limits which are determined either by competition, predation, territory or self-regulatory mechanisms. For instance, as shown in Figure 3.7, the oyster catcher has a fairly stable population. A variety of food sources, cockles, worms and mussels (as well as oysters!), buffers its population against environmental variations. However, very severe winters will reduce even this wide range of food supply and cause a certain amount of fluctuation in the oyster catcher population. On the other hand, population fluctuations in the hare and lynx are more marked. The greater amplitude of these latter swings is primarily the result of a close predator/prey relationship, although recent evidence has suggested that the quality of forage may strongly influence the population numbers of the hare (and, therefore, of the lynx). Populations of the pine moth are generally kept in check at low levels by a variety of ecological factors, e.g. bad winters, parasitic attack, lack of food supply. However,

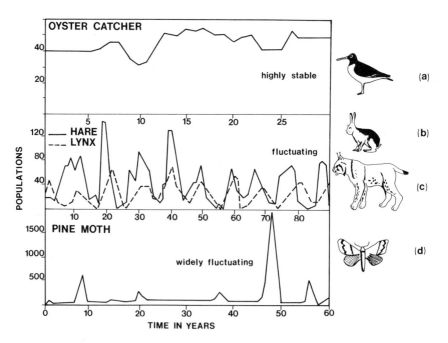

Figure 3.7   Types of fluctuation in animal populations (After R.H. Whittaker, 1975)

when factors such as favourable winters, lack of parasites and predators, good food supply, etc. are combined, high growth rates are achieved and very marked population peaks result.

In contrast, humans appear to differ from other animal populations in the long-term upward trend in their numbers, at a uniquely high and, until very recently, an increasing exponential rate. This is reflected in the rapid decrease in time taken for the world population to double itself (see Table 3.1).

Table 3.1 Decrease in doubling time of world population (After P.R. Ehrlich *et al.*, 1977).

Date	Estimated World Population (millions)	'Doubling Time' (years)
8000 BC	5	—
1650 AD	500	1500
1850	1000	200
1930	2000	80
1975	4000	45

This rapid increase in the rate of human population growth is, however, a relatively recent phenomenon. Until about three to four hundred years ago, it was more comparable to that of animal populations in being subject to more frequent and marked fluctuations and probably to comparable environmental constraints.

2. Stages in human population growth

Three stages in the growth of human population which can be correlated with technical and social evolution have been identified. They are: (a) the early food-collecting and rudimentary tool-making period when the human population was small and humans were little more than another predatory animal. Their numbers would have been limited, and have fluctuated in relation to the abundance and availability of food, and other environmental hazards. Average death rates were probably just below birth rates and increase in numbers was slow. (b) The stage marked by a shift from gathering and hunting to food producing took place during the so-called Neolithic Revolution initiated about 9000–7000 BC. It is assumed that more people could be supported as a result of an increased and more assured food supply. Numbers increased but probably stabilised at a higher level, with relatively little change in the ratio of birth to death rates, and fluctuations of population dependent on the occurrence of periodic famine, war and epidemic disease. Limits to population growth in these two stages are characterised by the classical Malthusian checks to population — famine, pestilence, disease and war. (c) The final state is that of modern scientific technical development during the last 400 years, which has been characterised by the rapid increase in the rate of world population growth (see Table 3.2).

Table 3.2   Rate of world population growth: approximate average annual per cent per decade (After P.R. Ehrlich *et al.*, 1977)

1650–1750	c. 0.3 per cent/annum
1750–1850	c. 0.5
1850–1950	c. 0.8
1950–1960	c. 1.8
1960–1970	c. 2.0

The main reason for this recent upsurge of population growth has been the decline in death rates and the increase in life expectancy, without a corresponding decline in birth rates. It has been the result, primarily, of human ability to control famine and disease through the development of scientific, particularly medical skills, combined with the evolution of modern agricultural techniques and greater food production. What Marston Bates has called the 'ecological death' of animals resulting from environmental hazards has been replaced by 'physiological death' from old age in humans. Total world population has, up to this decade, grown at an increasing exponential rate. In the period 1960—1970 it attained a maximum of 2 per cent per annum. Recently, however, there have been suggestions that it may be starting to decline.

3. Recent trends in human population growth

The beginning and continuation of this high and increasing exponential growth has varied from one part of the world to another. In the first part of the modern period of population growth, between 1650 and 1850, the rate was faster in the early industrialised area of Europe (including Russia) than anywhere else in the world except Asia (more particularly China in the period 1650—1750). In the more recent century (1850—1950), however, growth in Latin America (five times) and North America (six times) exceeded that in Europe (more than twice), Africa (more than twice) and Asia (more than twice) (Ehrlich *et al*, 1977). At the same time, however, as death rates were beginning to fall in the more developed countries, birth rates were also falling; in consequence, the rate of growth began to slow down. Figure 3.8 reveals very strikingly that the continued high exponential rate of world population growth, particularly since 1940, has been sustained by the phenomenal growth in the less developed world where decreasing death rates have been combined with high or increasing birth rates.

Opinions are divided as to what the future form of the world's population growth curve will be. Some maintain that it will stabilise at or below its present level and hence eventually assume the characteristic 'S' curve of most animal populations. Others believe it is an extended 'J' curve which will, in time, overshoot the carrying capacity of the biosphere and be followed by a catastrophic decline in population. In addition, as Figure 3.9 shows, per capita consumption of resources, consequent on growing affluence and de-

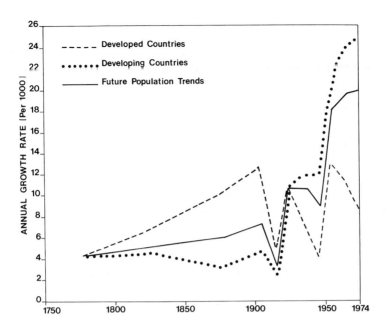

Figure 3.8 Annual population growth in the more developed, less developed countries and future world trends (After A.J. Coale, 1974)

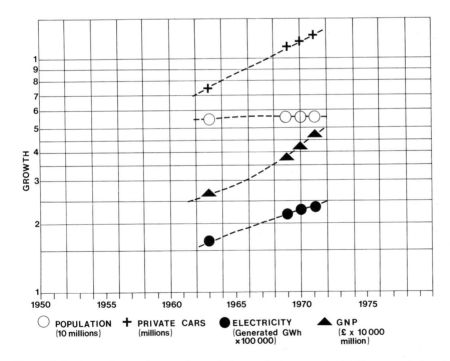

Figure 3.9 Annual growth rate of population, private cars, electricity generated and the Gross National Product (GNP) in Britain 1955–1972 (After Open University Press, 1974)

mand for consumer goods, particularly in the more developed countries, is increasing at a rate greater than that of population growth.

In the human-modified ecosystem 'run-away' or positive feedback mechanisms (refer back to Chapter 1) have increased and have become more pervasive than negative feedbacks, by which the ecosystem regulates itself. The 'trigger' to positive feedback has been the increase of human births over deaths. This has lead to the phenomenal and increasing population which previous negative feedback mechanisms can no longer control effectively. In addition, the effect of human activity either in terms of what is being added to or subtracted from the ecosystem, is bringing about changes at a scale and rate which 'Doomsday' exponents predict will disrupt the world ecosystem or life-support system completely. Figure 3.10 shows a predicted relationship between exponential population growth, resource availability and use, and environmental pollution. It is based on computer calculations made by a team of scientists from the Massachussets Institute of Technology headed by Professor Meadows.

The problem is made more difficult because the technical evolution of humans has been more rapid than that of their biological, social or cultural development. It should, however, be borne in mind, that since humans first emerged as a distinct species of animal their role in the ecosystem has not

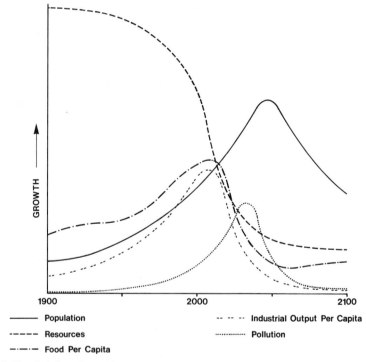

Figure 3.10   Predicted world trends in population growth, resource use, consumption of food per capita, industrial output per capita and industrial pollutants (After D.H. Meadows *et al.*, 1972)

changed so much in kind, as in intensity and geographical extent. The aim of the next four chapters is to demonstrate how humans have modified and, in some cases, disrupted the structure and function of the ecosystem.

ASSIGNMENT

Study Figures 3.11 and 3.12. Compare the two maps and comment on the relationships between density and rate of population growth.

Key Ideas

A. Humans as the ecological dominants
1. Ecological dominance is dependent on the ability of organisms to compete more successfully than others for the essentials of life.
2. Human ecological dominance is related to intelligence linked to population numbers.

B. Humans as tool making animals
1. Ecological dominance has been attained through the ability to use and make tools.
2. The early use of fire has assured humans of an ecological dominance, independent of, and out of proportion to, their numbers.
3. The use of tools has allowed humans to cultivate their own food.

C. Humans as robber animals
1. Humans make greater use of the ecosphere than any other organism.
2. Humans shorten food chains by eliminating those plants and animals (the weeds and pests) which compete for and diminish the particular food supply they have produced.
3. Humans tend to overexploit ecosystems by overcropping and overgrazing.
4. Ecosystems are exploited for non-consumptive purposes.

D. Humans as agents of evolution
1. Humans have exerted a powerful influence on the course of evolution as a result of:
   (a) the domestication of plants and animals
   (b) the creation of new habitats
   (c) the worldwide dispersal of plants and animals.

E. Humans as dirty animals
1. Humans are the only animals that pollute their own habitat.
2. The main sources of their pollutants are domestic, agriculture, manufacturing, transport and recreation.
3. The three main types of pollutants are solid, gaseous and liquid wastes.

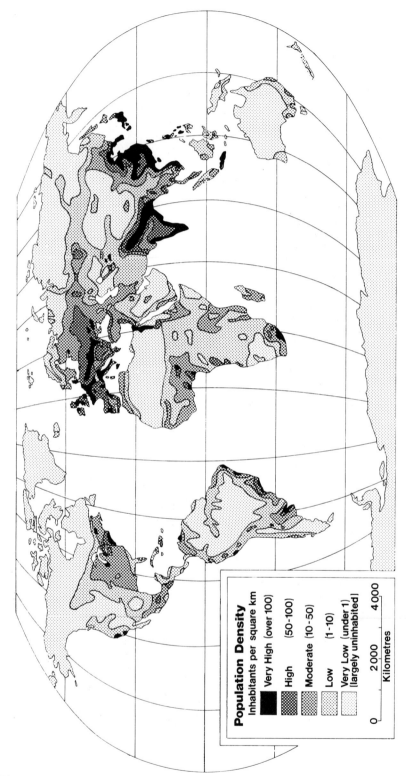

Figure 3.11 Density of world populations (After G.T. Trewartha, 1969)

Population Density
Inhabitants per square km

Very High (over 100)

High (50-100)

Moderate (10-50)

Low (1-10)

Very Low (under 1)
(largely uninhabited)

0   2000   4000
Kilometres

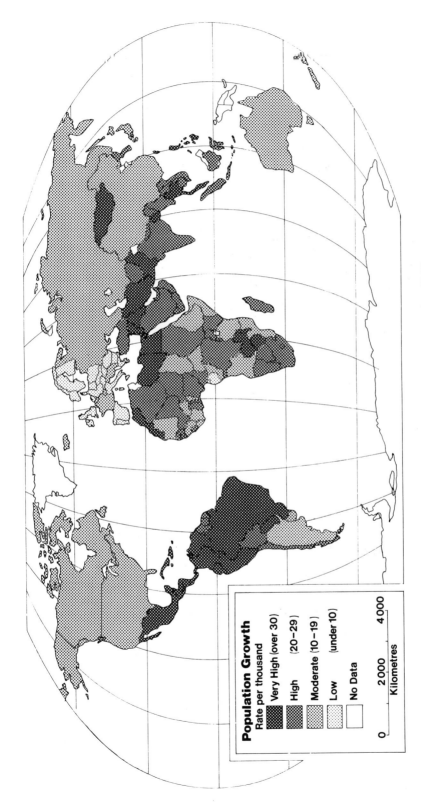

Figure 3.12 World distribution of the rate of population increase (After G.T. Trewartha, 1969)

Population Growth
Rate per thousand

■ Very High (over 30)
▨ High   (20 – 29)
▦ Moderate (10 – 19)
▨ Low   (under 10)
□ No Data

Kilometres
0   2000   4000

F. Humans as animals with a sustained rate of population growth
1. Human population growth, in contrast to that of other animals, has been characterised by an increasingly high exponential rate.
2. The characteristics of human population growth can be related to technical and social evolution.
3. At present, high exponential rates of world population growth are maintained more by the less developed than the more developed countries.
4. Increasing population growth is associated with increasingly high rates of resource use.
5. If human population growth continues unabated, it may be ultimately controlled by the carrying capacity of the biosphere.

Additional Activities

1. (a) Give an example of a domesticated plant or animal which has or has had: a sacred; sacrificial; medical; patriotic; ornamental; narcotic purpose. (See *Plants and Civilization* by H.G. Baker, 1964, and *Animals for Man* by J.C. Bowman, 1977)
   (b) What morphological features enable the following plants to survive or regenerate after fire: heather; bilberry; rose-bay willow herb; cork oak; ponderosa pine; lodgepole pine; acacias? (See Chapter 7 in *Plants and Environment* by R.F. Daubenmire, 1974)

2. *Field Project*

In a selected area:
(a) Identify, classify and map man-made habitats.
(b) Select one* for detailed study under the following headings:
   (i) Date of, and reason for, origin;
   (ii) Present use;
   (iii) Describe the characteristics of the physical habitat (where relevant measure pH of substrate, oxygen and suspended solid content of water, depth and texture of weathered mineral matter, depth of organic layer);
   (iv) Identify and, where possible, map the distribution of dominant types of plant and animal; and make a list of any others found;
   v) Conclusion:
      a) What features of the physical habitat might account for the presence of the organisms?
      b) How far are these organisms characteristic of the habitat?
(*recommended in the interests of comparative studies that two or more habitats be chosen by any one group)

3. Using the data shown in Figure 3.9:
   (a) Examine the general slope of the graphs. Make a quantitative com-

parison of the rates of growth of the four items shown. Rank the four variables in order of relative magnitude.
(b) Calculate the absolute amounts of increase of the four factors over the given period.
(c) Calculate: (1) the absolute growth in motor cars per capita; and (2) the absolute growth in electricity generated per capita over the same period.
(d) To what extent do you think that stabilisation of population in Britain would solve the problems arising from exponential industrial growth?

4. (a) Using the data in Table 3.3, plot on logarithmic paper similar graphs

Table 3.3 Rate of growth of population, private cars, electricity generated and the Gross National Product (GNP) 1950–1972 in New Zealand, Nigeria and India (After Open University Press, 1974)

Year	Population (millions)	Number of private cars (thousands)	Electricity generated (GW h)	GNP
A. *New Zealand*				($NZ × 10^6$)
1950	1.9	251	3125	1396
1960	2.4	502	5200	2622
1970	2.8	862	13750	5432
1972	2.9	968	15200	6260
B. *India*				(Crores)
1951	361	148	5858	n.d.
1956	n.d.	188	9662	n.d.
1961	442	256	16937	14029
1965	487	342	29563	21176
1969	537	443	47434	30329
1970	550	n.d.	n.d.	33019
C. *Nigeria*		+		(£ N)
1950	n.d.	n.d.	n.d.	514
1951	n.d.	n.d.	78	n.d.
1952	29	n.d.	n.d.	n.d.
1955	n.d.	14	n.d.	n.d.
1957	n.d.	n.d.	n.d.	910
1960	n.d.	31	n.d.	n.d.
1962	n.d.	n.d.	649	1181
1963	43	n.d.	n.d.	n.d.
1967	n.d.	48	n.d.	1639
1970	51	n.d.	n.d.	n.d.
1972	n.d.	n.d.	1509	2899

n.d. = no data
GNP = Gross National Product uncorrected for inflation
Crores (1 crore = 10^7 rupees: 20 rupees ≈ £1)
+ Fall off in 1967 probably due to onset of civil war

to those in Figure 3.9 for each of the three countries shown.

(b) Use the method shown in Assignment 3 to analyse the similarities and differences indicated between the less developed and the more developed countries.

5. (a) Locate and map all types of sewage treatment plants in your local area.

(b) Classify the plants in terms of the nature of the processes involved.

(c) Comment on the significance of your findings for water pollution.

4 Ecosystem Components

A. Ecosystem Components and Humans

All ecosystems are made up of two basic types of components: abiotic or inorganic, and biotic or organic.

1. Abiotic components

These include (a) air which, above or below ground, is the main source of oxygen, carbon-dioxide and nitrogen; (b) water which occurs as liquid or vapour in the air and in the soil; and (c) mineral elements produced by the weathering of rocks, which are the source of certain essential nutrients such as phosphorus, potassium, calcium and magnesium. Together these determine the nature of the physical environment.

2. Biotic components

These include living plants and animals (total biomass, see page 14) and dead or decaying organic material (DOM).

Organisms which occupy a particular habitat will be those capable of 'living together'. The dominant plants, as we have already noted, comprise the bulk of the biomass. They modify microclimatic and soil conditions to a greater extent than other plants. Only those species which can tolerate the modified habitat conditions will be able to accompany them. In fact, the interaction between the organic and inorganic components is such that organisms tend to produce their own particular habitats somewhat in the way that humans create distinctive homes within the physical framework of a house.

3. The effect of humans

As has been indicated in the previous chapter, humans are now the most powerful agents of change in the ecosystem. Their impact can be accidental or deliberate, direct or indirect. In some instances their activities have altered the volume, composition and structure of the organic components and, consequently, the nature of the physical habitat. In others, they have so modified the physical environment as to bring about changes in organic matter. However, the relationship between organisms and their physical environment is so close that it is almost impossible to understand the organic in isolation from the inorganic components of an ecosystem. Any change in the composition and structure of one will inevitably have repercussions on that of the other. It is, therefore, rather artificial to separate cause from effect under these circumstances. However, in order to illustrate the implications of human disturbance of ecosystem components, examples of changes initiated in both the organic and inorganic components, will be illustrated in the following sections.

ASSIGNMENT

Suggest, in general terms, how the following atmospheric conditions within a mature deciduous wood might differ from those in the open: light intensity; temperature; humidity; air movement. Keep a note of your suggestions and compare them later with Figure 4.1.

B. Change in Biomass

1. Deforestation

One of the most dramatic and extensive changes in the volume of the earth's biomass has been effected by deforestation. It has been estimated that perhaps something of the order of 35–40 per cent of the original forest and woodland cover has been removed either directly by felling or burning, or indirectly by the prevention of seedling regeneration by either grazing and/or burning. The pre-existing forest cover has been replaced by a smaller and often more variable biomass composed of either agricultural crops, grass, heath or scrub land, second-growth forest or human-established plantations. Until recently, the impact of deforestation has been greatest in temperate latitudes, the Mediterranean lands and in monsoon Asia. In China, for instance, there is evidence that despoilation of forests was well advanced as early as the third century B.C. Today, the rate at which inroads are taking place in the two largest remaining forest areas, the north boreal and the tropical rain forests respectively, is attracting growing attention and concern.

Microclimatic and hydrological effects of deforestation

Apart from the reduction in the flora and fauna formerly associated with the forest ecosystem, the most serious direct effect of deforestation is change in microclimatic conditions. Figure 4.1 gives some idea of the ways in which microclimatic conditions inside a forest tend to differ from those in the

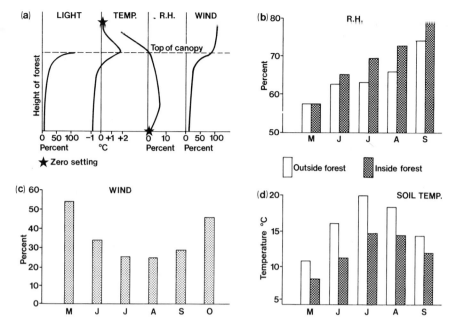

Figure 4.1 Microclimatic conditions inside and outside a forest: (a) solar radiation, temperature, relative humidity and wind speed below and above a solid forest canopy during a summer day, graphs show deviation from a set point (★); (b) average relative humidity measured at 5 pm inside and outside a deciduous forest during the summer months; (c) ratio of average daily wind speed inside and outside a deciduous forest measured at 6 m above the ground; (d) average daily soil temperature at a depth of 15 cm inside and outside a deciduous forest (After H. Riehl, 1978)

open, above and beyond it. Obviously the extent of change will vary, particularly according to the density and composition of the forest in question together with the season of the year, the time of day and whether mean or extreme values are taken. However, generally speaking, wind speed, light conditions, the maximum and the range of air and soil temperature tend to decrease, while relative humidity, average and minimum air and soil temperature tend to increase inside, compared with outside, a forest. One of the most important and far-reaching implications of deforestation is its effect on the hydrological cycle or the circulation of water between the atmosphere and the land and water bodies. The effects of forest removal on the routes by which water circulates are shown in Figure 4.2. The amounts by which the inputs and outputs of water will be changed as a result of deforestation will depend on: (a) the size of area affected; (b) the nature of the remaining ground-surface vegetation; (c) the nature and amount of soil organic matter; (d) the prevailing macroclimatic conditions; (e) the slope of the land; and (f) the soil texture.

In some cases deforestation can result in increased soil wetness, even saturation, and the consequent development of peat, because in the oxygen

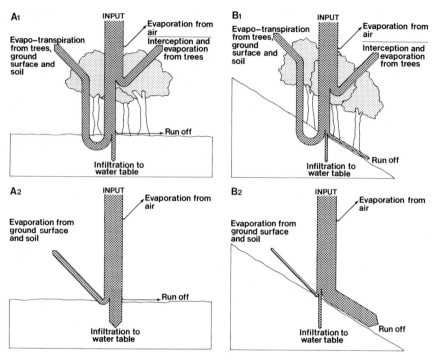

Figure 4.2   Hydrological cycle (1) before and (2) after deforestation; (A) flat ground (B) sloping ground

deficient conditions organic decomposition is retarded. For instance, the widespread occurrence of peat and peaty soils in Scotland has been attributed to the clearance of a former woodland cover in association with high rainfall and low evaporation. In other cases, deforestation may be followed by greatly increased surface run-off, accelerated soil erosion and an increased frequency of flooding in lowland areas. Disruption of the hydrological cycle can lead, over a long period of time, to changes which may either be difficult or impossible to reverse. For instance, destruction of the former forest cover in the Mediterranean uplands has resulted in increased surface run-off and soil erosion exacerbated by torrential rain. In addition, infiltration has been reduced and surface evaporation increased. This has produced soil aridity which, combined with lack of shelter, has made it difficult for tree seedlings to establish themselves. These soil and microclimatic changes, together with grazing pressures, have resulted in the replacement of the previously existing evergreen-oak forest by either a scrub (garrigue or maquis) or a poor grassland ecosystem.

2. Fire

As extensive as deforestation, though less drastic and more indirect in its effects on biomass, is the occurrence of fire. The use of fire is nearly as old as the human race. As has been noted in the preceding chapter, fire was the earliest tool by which humans not only modified, but deliberately managed ecosystems for their own particular ends. One of the principal uses of fire has been, and still is, to regulate the amount of biomass that can be directly used as forage for domestic or game animals. Periodic burning of the 'natural' vegetation is a long-established practice in many parts of the world, particularly in the tropical grasslands, and in heaths and moorlands in Britain. The aim in both areas is the same: to clear plant litter and reduce the proportion of less nutritious woody and fibrous tissues and increase that of the more nutritious and palatable young green foliage.

(a) The effect of burning

The effect of regular and controlled burning is to give a competitive advantage to more fire-resistant species, i.e. the *pyrophytes* (see page 35). Among these are plants whose seeds have hard protective seed coats. Some seeds will only open and germinate after a fire, either because the high temperatures produced are necessary to crack the seeds or seed-containers, such as cones, or because the fire leaves a warm seedbed which promotes rapid germination temporarily free of competition. Some plants have fire-resistant foliage and/or bark. Others have underground stems or root stocks which carry overwintering buds whose growth is stimulated by the removal of the above ground parts of the plant. In contrast, other species — particularly trees and shrubs — are very vulnerable to destruction because of the volume of inflammable woody material, and unprotected seedlings.

(b) Heather burning (muirburn)

One of the most important consequences of fire has been to produce and to maintain types of ecosystems which would not otherwise have existed. An outstanding example is that of heaths and moorlands in Europe and more particularly in Britain. The dominant component is a woody shrub, heather (*Calluna vulgaris*). It has a wide range of tolerance of climate and soil. Under natural conditions it can grow to a maximum altitude of about 500– 600 m, depending on environmental conditions. Originally, it was probably a widespread but minor element of forest and woodland on acid soils. However, it is unlikely that it would have dominated many areas other than those where exposure or extreme soil conditions inhibited tree growth.

The spread of heather-dominated areas started early with the clearance of forests and was further aided by the increase in number of domestic grazing animals (particularly cattle and sheep) which very effectively prevented the regeneration of tree seedlings. Heather, and many of its associated species, is a particularly valuable evergreen forage plant. It is the staple diet of the red grouse and one of the major food sources of the hardier breeds of hill sheep (e.g. the Scottish Blackface). For at least 200 years in Highland Scotland, and probably longer elsewhere, burning has been the main means of

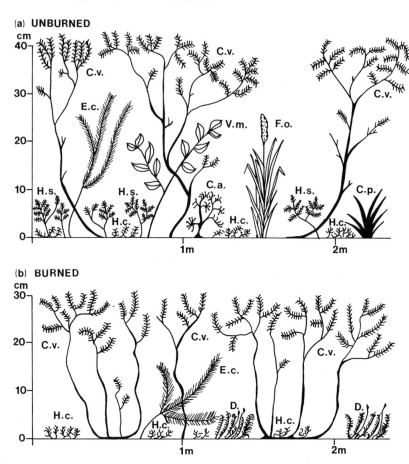

Figure 4.3   Composition and structure of (a) an unburned and (b) a burned heather stand (After C.H. Gimingham, 1972)

C.a. = *Cladonia arbuscula* (lichen)
C.p. = *Carex pilulifera* (sedge)
C.v. = *Calluna vulgaris* (heather)
D.   = *Dicranium scoparium* (moss)
E.n. = *Empetrum nigrum* (crowberry)
E.c. = *Erica cinerea* (bell heather)
F.o. = *Festuca ovina* (grass sheep's fescue)
H.c. = *Hypnum cupressiforme* (moss)
H.s. = *Hylocomium splendens* (moss)
V.m. = *Vaccinium myrtillus* (bilberry)
V.v. = *Vaccinium vitis-idaea* (whortleberry)

maintaining heather as one of the dominant forage plants of rough grazings in Britain.

The object of burning is to keep as much of the heather as possible at its most productive stage; that is, when the proportion of edible green shoots is at its highest. The total area burnt in any one year depends on the length of the rotation. It is usually done in small areas of about one hectare, in order to provide sufficient cover as well as feeding within the territory of each pair of breeding grouse. The result is the distinctive patchwork quilt pattern of heather at various stages of growth after burning (see Plate 6.1). Repeated burning tends eventually to produce a virtual monoculture of heather. Figure 4.3 illustrates the differences in composition and structure between a stand of burned and unburned heather. The result is an ecosystem which owes its distinctive composition and structure to burning. In this instance fire is the main factor controlling or limiting biomass development. It has been shown, in areas where grazing and burning have been discontinued, that heather moorland can eventually be colonised by trees.

ASSIGNMENTS

1. *Study Figure 4.1. Make a note of and account for the ways in which micro-climatic conditions inside forests differ from those outside.*
2. *Refer back to Figure 4.2 and explain the changes in relative importance of the routes in the hydrological cycle before and after deforestation.*
3. *Study Figure 4.3 and tabulate the differences in (a) the composition and (b) the structure between the stands of burned and unburned heather.*

C. Change in Dead Organic Matter (DOM) and Soil

1. Change in DOM

It has already been noted (see page 16) that the amount of DOM can equal or, more frequently, exceed that of the combined above and below ground biomass in many ecosystems. Human impact on this important component has been as great, though perhaps not so obvious, as that on the plant biomass. Deforestation, burning, grazing and cultivation have all served to reduce both the main source (i.e. the plant biomass) and the amount of DOM. In some cases, the rate of organic decomposition has been accelerated because of its exposure to air, light and heat. In others, it has been completely removed by erosion, following woodland clearance, over-burning, and/or overgrazing. In addition, continuous monoculture has completely depleted many cultivated soils of their former store of DOM. Nevertheless, there are situations where humans have, either accidentally or deliberately, increased the DOM in an ecosystem. For instance, the build-up of peat as a result of deforestation and consequent soil saturation has already been noted. The very liberal application of human sewage to Chinese paddy fields and the accumulation of organic matter promoted by a grass crop are other examples. However, of particular ecological significance is the effect on soil formation of the changes in DOM caused by the substitution of one type of vegetation cover for another.

2. Change in soil type

The effect of DOM changes are very strikingly illustrated in the woodland —heather moorland—bracken sequence characteristic of many upland areas in Britain, where the existing heather moorland has replaced a former oak/birch or pine cover.

(a) Mull humus soil

In the case of the oak/birch woodland, a relatively large quantity of nutrient-rich DOM would have been produced. Because of the large population of burrowing animals, especially worms, the DOM would have been efficiently broken down and incorporated with the mineral particles in the soil. This could support a large fauna of other soil animals and, in consequence, be relatively easily and rapidly decomposed to a mild, slightly acid *mull* type of *humus*. Humus, the end product of the process of decomposition, is an amorphous, black to brown organic material of very complex chemical composition. Its properties, particularly of the richer mull humus, are very comparable to those of clay particles. It is a finely divided colloidal substance capable of retaining both water and nutrients in the soil.

The presence of this mull humus helps to bind mineral particles together. It also reduces the effect of *leaching* or washing out of the more soluble nutrients (calcium, nitrogen, phosphorus, potassium) by water percolating down through the soil. The physical characteristics of the resulting mull humus soil are illustrated in Figure 4.4a.

(b) Mull to mor soils

The replacement of the oak/birch woodland ecosystem by a heather monoculture, such as has been described in the preceding section, has two important consequences. First is a marked reduction in the amount of DOM and second is the production of a particularly tough nutrient deficient, acid plant litter. As a result, there is an absence of worms—not only is the soil population smaller than in the richer mull, but the more efficient bacterial decomposers are replaced by a higher proportion of the less efficient fungi.

Decomposition is slow and incomplete and consequently dark, acid, peaty *mor* humus is produced. In the absence of worms, it is not mixed with the mineral matter below. During its formation, strong organic acids are released. These accelerate leaching and render iron oxides soluble; they also bring about *podsolisation*. This is the process by which clay/humus particles are both physically and chemically broken down. They become mobile and the aluminium oxides released go into solution and can, in turn, be leached through the soil.

The upper mineral layers (horizons) of the soil are, therefore, intensely leached, not only of the more soluble nutrients, but also of normally less soluble and mobile materials such as organic acids, clay particles and iron and aluminium compounds. The materials leached from the upper horizons are eventually deposited further down or are removed completely from the soil profile. Figure 4.4b summarises the characteristics of a mor humus, podsolic soil resulting from these processes. In some cases, the deposition of

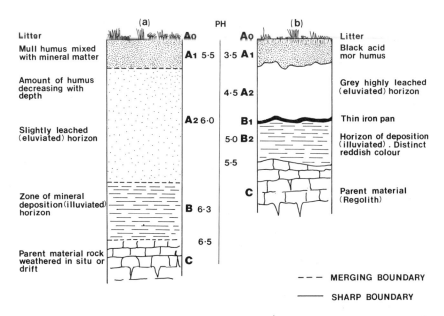

Figure 4.4   Characteristic profiles of (a) mull (acid brown forest soil, brown earth or inceptisol) and (b) mor (podsol or spodosol) soil with iron pan

iron, together with humic matter in the B-horizon, can be so concentrated as to form a thin, hard, indurated or cemented layer called an *iron pan*. This can very effectively block root penetration and the heather root system becomes concentrated in the DOM layer. Perhaps more seriously, the pan can impede the downward drainage of water. This can lead to soil saturation in the upper horizons and, eventually, to the accumulation of peat, resulting in a peaty podsol with iron pan soil.

(c) *Mor to mull soils*

There are, however, many areas where, as a result of overburning and accelerated soil erosion, the bracken fern (*Pteridium aquilinum*) has invaded formerly heather-dominated moorland. There is now sufficient evidence to demonstrate that the DOM produced by bracken can check the process of podsolisation, and produce a soil more comparable to that which would originally have formed under an oak/birch woodland. Figure 4.5 illustrates the main soil changes involved in this process.

Bracken litter, although acid and nutrient deficient, is not as tough and fibrous as that of heather. However, it produces a much larger amount of DOM annually. This decomposes relatively rapidly and has a lower water-holding capacity than that of the rather spongy mor humus produced by heather. The large, deeply ramifying bracken rhizomes facilitate soil aeration and drainage, and mechanically break down the iron pan. They also contribute a large quantity of DOM below the soil surface, particularly in

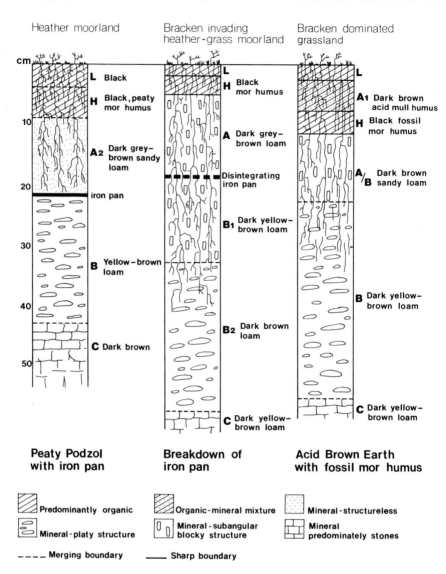

Figure 4.5   Modification of heather dominated mor soils by colonising bracken (After J. Mitchell, 1973)

the formerly depleted A-horizon of the heather podsol. Since the rhizomes penetrate to greater depths than heather roots, they can draw on nutrients available in the lower soil horizons. The result is the eventual transformation of what was a podsol into a slightly acid brown forest soil.

ASSIGNMENTS

1. (a) *With the aid of Figure 4.4, compare acid brown forest soils with podsols under the following headings: general depth of soil; acidity or pH variation; type, amount and distribution of humus; nature of horizon*

Table 4.1 Characteristics of mull and mor humus (After P. Duchaufour, 1965)

Type	Horizon	pH	Carbon: Nitrogen ratio	Initial mineralisation	Humification	Conditions of formation
Calcareous Mull	A₀ very thin A₁ thick, black-brown	neutral 7.5–8.5	10	rapid	Slow with good production clay/humus complex	Grass on chalk/ limestone; chernozem soils
Forest Mull	A₁ fairly thick, grey-brown	5.5	< 20 (12–15)	rapid	Fairly slow; fair development humus complex	Deciduous woodland
Moder (transitional)	A₀ 2–3 cm A₁ 10 cm (black sharp boundary)	4.0–5.0	(15–25)	moderate	Limited development humus complex	Deciduous forest on acid material
Mor	A₀ 5–20 cm A₁ 2–5 cm (black sharp boundary)	3.5–4.5	A₀ 30–40 A₁ 25	slow	Slow with production of organic acids	Coniferous forest; heather and moorland

*boundary; nature and degree of leaching; nature and degree of miner-
al deposition; aeration and drainage.*

(*b*) *Which soil offers the better medium for plant growth? Suggest why.*

2. *With the aid of the text and Table 4.1, analyse the differences between
mull, moder and mor humus.*

D. Change in Inorganic Components

1. Microclimatic modifications

The preceding section should have made it clear that any changes humans
make to the organic components of the ecosystem will have repercussions on
the inorganic components. They also deliberately set out to modify or alter
the physical habitat for particular purposes. For instance, many efforts have
been made to control the condition of the atmosphere. The greatest success,
however, has been on a small scale near the surface of the ground.

Shelter belts

One of the main means by which the microclimate is deliberately modified is
by the use of trees to provide shelter and/or shade (see Plate 4.1). In Britain
the need for shelter is usually the greater. Lines or blocks of trees (shelter
belts) are purposely designed to check high wind speeds which increase
evapo-transpiration, reduce air temperatures and may cause physical damage to plants and constructions. The composition, structure and shape of a
shelter belt will depend on its particular purpose. A shelter belt can reduce
wind speed in two ways: the air which flows parallel to the ground is deflected up and over the belt, and its speed is consequently reduced by the
frictional drag and the eddies that occur in contact with the surface of the
trees; and, air flow is slowed down in its passage through a stand of trees.
The effectiveness with which it will check wind speed is, therefore, dependent on four main characteristics: penetrability; height; shape; length.

The penetrability of a shelter belt is determined by its density (a function
of the types of tree as well as their spacing) and its width. Figure 4.6
illustrates the effect of varying degrees of penetrability on wind speed and
direction. The extent of the area sheltered is related largely to the height of
the belt. There is a known relationship between the height of a shelter belt
and the distance in its lee which will be affected. The ratio is 1:30; that is to
say, the distance sheltered will be about 30 times the height of the belt.
There are some cases where the ratio can be as high as 1:40–50 (Figure
4.7), and it can vary particularly with exceptionally high wind speeds. Width
obviously will reinforce the effect of penetrability and height; this is, however, usually determined by the availability of land and degree of exposure.

The shape and, more particularly, the cross profile of the belt is also important. Experiments have shown that a slope of about 20° on the wind-

Plate 4.1 Shelter belts (mainly Cyprus) across the Rhône valley in the Department of Bouches du Rhône, France, to protect horticultural crops from the desiccating northerly Mistral wind. (*French Government Tourist Board*)

ward side will produce the maximum effect. Finally, length must also be considered, because, if the belt is too short, the eddies and turbulence which occur where the air flows around its sides may increase wind speed. To cut down the effect of gustiness to a minimum, a length of at least 12 times the height is considered necessary. Linear shelter belts, at right angles to either

1. Impenetrable fence or wall

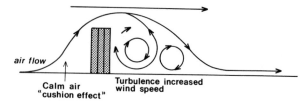

air flow

Calm air
"cushion effect"

Turbulence increased
wind speed

2. All evergreen

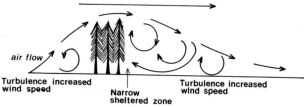

air flow

Turbulence increased
wind speed

Narrow
sheltered zone

Turbulence increased
wind speed

3. Mixed evergreen and deciduous

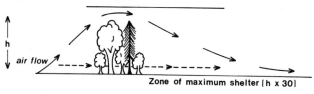

h

air flow

Zone of maximum shelter (h x 30)

4. Winter deciduous

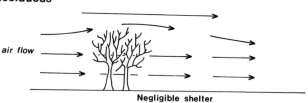

air flow

Negligible shelter

Figure 4.6 Effect of shelterbelt density and composition on wind direction and velocity

the prevailing or strongest winds, are a common feature of exposed upland farm land, and in lowland or fruit growing areas. In the latter case, the flowering stage is vital to successful fruit production and can be very vulnerable to only a moderate or low degree of exposure. More compact rectangular blocks of trees tend to be used when the aim is shelter for stock, and where total length and aspect is more important than the width of the sheltered zone.

ASSIGNMENT

From Figures 4.6 and 4.7, what can you deduce about the relationship between shelter belt thickness and wind speed reduction?

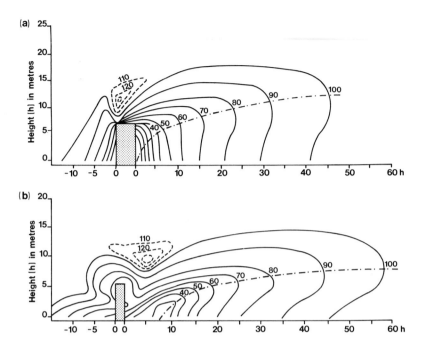

Figure 4.7   Percentage wind speed change from undisturbed conditions at the same level caused by (a) a thick and (b) thin forest belt at Kirov, USSR. Distance along ground, expressed as multiples of forest belt height (h) (After R.F. Munn, 1966)

E. Agro-Ecosystems

1. General nature of agro-ecosystems

Human impact on ecosystem components is greatest in those which are deliberately managed in order to maximise the output of a particular product. In this respect, the effect is most marked in crop production. What have become known as *agro-ecosystems* are the most highly developed and widespread of all man-made ecosystems (see Plate 4.2).

The dominant components are plants (and animals) selected, propagated, tended and harvested by humans for a particular purpose. In comparison to unmanaged ecosystems, their composition and structure are simple. The plant biomass is composed of stands usually dominated by one major crop plant within well-defined field boundaries. While one crop may be under-sown with another, as in the case of grass under cereals or field crops or grass under orchard trees, there is normally only one layer or strata formed by the crop itself (see Figure 2.2).

Diversity of composition, however, can vary. In tropical garden cultivation, a wide range of different food crops may be intersown on one small area; this has the advantage of providing a continuous food supply in areas with a year-long growing season and where, in the humid tropics, the basic

Plate 4.2 Man-made land reclaimed from the sea in 1942 on the Noord Oost Polder, Netherlands. (*Aerofilms Ltd*)

food crops such as yam and cassava are not easy to store. It also furnishes a reasonably continuous protective cover for the soil, which is particularly susceptible to erosion in these areas. Modern, technically advanced agro-ecosystems are, in contrast, characterised by very large areas often devoted to the cultivation of a particular variety or strain of one crop. In most cultivated areas of the world, selection has favoured crop plants that give a high return of storable material and which will also satisfy basic human nutritional requirements for energy (carbohydrates) and growth (protein). The number of species which have been selected is remarkably few given the diversity of the world's organic resources. Only some eleven plant species account for about 80 per cent of the world's food supply. Among these, the cereals have dominated the development of agriculture. They provide over 50 per cent of the world's production of protein and energy; over 75 per cent if grains fed to animals are included. In comparison, field crops, grass/legume forage crops and tree crops cultivated for food or forage, represent a relatively small proportion of the total agricultural biomass.

2. Crop plants

A high proportion of crop plants are annuals and are also light-demanding (i.e. they are *heliophytic*). They are characterised by high yields of that part of the plant humans wish to use, be it the seed, the leaves, stem, root or fruit. The biomass of the standing crop at harvest time is comparatively small, particularly in areas formerly forested. However, in those regions where the original vegetation was grassland, the cultivated biomass is greater at its maximum period of growth. The crop biomass contrasts in two other ways with that of previously existing ecosystems: first, the proportion above ground is usually greater than that below; and second, except in those parts of the world where multiple cropping is possible, seasonal variation is normally greater in cultivated than in non-cultivated ecosystems, with the result that the bare soil can be exposed for several months of the year.

As indicated in Chapter 3, the most important food crops, the cereals, have undergone a very long period of domestication. Many have no known wild counterparts. They have evolved as a result of selection and breeding. Many could not propagate themselves without human aid and, hence, could not survive in the wild. Crop breeding has been directed primarily towards the production of varieties and strains which will give as high a yield as possible under prevailing environmental and, particularly, climatic conditions. In recent years, much publicity has been given to 'The Green Revolution' — involving the production of very high yielding hybrid varieties of rice and wheat adapted to the particular environmental conditions in the poor, hungry areas of the Third World. Also, plant breeding has been directed towards the production of machine crops, i.e. those adapted by reason of uniform height, flowering, fruiting or seeding, as the case may be, to mechanised cultivation, harvesting and packaging. One of the principal consequences is that crop stands have become simplified to such an extent that areas large enough to make use of expensive machinery are now dominated not just by one particular crop but by varieties so highly bred as to be genetically uniform. All the members of the population may be equally cold, drought or disease resistant. In other words, they all have the same range of tolerance to environmental conditions and changes which exceed their limit of tolerance will be disastrous to the whole population. Agro-ecosystems, in contrast to unmanaged ecosystems, are characterised by a 'man-made' physical habitat. Cultivation involves a wide range of physical processes including tillage, planting, fertilising, draining, irrigation, weeding and finally harvesting, all of which are designed to give optimum conditions for crop production.

3. Weeds

In creating agro-ecosystems humans have also provided habitats for other organic components. These are the weeds and pests of cultivation. Both weeds and pests can only really be defined as organisms existing where they are not wanted. Both are exclusively associated with humans and their activities; they occupy habitats created partially or wholly by them, the most extensive of which is that produced by cultivation.

Weeds have a long history. They appear to be particularly well adapted to open, exposed, nutrient deficient and physically stressed conditions such as occur naturally on coasts, river banks and screes. Among the characteristics shared by many weed plants are high seed production, successful germination, an ability to spread vegetatively and a tolerance of a wide range of environmental conditions. Cultivated ground has extended their potential habitat and provided one in which, because of nutrient enrichment, they can grow with even greater vigour than before. Indeed, the one characteristic common to all weeds is their ability to survive in cultivated land where they are disturbed and often battered, by machines as well as natural agents.

A considerable number of weeds are virtually cosmopolitan and their dispersal is, to a very large extent, a direct result of human activities and the transportation of agricultural materials from one place to another. The most important means of weed dispersal is as contaminants in seed crops. While they are characteristic components of agro-ecosystems, weeds compete with crop plants for space, water, light and nutrients, and some produce toxic substances. Weeds also act as hosts for pests and diseases. As a result, an integral process in cultivation is that of 'weeding', orginally involving considerable labour and now, in advanced agricultural technologies, the use of chemical herbicides.

4. Pests

Pests are the animal counterpart of weeds. The two most important groups are the parasitic fungi, which cause serious diseases in cereals and fruit trees, and the insects. The increase in pest populations has been, in the first place, the direct result of large-scale monoculture of the crops on which these particular organisms depend. Another contributory factor has been the accidental transport of pests from their areas of origin to those with an abundance of food, combined with an absence of their natural predators and/or parasites. Figure 4.8a illustrates the spectacular increase in the incidence of the Colorado beetle following the introduction and large-scale production of the New World potato in the Old World. The fungi that cause potato blight, the Dutch Elm disease and the phylloxera fungi which decimated vines in France at the end of the nineteenth century, are other examples of pest outbreaks.

In addition, modern large-scale, highly mechanised agriculture has resulted in the destruction of many wildlife habitats such as hedgerows, wetlands, water channels, and the number of native predators that orginally would have helped to keep pest populations under control has, consequently, been reduced. Moreover, the use of chemical pesticides since 1940 has also often resulted in the destruction of predatory populations. It is significant that the increase in pest populations in agro-ecosystems is

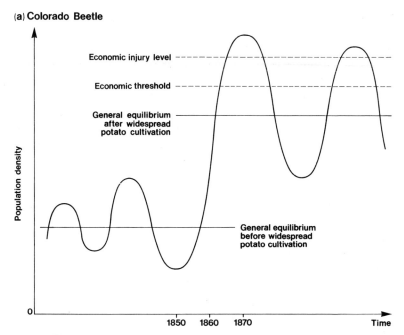

Figure 4.8a The growth and increase in amplitude of population fluctuations of the Colorado Beetle as a pest after the introduction and widespread cultivation of the potato in Europe (After R.L. Rudd in W. Murdoch, 1975).

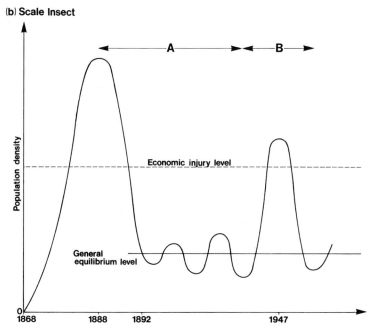

Figure 4.8b Changes in population density of the Scale Insect pest in citrus orchards in California showing effect of: (A) biological methods of control, i.e. the effect of the introduction of the ladybird beetle and (B) chemical methods of control i.e. the resurgence produced by DDT in the San Joaquin Valley (After R.L. Rudd, 1975)

accompanied by a reduction in the richness of the fauna. Studies which compared the insect fauna in virgin and ploughed steppe in the Kazakhstan region of the USSR revealed that, while the density of insect population in the latter was twice that in the former, there were twice as many species in the virgin steppe as in the wheat fields. It was also shown that the number of dominant and constant insect species in the virgin steppe was twice that in the wheat fields. However, in the former, insects comprised only half the total fauna, while they accounted for 94 per cent in the latter. The virgin steppe, therefore, had not only a greater variety of species but also a more even balance of populations. In contrast, in wheat fields only a few species became dominant, most of which were economically significant pests. It is notable that these differences were established in the short space of only two years.

ASSIGNMENTS

1. *Compare the components of agro-ecosytems with wild or unmanaged ecosytems.*
2. *Study Figure 4.8a and b. Suggest reasons for the variations in population density of the Colorado beetle and the Scale insect, respectively.*

Key Ideas

A. Ecosystem components and humans
1. All ecosystems are composed of a close interacting set of living and non-living components.
2. The interrelations between these components is such that any change effected by humans on one will have repercussions on that of all others.

B. Change in biomass
1. Two of the most extensive changes in biomass have been effected by deforestation and burning.
2. The major impact of deforestation is on the hydrological cycle, but microclimatic change is also important.
3. The most important effect of fire is to control the type and amount of biomass.
4. By giving a competitive advantage to fire-resistant species, regular and controlled burning gives rise to a type of ecosystem which either would otherwise not have existed or would not have been so extensive.

C. Change in dead organic matter (DOM) and soil
1. Change in type and amount of DOM is one of the major factors in soil development.
2. Mull (brown earth) to mor (podsolised), or mor to mull soils can be brought about by human-induced changes in vegetation.

D. Change in inorganic components
1. One of the most successful means of changing the physical environment has been by the use of shelter belts to modify microclimate for particular purposes.
2. The effectiveness of the shelter belt depends on its dimensions, combined with its species composition and structure.

E. Agro-ecosystems
1. Maximum change in both organic and inorganic components has been effected in the creation of extensive managed systems for agriculture.
2. Agro-ecosystems are characterised by relatively uniform habitats and simplified organic components.
3. Agro-ecosystems provide new habitats for the proliferation of weeds and pests.

Additional activities

1. *Field Project A*

   (a) In a selected area, map woodlands classified by composition (dominant tree(s)) and use(s).
   (b) For each type of woodland, record the number of strata that can be identified and the average height and composition (dominant type of plant) of each.
   (c) How far can the structure of the woodlands be correlated with their composition, and what other factors may account for the structural variations recorded?

2. *Field Project B*

   (a) In each of the following habitats, dig a soil-pit 1 m square to a depth sufficient to expose the whole of the organic layer: old (25 years) coniferous plantation; deciduous wood; heath or moorland.
   (b) For each profile record:
      i) depth or organic layer.
      ii) depth of undecomposed litter, decomposing litter and completely decayed organic matter.
   (c) Take samples (approx. 0.25 kg weight) at the surface, 5 cm and 10 cm below the surface from each profile.
   (d) Measure in a laboratory the pH, percentage water and organic matter content of each sample.
   (e) Draw profiles to illustrate your results; note the main points of variation between profiles; and suggest what the effect of the organic material on soil development might be.
   (See *Soil Survey Manual: Soil Survey of England and Wales*, Rothamsted, for field methods).

3. Assign the following types of vegetation to one of the three types of humus: Sitka spruce plantation; oak wood with bilberry field layer; moor mat grass (*Nardus stricta*); Fescue/Agrostis grassland; Sphagnum moss; willow/alder woodland; larch with bracken undergrowth.

4. *Field Project C*

   On a selected farm:
   i) Make a list of weeds present and note where they occur;
   ii) Ask the farmer what methods of weed control are used, and why;
   iii) Ask the farmer if there are any weeds particularly difficult to eradicate and why. (For comparative purposes it is suggested that two or more different types of farm be visited.)

5. Make notes on the history and spread of six well-known pests (insect, bird or animal), three of which have been subsequently subject to chemical techniques of control and three to biological methods. What conclusions can you make as to the advantages and disadvantages of these two different methods of control? Useful texts on this subject include those by C.S. Elton (1972), V.L. Delucchi (1976), F.H. Perring and K. Mellanby (1977) and H.F. Van Emden (1974).

5 Humans and Energy Flow

As was explained in Chapter 2, the two most fundamental processes common to all ecosystems are the flow of energy through the system and the circulation of materials within it. The aim of this and the succeeding chapter is to analyse the ways in which humans have disturbed these processes and the environmental consequences of their deliberate or accidental actions.

A. Humans and Energy Flow

One of the most important impacts of humans on the biosphere relates to their ability to channel an ever-increasing proportion of solar energy through themselves, but it is difficult to measure the precise amount involved. Odum (1975) estimates that direct human consumption of food is about one per cent of the total net productivity of the biosphere (about 21×10^{15}MJ/year). On the other hand, Borgström (1973) has pointed out that the global standing crop or biomass of domesticated livestock represents about four times that of human beings in terms of equivalent food energy requirements. Inspection of Figure 5.1 shows that there are over 18 000 million human population equivalents (PE units) in the world today. An analysis of livestock categories reveals a cattle biomass twice that of humans; hogs (pigs) are close to half; and sheep, poultry and buffalo each equal around 1000 million PE units. Further, it has been implied, mostly by vegetarians, that if the tremendous biomass of livestock (14 405 million PE units) were removed, the earth could feed that many more people. Although substantial increases could be accommodated it should be kept in mind that livestock do not always compete directly with humans. Domestic ruminants can digest plant ingredients such as cellulose, hemi-cellulose and other materials with which the human gastric system cannot cope. Consequently, they can graze and produce food from land normally regarded as too poor to cultivate. The extent and possession of such poor land by individual countries explains to a large degree the wide national variations in livestock/humans ratios found over the globe (see Table 5.1). However, it should not be forgotten that variations in social, economic and political conditions also have an important effect on the types of rural economy found in individual nations, to say nothing of their influence on human population numbers (see Chapter 3).

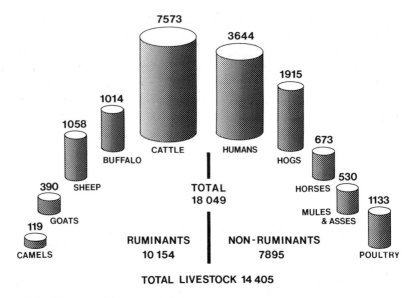

Figure 5.1 Biomass of humans and their domesticated livestock in human population equivalents (P.E. units) (After G. Borgström, 1973)

It has been contended that humans, together with their animal stock, already consume at least 11 per cent of the net primary productivity of the land. In addition, they consume indirectly large quantities of primary produce in the form of industrial fibre (wood, cotton, paper) so that there is very little of the land surface from which something is not harvested.

Table 5.1 Population equivalents (in millions) and ranking of ratio livestock to humans (1967) for selected countries (After G. Borgström, 1972).

	Livestock	Humans	Total	Ratio Livestock/Humans
Japan	65.2	99.9	165.1	0.65
Indonesia	127.7	110.9	238.6	1.20
Nigeria	98.9	62.0	160.9	1.60
China	1589.0	797.8	2386.8	2.0
Pakistan	304.1	120.2	424.3	2.25
India	1476.0	511.6	1987.6	2.90
United Kingdom	160.0	55.1	215.1	2.90
France	271.6	49.9	321.5	5.4
USSR	1287.2	235.5	1522.7	5.5
USA	1172.0	199.0	1371.0	5.9
Canada	131.5	20.4	151.9	6.4
South Africa	138.4	18.7	157.1	7.4
Ethiopia	241.9	22.1	264.0	11.0
Brazil	1148.5	85.7	1234.2	13.4
Argentina	526.3	23.3	549.6	22.6
New Zealand	125.3	2.73	128.0	46.0

Moreover, it has been estimated that about 20 per cent of the NPP of the oceans provides food for humans. Indeed, most fishing experts believe that everything possible is already being harvested from the sea. Humans are currently dependent on between 10–20 per cent of the total NPP of the globe. This enormous energy demand is all the more astonishing in view of the fact that the total human biomass (250–300 × 10^6 tonnes) is only a small fraction of one per cent of that of the biosphere (177 000 × 10^6 tonnes).

ASSIGNMENTS

1. *Look at Figure 5.1 and note the global livestock/humans ratio.*
2. *Study Table 5.1 and suggest reasons for the regional variations shown.*

B. Humans and Global Net Primary Productivity

1. Global variations in NPP

Humans have quite significantly reduced the amount of solar energy fixed by photosynthesis, but it is not easy to assess where, or by how much, this has happened. It is only within recent years that data have become available by which the contribution of various ecosystems to the global NPP can be assessed; these are summarised in Figure 5.2. This shows that the mean NPP ranges from as little as 0.1 to 0.2 kg/m^2 year for land deserts and the open oceans, to almost 3 kg/m^2 year in the tropical rain forest. It is also interesting to note that although marine ecosystems occupy nearly two-thirds of the earth's surface, they contribute only about a third of the world's total production. On the land, the combined forest ecosystems contribute nearly half (46 per cent) and the rain forest alone over a quarter (27 per cent).

2. Reduction in global NPP

It would seem reasonable to assume that widespread deforestation will have reduced energy flow into the biosphere. For instance, Eyre (1978) has estimated that NPP of all pasture land has been reduced to one third of that previously forested, and NPP of all cropland from one half (in mid latitudes) to one quarter (in tropical areas). On this basis he concludes that the total potential NPP of the land has probably been reduced by about a third from 120 × 10^9 to an actual of 80 × 10^9 tonnes. These figures, however, vary considerably from the recently revised International Biological Programme (IBP) figures of 122 × 10^9 tonnes for actual production. However, the ratio of above to below ground NPP (3:1) is thought not to have altered much as a result of human activities; indeed the reverse may well have occurred. Many arable crops, especially those grown in the most fertile soils, have no more than 10–15 per cent of their dry weight below ground. However, others grown in poorer soils, some tree crops and pasture land, all produce at least 25 per cent of their biomass below ground.

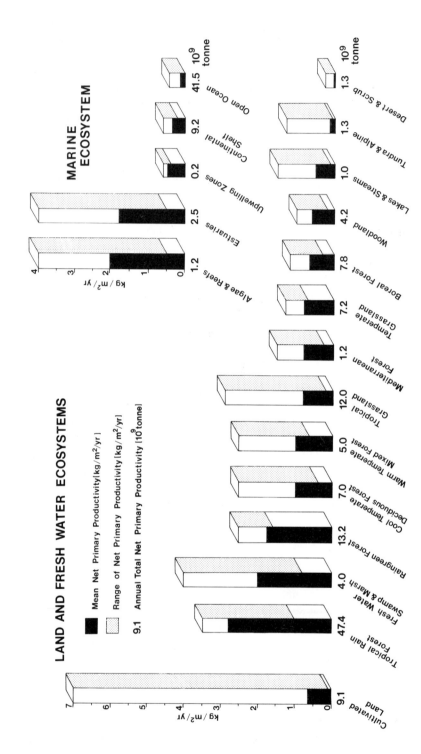

Figure 5.2 Net primary productivity of the major land, freshwater and marine ecosystems of the world (After H. Leith, 1975)

Further, it is interesting to note on Figure 5.2 that, whereas the mean NPP of cultivated land is generally less than that of wild forest and grass land, certain localised and specialised cultivated systems may achieve rates of productivity greatly in excess of natural systems. The highest yielding tropical crops with all year round growth (such as sugar cane and Napier grass) may yield about 6–8 $kg/m^2/year$ dry weight with a photosynthetically active radiation (FAR) efficiency of about 4–5 per cent. This compares very favourably with the maximum productivities of about 4 $kg/m^2/year$ dry weight and efficiencies of 1–2 per cent for the most productive of the world's ecosystems such as tropical rain forest, freshwater swamp and marsh, estuaries and algal reefs.

3. Wild and human-controlled ecosystems

A large proportion of the primary production of *wild ecosystems* is of little direct use to humans at present. The greatest demand is for particular organic products, such as digestible carbohydrates, plant and animal proteins and fibres. The productivity of these materials bears very little relation to that of the total ecosystem NPP. Hence, wherever possible, wild and semi-wild ecosystems have been supplanted by *human-controlled* systems.

The major human-controlled or regulated ecosystems include cultivated land which provides food, beverages and fibre (cotton, jute, wood), together with grazing land for fodder, which in turn furnishes humans with livestock products. It should be noted that such systems are not mutually exclusive; products from cultivated land may support or supplement livestock feeding and several fibres useful to humans (wool, hides) come directly from animals.

According to Ayres (1965) cultivated land, although providing only about 7.8 per cent of total terrestrial productivity, furnishes humans with more than 70 per cent of their food consumption. Grazing lands with their associated livestock are responsible for 18.7 per cent of the total carbon assimilation and contribute about 15 per cent of human food. In contrast, forests which, despite their substantial global productivity (47 per cent total) and their importance for timber supply, can at a maximum supply only about 10 per cent of human food.

ASSIGNMENT

Using the data given in Figure 5.2 and information from world maps of vegetation (atlas, textbooks), map the global land distribution of NPP. Comment on possible reasons for the major variations revealed.

C. Humans and Food Production

Increasing demands on the biosphere have been met by (a) increasing the net productivity or yield of those plants which are of most value to humans, and (b) by channelling the flow of energy from this increased yield along as short food chains as possible.

1. Increased yield

There are two principal ways of increasing the NPP of usable products or yield. The first involves the *selection and breeding of high yielding plants and animals*, i.e. those with the potential to convert as large a proportion of the available energy as possible into required products under given environmental and farming systems. These are the domesticated plants and animals referred to in the preceding chapters. The second is by *increasing inputs into the ecosystem* in the process of cultivation and thereby producing environmental conditions within which crop plants and animals achieve their highest yields.

As Figure 5.3 demonstrates, these inputs can be thought of as subsidising the input of solar energy. They comprise, on the one hand, the direct input of energy in the traditional forms of human or draught animal power, and that derived from fossil fuels. The latter now includes oil, the basic fuel for farm machinery. On the other hand, there are also indirect energy subsidies in the form of seeds, fertilisers, herbicides and pesticides, machinery and water (see Plate 5.1). All these inputs have in common the ability to buffer production against environmental constraints, which may be both natural (climate and soil) and human-created (land tenure, capital, economic cli-

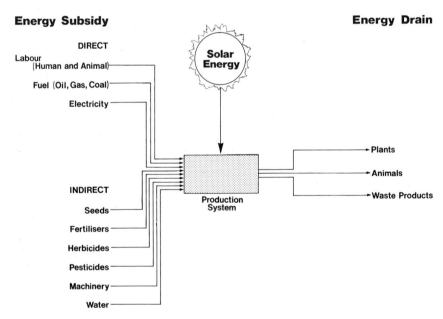

Figure 5.3   Energy subsidies and drains in human agricultural production systems (After M. Slesser, 1975)

Plate 5.1 Spray irrigation of early potatoes in late spring in Fife. (*Scotsman Publications Ltd*)

mate). In food and fibre producing systems they improve solar energy utilisation and thus help to increase yields by reducing respiratory maintainance. For instance, plants will expend less energy of gross primary productivity (GPP) searching for nutrients, and in 'fighting off' parasites and predators, if a ready supply of fertilisers and pesticides are made available to them.

The human population is now about 4 000 million, with a doubling time of about 35 years (see Chapter 3). Table 5.2 illustrates very clearly the positive relationship between food yields and fuel-subsidised agro-ecosystems. The ability of energy-driven technology to raise the energy and protein productivity of the land (on occasion to over 100 times per hectare that of natural systems) is fundamental to continued human existence.

Table 5.2 Food energy return per annum to humans from unsubsidised and highly subsidised systems (After E.P. Odum, 1975)

	Energy kJ/m²/year
Primitive food gathering	0.8– 42.0
Agriculture: without fuel subsidy	104.5– 4185.0
Fuel-subsidised grain agriculture	4185.0– 41850.0
Theoretical fuel-subsidised algae culture	41850.0–167400.0

2. Energy efficiency

(a) Calculation of energy ratio (Er)

Each type of energy used in making every identifiable input of production can be converted into an equivalent energy or heat value. If the energy equivalents of all inputs are added together, the Gross Energy Requirements (Slessor, 1975) of the production process can be obtained. The GER per hectare of land provides a measure of the energy density of the particular system. In addition, the energy ratio of the food products from any area of land can be calculated as follows:

$$\frac{\text{Energy (food output) per hectare}}{\text{Energy density (input) per hectare}} = \text{Energy ratio (Er)}$$

Such energy calculations may be based on the product before it leaves the farm gate or dockside, or on the whole farming industry, including not only the production, but also the preparation, packaging, retail and distribution of the food to the consumers shop and table. For instance, as shown in Figure 5.4, energy ratios may be calculated for a field crop such as cassava

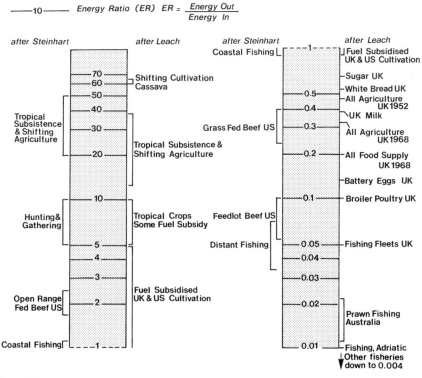

Figure 5.4   Energy ratios of different foods and farming systems (After G. Leach, 1976 and S.S. Steinhart, 1974)

grown under subsistence agriculture (Er about 70), or for processed foods such as UK sugar and white bread (Er = 0.7 and 0.55 respectively). Moreover, the energy ratio of all UK agriculture in 1968 was around 0.35, while that for the whole food industry was 0.20.

(b) Variations in energy efficiencies

A comparison of the energy ratios for different foods and cropping systems can be obtained from Figures 5.4 and 5.5. These reveal: (i) how inefficient industrial forms of arable food production (Er = <1.0–5.0) are compared to semi-industrial (Er = 2–10) and, especially, subsistence agricultural systems (Er = 10–70); (ii) that most livestock production systems (Er = 0.05–1.0) are inefficient users of energy subsidies in comparison with plant production systems (Er generally > 1.0); (iii) that most (i.e. distant) forms of fishing (Er = 0.004–0.05) are particularly inefficient.

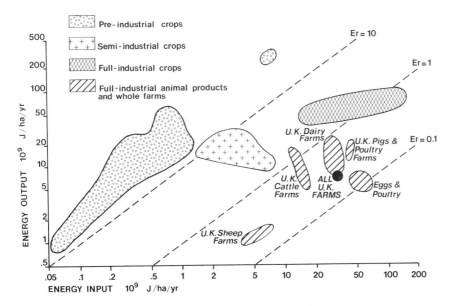

Figure 5.5 Relationship between energy density and food energy output per hectare per year for different farming systems (After G. Leach, 1975)

3. Shortening the food chain

In view of the large loss of energy each time food passes from one trophic level to the next (see Chapter 2), it is not surprising that humans attempt to establish short, reasonably linear, food chains between themselves and their desired harvest. They obtain the maximum food energy when they crop at the second trophic level. However, since protein availability is as important

Table 5.3 Food production from (A) a crop and (B) a livestock food chain.

Chain A: Potatoes (T_2)		Chain B: Livestock (T_3)	
GPP/ha	100%	GPP/ha	100%
R_A	37%	R_A	34%
Unharvested vegetation	15%	Unharvested vegetation	11%
Post-harvest loss	9%	Uneaten grazing	14%
Household waste	9%	Faecal loss	14%
Net human food	30%	R_H	17%
		Tissue conversion loss	4%
		Slaughter and household waste	2%
		Net human food	4%

GPP = gross primary productivity
R_A = Plant respiration
R_H = livestock respiration
T_2 = second trophic level
T_3 = third trophic level
(After A.N.Duckham and G.B. Masefield, 1970)

as calorie or energy content, they also crop at the third trophic level as a primary carnivore. The significance of moving from (T_2) to (T_3) for food production is demonstrated in Table 5.3.

In Chain A, a third of the total GPP is converted into human food; only four per cent in Chain B. Put starkly, this means that more people could be fed at a given level from a hectare of wheat or rice than from the meat produced on the same area. These figures should also serve to emphasise the low energy returns which must accrue to humans when they crop further up the food chain, at T_4 and T_5 in fishing.

Although the human species has become a major factor in channelling energy flow, it should not be concluded that energy diversion along un-wanted food chains has been reduced to negligible proportions. It is well known that, in modern industrial farming systems, insects, pests and pre-dators consume in the region of 20–25 per cent of a crop before harvest, and a similar proportion is lost in post-harvest operations. In the production of potatoes in the UK (Table 5.3), for instance, harvest loss, together with other wastage, accounts for about 50 per cent of the net yield. In these developed systems, therefore, a lot of *cultural waste* occurs because perfectly edible or usable material is discarded; for instance, tubers are peeled before eating and the above ground parts are burnt. In the tropics, human food chains are not characterised by such waste to the same degree. However, in the absence of chemical control, they are particularly susceptible to the biological depredations of weeds, pests and predators. As a result, total losses can on occasion be well in excess of the 50 per cent suggested for industrialised farming systems.

1. *Refer back to Figures 5.4 and 5.5. What does 5.5. tell you about energy efficiency that 5.4 does not?*
2. *For each of the four major farming systems shown on Figure 5.5, construct an energy diagram based on the general model given in Figure 5.3.*
3. *With reference to Table 5.4:*
   (a) *Calculate the total percentage loss from pests, disease and weeds for the crop groups shown in section 1. Comment on the size and variation of such losses.*
   (b) *Note the percentage differences in crop losses from pests, disease and weeds for the more developed and the less developed countries shown in section 2 and discuss the variations shown.*

Table 5.4   Estimated annual biological losses of crops to pests, diseases and weeds in selected regions. Cultural and other wastage not shown (After T.A. Hill, 1977)

1.	Crop	Potential production in millions of tons	Losses due to Pests	Losses due to Diseases	Losses due to Weeds
	All cereals	1468	204	135	167
	Sugar beet and sugar cane	1330	228	232	175
	Vegetable crops	280	23	31	24

2.	Region	Percentage of potential value of all crops	Percentage losses due to Pests	Percentage losses due to Diseases	Percentage losses due to Weeds
	(a) Worldwide	100%	14%	12%	10%
	(b) Europe	100%	5%	13%	7%
	(c) North & Central America	100%	9%	11%	8%
	(d) Africa	100%	13%	13%	16%
	(e) Asia	100%	21%	11%	11%

D. Methods of Energy Diversion by Humans

1. Methods of cropping and nature of energy flow

There are four basic ways by which humans divert or channel photosynthetic energy for their own needs. Expressed in another way, we can say that there are four main types of crops which they take out of the biosphere. They can be simply categorised: arable food, fodder and 'industrial' crop plants; domestic animals and animal by-products; fish; wood.

Plate 5.2 Glasshouse landscape near The Hague, Netherlands. (*Aerofilms Ltd*)

The methods by which these crops are obtained determine the particular patterns of energy flow. First, the energy flow *routes* differ, between the very short, annual food crop to humans, the longer forage or fodder crop via animals to humans, and the very much longer plant-fish-human route. Second, they vary in the *rate* of energy flow involved; in annual crops it can be very rapid or short-run, especially in the case of those with a short growing season. In animals, where the build-up of tissue takes longer and their age and rate of reproduction is slower, the energy flow is obviously slower. Wood production, in contrast, involves a particularly slow, long-run rate of flow since accumulation usually takes many years. Third, energy flow routes vary in the amount by which solar input is subsidised or in what we may call the *intensity of energy use*.

The amount of energy subsidy is much less in wood production and live-

Plate 5.3 Three combine harvesters in the extensive wheat prairies of Iowa, USA. The harvesters are 4 m wide and nearly 11 m long, they have 119 kW (160 DIN/hp) engines, and a grain tank capacity of 6400 litres. (*Massey-Ferguson (UK) Ltd*)

stock which feed on rough uncultivated forage, than in the production of high yielding annual crops. Also, the type of energy subsidy varies with technological development. In the past, cropping the biosphere mainly involved increasing amounts of human and animal energy and the addition of organic fertilisers. Modern intensification of cropping, in all systems, has been accompanied by the substitution of human labour by oil-fuelled or electrically powered machinery, and organic by inorganic fertilisers. The most highly energy subsidised type of cultivation is that of the controlled environment of the glasshouse (see Plate 5.2).

Three stages in the process of energy intensification have been recognised (Leach, 1976), examples of which can be found in different parts of the world today; (i) *pre-industrial* with only relatively low inputs of human labour; (ii) *semi-industrial*, with high inputs of human and animal-power; and (iii) *full-industrial*, with very high inputs of fossil fuels and machinery (see Plate 5.3). Figure 5.6 illustrates the decline in human power associated with the rapid energy intensification of farming in the USA during the last fifty years. This process of intensification has, as we have already explained, also been accompanied by an increase in energy density. Table 5.5 shows how the different systems of agriculture, from primitive to modern intensive, can be ranked or 'classified' on this basis. In the next section we will look in more detail at the energy-flow characteristics in the main types of managed cropping systems with a view to finally assessing their total environmental implications.

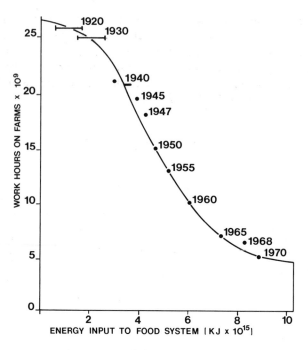

Figure 5.6   Relationship between work-hours on farms and energy input to the US food system (After S.S. Steinhart, 1974)

Table 5.5   Agricultural taxonomy based on energy density and protein yields (After M. Slesser, 1975)

	Energy Density (GJ/ha)	Protein Yields (kg/ha)
Hunter-gatherer	Zero	–
Andean village (Peru)	0.2	0.5
Hill sheep farming (Scotland)	0.6	1–1.5
Marginal farming	4.0	9
Open range beef farming (New Zealand)	5.0	130
Mixed farming in developed country	12–15	500
Intensive crop production	15–20	2000
Feed-lot animal production	40	300
Algae manufacture	1600	22000

2. Farming

As has already been noted, the main objective of farming is to obtain the maximum output or yield of the product required. All farming systems are characterised by their short-route, short-run energy flows to humans either directly via the arable crop, or indirectly via the domestic animal. In the case of arable crops, the highest yield per unit area will be obtained when they are grown under optimum environmental conditions of climate and soil. However, productivity can vary with the type of crop and the length of the growing season (see Table 5.6).

Table 5.6   Length of growing season and yield for selected temperate and tropical cereal and root crops (After J.P. Cooper, 1975)

Temperate regions		Country	Latitude	Growing season (in days)	Yield (t/ha)
Cereals	Barley	UK	52°N	148	7
	Spring Wheat	UK	52°N	160	5
	Maize	USA (Iowa)	42°N	141	16
	Maize	USA (Kentucky)	38°N	127	22
	Rice (wet)	Japan	37°N	123	7
Roots	Sugar beet	USA (Washington)	46°N	240	32

Tropical regions					
Cereals	Rice (wet)	Philippines	15°N	115	7
	Sorghum	Philippines	15°N	80	7
Roots	Cassava (manioc)	Malaysia	3°N	270	38
Multiple Cropping (4 crops)					
	Rice	Philippines	15°N	115	5
+	Sorghum	Philippines	15°N	90	6
+	Sorghum (ratoon)	Philippines	15°N	80	7
+	Sorghum (ratoon)	Philippines	15°N	80	5
Total for year				365	23

(a) Arable farming

Productivity of arable crops also depends on the types and amount of energy subsidy. The variation in energy subsidies and stages in energy intensification are very clearly brought out in Table 5.7. A comparison of the energy budgets for corn (maize) production in Mexico and Guatemala with those in the USA reveals a number of important points. The yield in the latter is about three to five times that in the former. Also, as human labour is progressively replaced, first by animal power, and then by fuel and machinery, the energy density increases nearly 30 times. The most outstanding feature of the high-energy intensive corn growing system is that the contribution of human labour is negligible, while the gross energy requirement for nitrogen fertilisers is greater even than that of all the direct fuel used in production.

Table 5.7   Energy budgets for corn (maize) crops grown under different stages of energy intensification (After G. Leach, 1976)

Pre-industrial stage

A *Corn: Mexico*   GJ/ha-yr

Inputs
Labour 1144 × 0.8 MJ/h   0.915
Axe and hoe 10 kg × 90 MJ/kg   0.045
　　　　　　　　　20 year life

Total   0.96

Outputs
1934 kg corn/ha (184 kg Protein)   29.4

Ratios
Energy input/protein output = 5.22 MJ/kgP
Energy output/energy input = Er = 30.6

B *Corn: Guatemala*   GJ/ha-yr

Inputs
Labour 1414 h × 0.8 mJ/h   1.132
Axe and hoe as A   0.045
Total   1.18

Outputs
1056 kg corn/ha (100 kgP)   16.0

Ratios
Energy input/protein output = 11.8 MJ/kgP
Energy output/energy input = Er = 13.6

Semi-industrial stage

C *Corn: Mexico*   GJ/ha-yr

Inputs
Labour 383 h × 0.8 MJ/h   0.306
Oxen 198 h × 8 MJ/h   1.584
Machinery 225 kg × 90 MJ/kg   1.013
　　　　　　　　　20 year life

Total   2.903

Outputs
931 kg corn/ha (88.4 kgP)   14.15

Ratios
Energy input/protein output = 32.8 MJ/kgP
Energy output/energy input = Er = 4.87

D *Corn: USA 1970*   GJ/ha-yr

Inputs

Labour 22 h × 0.8 MJ/h	0.018
Fuel 206 litres × 43.3 MJ/litre	8.92
Machinery	4.343
Fertiliser N, 125 kg × 80 MJ/kg	10.00
P + K, 102 kg × 11 MJ/kg	1.120
Irrigation	0.786
Insecticides 1.12 kg × 100 MJ/kg	0.112
Herbicides 1.12 kg × 95 MJ/kg	0.106
Drying	1.241
Electricity	3.205
Total	29.85

Outputs

5060 kg corn/ha (481 kgP)	76.91

Ratios

Energy input/protein output = 62.1 MJ/kgP
Energy output/energy input = E_r = 2.58

(b) *Livestock farming*

In contrast to arable crop production, that of livestock and livestock products involve longer-route and longer-run energy flows. Also, as we have already noted, the production of animal protein is extremely expensive in terms of photosynthetic energy costs, because of the high loss of energy in its conversion from plant carbohydrate to animal protein. As with plants, productivity, whether expressed in units of land, time or livestock, is dependent on animal nutrition on the one hand, and on the efficiency of conversion of plant into animal tissue on the other. Figure 5.7 shows the efficiency with which the commonest types of livestock convert crude protein and energy consumed into products edible by humans. Although cattle and sheep have relatively low efficiencies, they can be maintained on diets composed of plant material high in cellulose (i.e. roughage) that is inedible by humans. On the other hand, poultry and pigs have diets more comparable to that of humans. Where high-protein (i.e. concentrated) fodder is in short supply, as in the poor agricultural countries of the world, it will generally be reserved for the most efficient converters — hens and pigs.

The simplest form of livestock production is that where the main food input is from wild, semi-natural forage, as in the case of hill sheep in Britain or open-range feeder (store) cattle in the USA. Although output is low, this system of meat production involves a very small input of energy other than solar radiation. Stocking rates are low; in Scotland from 1–4 hectares per breeding ewe, in the semi-arid grasslands 30–40 hectares per breeding cow,

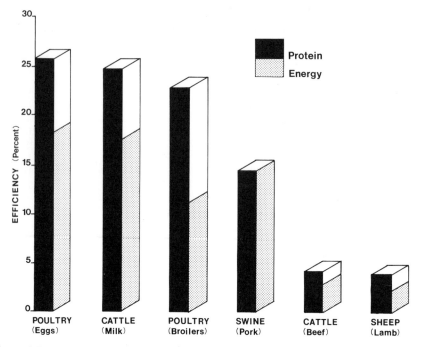

Figure 5.7   Efficiency of livestock in the conversion of dietary crude protein and energy to products edible by humans (After J. Janick, 1976)

dependent on the feeding value of the forage available. However, although energy subsidies and outputs are low, the efficiency of energy use is relatively high.

Nevertheless, these methods of livestock production are wasteful in some respects. It has been shown, for instance, that on the open range in the USA cattle only consume about one-seventh of the available herbage, the remainder goes to rival herbivores and decomposers. In addition, large respiratory and faecal losses are incurred by such stock, due to their necessary mobility on extensive/poor quality grazing land. The carrying capacity of such natural pasture, however, is determined by its ability to maintain stock throughout the year, and mean stocking levels are determined by the availability of winter feed. If numbers were increased in the growing season in order to make greater use of excess forage at this time, it would probably be necessary to bring in supplementary feed (as is done in some systems) during the winter months.

Increasing demand for protein foods has been accompanied in many parts of the world by increasing livestock production. To achieve this an increasing proportion of arable fodder crops have to be fed to livestock to fatten for meat and/or to increase their unit production of milk or eggs. In agriculturally rich countries, animal productivity has been increased by supplementing their diet with grain and high protein foods such as fish meal.

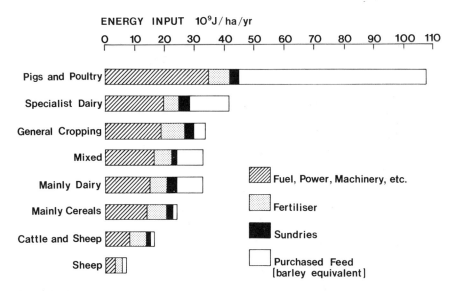

Figure 5.8 Size and composition of energy subsidies in selected farming systems (After M. Slesser, 1975)

Pigs and poultry consume nearly all nutrients in this concentrated form. Cattle are fattened on a diet supplemented with grain to increase their rate of weight-gain. Productive dairy cows receive from 20–50 per cent grain; with liberal grain feeding they can produce 45 kg milk per day; on forage of average quality they would not get sufficient nutrients to produce more than 5–10 kg per day. To achieve this high protein output has necessitated massive energy subsidies in the form of either purchased feed and/or plant and machinery as indicated in Figure 5.8. The most energy-intensive forms of livestock production are the all-year stall-fed dairy and cattle herds, and the battery hen systems. These are in essence livestock producing factories entirely dependent on the input of subsidised feeding as well as other forms of direct/indirect energy input. A higher proportion of energy is also expended in providing lighting and heating of buildings than in most traditional farm systems.

ASSIGNMENTS

1. *Turn back to Table 5.6 and for each country obtain mean monthly temperatures and rainfall figures for a station representative of the given latitude. Plot the data graphically and calculate the sum of the month degrees of accumulated temperature above 6°C (i.e. Σ monthly temperature −6°C) for each station.*
2. *How far does this data and that given on Table 5.6 explain variations in the crop yields shown?*

3. Using Table 5.7:
   (a) Indicate where the corn production systems A to D would occur on the diagram shown in Figure 5.5 by plotting the total energy inputs and outputs for each along the X and Y axes respectively. Do they fit the expected pattern? Note: 10^9 joules = 1GJ
   (b) Analyse the chief energy contrasts between pre-industrial, semi-industrial and full-industrial corn production from the data on Table 5.7.
   (c) Suggest a possible explanation for the relatively low corn yields in examples B (1056 kg/ha) and C (931 kg/ha) compared with A (1934 kg/ha) despite the use of greater energy inputs in the former.
   (d) With specific reference to examples C and D what do you think are the potential benefits of replacing human labour by draught animal power and machinery (apart from any direct effect which they may have on yield increase)?
4. (a) With the aid of the text, comment on the relationship between the composition and amount of energy subsidy in each of the livestock farming systems shown in Figure 5.8 with livestock protein and energy conversion efficiencies shown in Figure 5.7.
   (b) With reference to Figure 5.8, analyse the contrasts between arable and livestock farming in terms of the composition of energy inputs.

3. Fishing

(a) Fishing versus farming

Fishing differs from all but the most primitive farming systems in that humans directly exploit a natural, unmanaged ecosystem for food and, increasingly, for fodder. Fish-farming is still largely limited to fresh waters and to some specialised types of marine inshore products such as oysters. Although human exploitation of the marine ecosystem is largely a robber one, in that energy is taken out without being returned, it is nevertheless highly selective. Humans obtain their food/fodder energy from the higher trophic levels, near the end of the marine food chains, in the form of fish or detrital feeders such as the so-called shell fish. This is because all but a very small proportion of the plant biomass is composed of minute unicellular organisms, the *phytoplankton*, which are not as yet amenable to direct commercial exploitation. Also, many direct phytoplankton consumers (the marine herbivores or *zooplankton*) are very small animals, which form the basic food for larger animals. As a result, the marine plant-humans energy route (with the exception of whales) probably constitutes one of the longest food chains in the biosphere. On the other hand, fish have a relatively high reproductive capacity and, hence, permit a short-run energy flow to humans.

(b) Low intensity versus high intensity fishing

As an exploitive system, however, fishing compares very unfavourably in terms of energy efficiency with other cropping systems. This is largely because the mobile, elusive and variable nature of fish stocks in the sea forces humans to employ techniques of hunting rather than husbandry in their exploitation. The fact that fishermen, at times, have to travel long distances in search of their prey can be very extravagant in terms of energy inputs. In addition, the energy or calorific return (but not protein value) to humans from fish tends to be both low and variable. This is because of (i) the variability of the fish catches themselves — a function of marked variation in fish distribution in relation to environmental conditions in the sea; and (ii) the generally low edible or filleted energy value of most fish (Table 5.8).

Table 5.8   Dressing or edible percentage of different livestock and fish, i.e. proportion of food available after preparation for sale.

Livestock	Dressing or Edible Percentage
Poultry	70
Pigs	75
Cattle	60
Sheep	50
Fish	30–35 average (range 30–70) (filleted yield)

However, a distinction can be made in energy terms between low intensity fishing on the one hand with relatively high energy ratios, and high intensity fishing on the other with extremely unfavourable ratios.

Most of the world's fishermen from both the more developed and less developed nations work on a small scale, from small boats, without modern technical aids, and often do not fish far from their home shores. Such inshore fishing, especially when the energy of transport is derived from wind and/or human effort, is relatively conservative in its use of power. Calculations suggest that such low intensity fishing can have positive energy ratios (see Figure 5.4).

On the other hand, the bulk of the world's fish harvest is caught by the large-scale, highly mechanised, commercial fishing fleets, which use a high level of technological support and are thus both capital and energy intensive. Modern fishing technology is designed to allow the largest catches possible to be handled in a given time; to facilitate the location of fish shoals; and to aid navigation through the use of advanced electronic equipment. The ultimate expression of the modern industry is the large 'mother' factory ships which collect and process their own and/or the accumulated catches from auxiliary fishing vessels. Consequently, as boats have become larger and more powerful, higher indirect energy inputs are required.

However, these large fixed energy costs are often exceeded by substantial energy-demanding, running costs (see Table 5.9) in the form of fuel oil. This latter point can be better appreciated when it is realised that many modern fishing vessels may have to travel over 1500 km and be at sea for three to four weeks or more in order to obtain an economic catch. In view of such high fossil fuel energy inputs, it is not surprising that modern intensive fishing has extremely low energy ratios. Leach (1976) calculates that typical values may range between 0.05 (average UK) and 0.004, and are lower than for any other major form of food or fodder production.

ASSIGNMENT

(a) *Study Tables 5.9 and 5.10. Note the different ways of calculating energy ratios. Compare and contrast the energy ratios for shrimp with those for total UK fishing.*

(b) *Suggest possible reasons for the differences in energy ratios for shrimp fishing in the Gulf of Mexico and around Australia.*

Table 5.9 Energy budget for UK fisheries (After G. Leach, 1976) Note that, by convention here, no credit is given to fish meal and other by-products. Meal accounts for an additional 25 840 tonnes of protein and approximately 0.72 MGJ of energy (38 per cent and 43 per cent of output to humans respectively)

Fish: UK fisheries (1969) total catch

Inputs (MGJ)

Gas/diesel oil 0.4145 Mt × 51.7 GJ/t	21.43
Fuel oil 0.2123 Mt × 49.0 GJ/t	10.40
Shipbuilding and equipment £6.9 M × 107 MJ/£	0.74
Ice, approx. 2.5 Mt × 160 MJ/t	0.40
Total (rounded)	33.0

Outputs

		All	Demersal	Pelagic	Shellfish
Landed catch	Mt	0.954	0.728	0.175	0.051
For human consumption	Mt	0.420	0.313	0.093	0.014
Energy content, edible portion	MJ/kg	—	2.89	7.96	1.46
Energy output	MGJ	1.665	0.905	0.740	0.020
Protein content, edible portion	%		16	16	18
Protein output	10³ tP	67.48	50.08	14.88	2.52

Ratios

Energy input/total catch	34.6 MJ/kg
Energy input/edible kg for humans	78.6 MJ/kg
Energy input/protein for humans	489.0 MJ/kgP
Energy output/input	Er = 0.050

Table 5.10 Energy budgets for shrimp fishing in the Gulf of Mexico and off Australia (After G. Leach, 1976)

Gulf of Mexico (tonne shrimp)

Inputs (GJ)

8300 litres or 6.95 t gas-oil per t shrimps landed: total to dockside	359

Outputs and ratios

1 t shrimps, 65% edible weight, and 16% protein edible portion	3.38 MJ/kg
Energy input/edible kg	552.0 MJ/kg
Energy input/protein	3450.0 MJ/kgP
Energy output/input	Er = 0.0061

Australia (tonne shrimp)

Inputs (GJ)

573 litres or 0.48 t gas-oil per t shrimps landed	24.8
Vessel maintenance £105/t landed × 90 MJ/£	9.5
Vessel manufacture £41.8 per t landed = 90 MJ/£	3.8
Total to dockside	38.1

Outputs and ratios

1 t prawns, 65% edible weight, 3.38 MJ/kg and 16% protein edible portion	
Energy input/edible kg	58.6 MJ/kg
Energy input/protein	366.0 MJ/kgP
Energy output/input	Er = 0.058

4. Forestry

(a) Comparison with farming and fishing

The exploitation of forest products, particularly for wood, is the fourth major method by which humans tap the flow of photosynthetic energy. In comparison to either arable and livestock farming or fishing it is a short-route but very long-run system. It is, however, the largest and most productive source of energy directly available to humans. This is because trees combine a high photosynthetic efficiency with an ability to intercept a high proportion of the photosynthetically active radiation (FAR) and a long or all-year growing season. Their average annual levels of NPP at their period of maximum growth are high.

However, a large part of their net productivity accumulates each year, the bulk of which (about 75 per cent) is stored as woody tissue in the trunk, with lesser amounts in the branches, twigs and roots, and in the leaf litter.

The forest ecosystem is outstanding in the large accumulation of plant biomass and of dead organic matter (DOM) on and in the soil. Also, since woody tissues are rich in carbohydrates (particularly cellulose) and lignin relative to other materials, the plant biomass constitutes an exceptionally energy-rich store. Finally, the woody tissues are very durable. Only a few highly specialised fungi can digest the lignin-rich material; a very small proportion is eaten by consumer animals, so that the amount of the total energy available for use by humans is much higher than in other plant products. However, since it takes time for wood to accumulate it is inevitably cropped at much longer time intervals than any food product.

(b) Biological maturity and annual increment

The age at which a tree attains biological maturity varies according to the species concerned and the environmental conditions under which it is grown. It is usually taken to be when the current annual increment (CAI) or, literally, the trunk growth (CAI = NPP minus litter, i.e. leaves, twigs and branches) is at a maximum. After this, the annual increment decreases until growth becomes negligible and eventually, in its degenerate stage, the biomass may decline. From Figure 5.9 it can be seen that the oak reaches biological maturity (i.e. where the distance between NPP and litter produc-

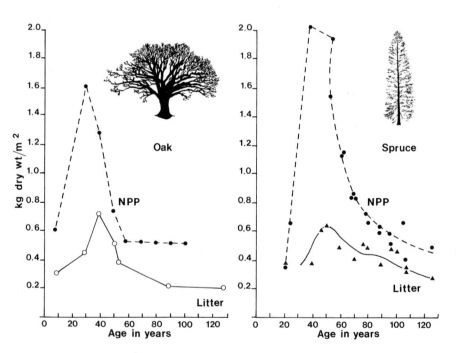

Figure 5.9   Annual net primary productivity (NPP) and litter fall in relation to forest age (After Open University Press, 1974)

tion on the graph is greatest) at around 25 years, spruce at 40 years. The age at which a tree is harvested for wood, however, is that when economic maturity is attained. This will be determined by the use to which the wood is to be put and, consequently, the size and quality of timber required. Felling will take place during the mature phase (see Figure 5.10), that is to say, before the degenerate phase in which the mean annual increment (MAI) falls to a level at which further increase in trunk biomass is negligible. The MAI is calculated by dividing the sum of NPP minus litter production for previous years by the number of years. Even for large timber, this will normally be well before the degenerate phase; it will usually occur when the MAI reaches a maximum, which is the forester's index of maturity.

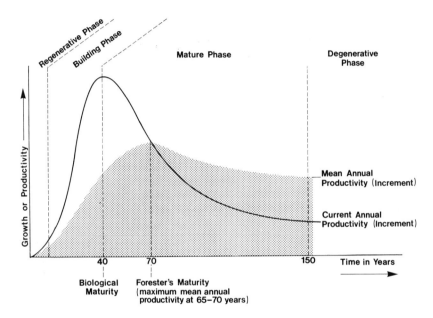

Figure 5.10   Growth phases and indices of maturity with time in Scots pine stand (After J. Cousens, 1974)

(c) *Economic yield*

Ideally, trees should be felled at their stage of maximum economic yield. As can be seen from Figure 5.11 this is when the difference between input cost and sales is greatest, represented by line A/B on the graph. However, in forest systems used for coppicing or pulp, felling may occur well before this when trunks are relatively thin (line E/F); while in those earmarked for the strong constructional timber of mature trees, cropping may be later (line G/H). In some instances, the economic age may be determined by environmental conditions, as in the case where trees over a given age and height are particularly susceptible to wind-blow.

105

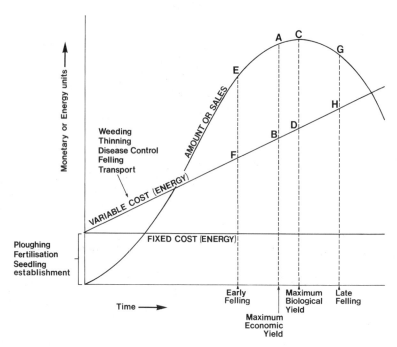

Figure 5.11   Stages in the economic maturity of a forest with time

Plate 5.4 Timber extraction by Timberjack Forwarder in Rheola Forest, South Wales. (*Forestry Commission*)

Plate 5.5 Fertiliser (gafsaphosphate) spraying of Sitka spruce plantation, Minard Forest, Argyll. (*Forestry Commission*)

As with farming and fishing, forestry has become increasingly mechanised, particularly at harvesting (see Plate 5.4). The inputs of seeds, fertilisers and insecticides have also expanded (see Plate 5.5). However, when the rapid accumulation of energy in forest ecosystems is considered in relation to both fixed and variable energy subsidies, very high energy ratios are obtained. For instance, Black (1971), although using only direct fuel and labour inputs, has calculated that the production of Sitka spruce in West Central Scotland could attain energy ratios (Er) as high as 58. This suggests that forestry may be more than twice as efficient in channelling energy to humans as both subsistence (Er = 3–34 calculated on a similar basis) and fuel-subsidised agriculture (Er = 9–32). Unfortunately, humans cannot eat wood!

ASSIGNMENTS

1. *Using the data in Figure 5.9, plot on standard graph paper (a) the current annual increment (NPP — litter production); (b) biomass (sum of NPP — litter production for previous years); and (c) mean annual increment (sum of NPP — litter production for previous years divided by number of years) for both oak and spruce on the basis of the model given in Figure 5.10.*

2. *Compare the biomass in each of the growth phases, and the age of biological and foresters maturity in the two species.*

E. Implications of Energy Diversion and Subsidisation

The diversion of a growing proportion of the energy flow in the ecosystem through humans, and their use of fossil fuels to subsidise food and fodder production have complex biological and socio-economic implications. The former have been discussed in this and preceding chapters; detailed analysis of the latter are beyond the scope of this book. However, the implications and problems ensuing from energy diversion and subsidisation differ markedly as between the more developed and the less developed countries. In the latter, the main problem is that of increasing food production at a rate commensurate with that of population growth; in the former, it is that of increasing the efficiency of energy use in highly productive agricultural systems. The one is exemplified by 'The Green Revolution', the other by 'Diminishing Returns' on energy investment.

1. The Green Revolution

Two-thirds of the world's population live in mainly intertropical areas where yields of staple food grains are low. Traditional, labour-intensive farming techniques, well adapted to native crop-plants and particular environmental conditions alike, have remained unchanged for a long period of time. To-day, continuing and exceptionally high population growth rates are combined with low standards of living and poor nutritional levels. The need to increase food production is urgent and has stimulated research designed to improve the performance of food crops themselves rather than investment in extremely costly land reclamation and/or irrigation schemes.

The traditional types of rice, wheat and sorghum are characterised by large leafy plants (which depress weed growth effectively) and extensive root systems which can tap the limited soil nitrogen sources as efficiently as possible. Their size inhibits close planting. The addition of fertilisers merely tends to stimulate leaf growth and hence mutual shading, and to produce an over-elongated grain stalk which is very susceptible to 'lodging'. To overcome these problems, new, high yielding, 'dwarf' hybrid varieties of rice, wheat and maize have been produced since the mid-forties. These new varieties have short upright leaves, a short, stiff straw capable of carrying a heavy head, and a shallow root system. Their yield, without the liberal addition of fertilisers, water, herbicides and pesticides, is no better than that of the older native species. The dwarf hybrids have been the basis of what has been called *The Green Revolution*, which would, it was hoped, provide a panacea for many of the Third World's agricultural problems.

Spectacular increases in wheat and rice yield have been achieved in Colombia, Mexico, the Philippines and parts of India and Pakistan. However, it is perhaps significant that the new, high yielding varieties have had their greatest impact in areas technically best suited to their cultivation, i.e. on the larger, owner-occupied farms, particularly in already irrigated areas. Overall, however, the programme has not fulfilled initial expectations. The success of the new crops depends on the rapid concurrent development of an intensive high-energy subsidised farming system. Odum (1975) suggests that a doubling of agricultural output per unit area requires a ten-fold increase in energy input and, thus, in the cost of fertilisers, pesticides and machinery. Not only are the input costs higher than the less developed countries can maintain in face of current price inflation, but the programme has resulted in the application of farming techniques better adapted to temperate than to tropical areas, with often undesirable environmental impacts which may defeat the desired end.

3. Diminishing returns

As has been demonstrated, high agricultural productivity has been achieved at the expense of high and ever-increasing energy subsidisation. In contrast to the less developed countries, where 60–80 per cent of the total energy expenditure is taken up in food production (including production, processing, distribution and preparation), the comparable proportion in the more developed countries ranges from 15–30 per cent. In the former, energy is provided mainly by humans and animals, in the latter, by that derived from fossil fuels. Although the USA uses only 16 per cent of its total energy in food production, this is more than the total fossil fuel energy expenditure in the whole of the Third World! It has been estimated (Leach, 1976) that three times as much energy is used *per capita* in food production than is expended per capita for *all* energy-consuming activities in the less developed countries.

However, as we have seen, although agricultural output per unit area and per work-hour has increased considerably, particularly since the 1940s, efficiency in terms of the ratio of energy output to input has decreased; to state it in simple terms, the energy-cost of food production has increased. What is even more serious is that there are indications in some of the most energy-intensive farming systems in the more developed countries that the point of diminishing returns has been reached, if not passed. In some extreme cases over-cultivation can cause an absolute decrease in yield. The need for energy conservation in intensive agricultural production is now urgent.

ASSIGNMENT

Using Table 5.11: (a) plot on standard graph paper energy inputs for labour, machinery plus fuel; all fertilisers combined; seeds; irrigation; insecticides and herbicides; electricity; and transport for each of the years indicated.

Table 5.11 Energy inputs and returns (1945–1970) in advanced corn production in the USA. All figures in GJ/hectare (After M. Slesser, 1975).

Inputs	1945	1950	1954	1959	1964	1970
Labour	0.30	0.24	0.23	0.2	0.15	0.12
Machinery	4.5	6.2	7.5	8.7	10.5	10.5
Fuel	14.0	15.5	17.2	18.0	18.9	19.9
Nitrogen	1.4	3.0	5.3	8.1	11.6	22.2
Phosphorus	0.25	0.36	0.42	0.58	0.64	1.12
Potassium	0.13	0.25	0.45	0.75	1.02	1.49
Seeds for planting	0.77	0.92	1.13	1.34	1.49	1.49
Irrigation	1.04	1.3	1.50	1.71	1.89	1.89
Insecticides	0	0.03	0.08	0.19	0.28	0.28
Herbicides	0	0.1	0.03	0.07	0.1	0.28
Drying	0.1	0.35	0.74	1.65	2.48	2.98
Electricity	0.8	1.35	2.5	3.47	5.02	7.67
Transportation	0.5	0.75	1.15	1.50	1.74	1.74
Total inputs	23.9	30.8	39.1	47.5	57.2	73.4
Corn yield (output)	77.5	86.65	93.5	123.1	155.0	184.7
$\dfrac{\text{GJ output}}{\text{GJ input}}$ = (Er)	3.24	2.81	2.39	2.59	2.71	2.52

Comment on variations in trends. (b) In the same way, plot corn yield, total energy inputs and Er on one graph. Comment on the relationships between the three variables.

Key Ideas

A. Humans and energy flow
1. Humans divert through themselves an amount of solar energy flow out of all proportion to their numbers.

B. Humans and global net primary productivity
1. The effect of humans on NPP is generally to reduce the productivity of wild systems and to increase that of cultivated systems.

C. Humans and food production
1. Humans exploit the biosphere by increasing their crop yield and shortening their food chains.
2. Increased crop yields are achieved by plant breeding and energy subsidisation of the cropping system.
3. The energy efficiency of food production from arable and livestock farming as well as fishing generally decreases as energy subsidisation increases.
4. Even in the shortest and most efficient of food chains loss of energy may be high.

D. Methods of energy diversion by humans

1 There are four main crops taken out of the biosphere: arable food, fodder and industrial crop plants; domestic animals; fish; and wood. The methods of cropping vary in terms of length of food chain, rate of energy flow and energy intensity.
2. Energy intensification in cropping has been accompanied by a substitution of fossil fuels for human and animal power.
3. Crop and livestock production is generally characterised by comparatively short-route, short-run energy flows and wide variations in energy intensity.
4. Increasing demand for animal protein is met only by very energy-intensive systems.
5. The lowest energy efficiencies are generally associated with intensive commercial fishing.
6. Forestry in comparison to farming and fishing, is, a short-route, very long-run system with a relatively low level of energy subsidisation.
7. In forest systems there is a varying relationship between crop maturity and economic return.

E. Implication of energy diversion and subsidisation

1. The implications of energy diversion differ as between the more developed and the less developed countries.
2. Increasing food demand in the less developed countries has resulted in the introduction of energy-intensive agricultural methods collectively known as *The Green Revolution*.
3. Increasing intensification of cropping in the more developed countries is being accompanied by decreasing energy efficiency and diminishing energy returns.

Additional Activities

1. *Field Project*

   (a) In a selected area locate three farms either of different type and/or of different size of the same type. Ask the farmer to give you the following information:
   a) acreage of farm
   b) total amount of fuel oil used on the farm
   c) total amount of all fertilisers used on the farm
   d) total amount of feedstuffs bought in to the farm
   e) total live weight of all animals sold off the farm
   f) total amount of animal products (milk, eggs, etc.) sold off the farm
   g) total weight of all crops sold.
   (b) Using Table 5.12, convert items b–g into joules.

Table 5.12 Energy equivalents for selected farm inputs and outputs (After G. Leach, 1976).

Inputs				Unit	Energy Unit (MJ)	Outputs	Metabolisable Energy (MJ/kg Dry Weight)
Diesel fuel				l litre	43.3		
Fuel oil				l litre	46.6		
Electricity				kW h	14.0		
	N	P	K ratios			*Crops*	
	13	13	20	kg	14.0	Roots	12.5
	20	10	10	kg	18.3	Hay	9.0
	29	5	5	kg	24.3	Barley	13.7
	15	15	21	kg	16.5	Maize	14.2
	22	11	11	kg	20.0	Oats	11.5
	9	25	25	kg	14.0	Wheat	14.0
	17	17	17	kg	17.8	Beans	12.8
	20	6	12	kg	18.0	Peas	13.4
	14	14	20	kg	16.7	Cabbage	10.4
	10	20	10	kg	11.6		
	12	18	12	kg	13.9	*Livestock Products*	
Lime (ground limestone)				kg	2.0	Meat	
Medium (50 hp 37 kW) tractor with 6000 hour working life				one	166,000.0	(cattle)	7.9
						(sheep)	10.17
Medium tractor depreciation				hour	27.6	Milk	12.81
Medium tractor use (depreciation, repairs, fuel, etc.)				hour		(separated)	14.1
Purchased feed				t	188.7	(whey)	14.5
Average grain drying				t	9570.0		
Barn hay drying				t	520.0		
Piped water				t	2360.0		
Sundry goods				£	9.1		
					180.0		

(c) For each farm calculate: (i) energy density; (ii) energy efficiency. Comment on, and suggest reasons for the main points of contrast.
2. Why does the marine ecosystem produce only about 2 per cent of human food? Discuss the problems of increasing food production from the sea. (See Joy Tivy, 1977).
3. Draw an outline (unlabelled) graph similar to that shown in Figure 5.11. List fixed and variable costs for the fishing industry and insert them on the diagram. Replace the time axis by numbers of producers and fishing intensity. Comment on the usefulness of this model to demonstrate the concepts of underfishing, maximum sustained yield, and overfishing.

6 Humans and Biological Cycling

A. Human Disturbance of the Biological Cycle

The biological cycle (see Chapter 2B) involves the continuous circulation of matter. Relatively simple inorganic elements, such as oxygen, carbon and hydrogen, derived from the physical environment are assimilated and converted into complex organic compounds in the bodies of plants and animals, and eventually released in the process of decomposition for re-use. The principal characteristic of the global biological cycle is that nothing is lost from the system; materials are converted from one form (inorganic) into another (organic) or transported from one place to another.

Human activities can disturb the biological cycle by altering either the *composition* and/or *amount* of the materials which naturally circulate through the ecosystem. These are largely nutrients, or any substance essential for the metabolism of an organism, and others which are non-essential for organic growth, some of which may be harmless, others harmful or toxic. Another important attribute which can be disrupted is the ease and hence *rate* with which materials circulate along the various routes between the nutrient pools or reservoirs previously illustrated in Figure 2.6. Humans can disturb the biological cycle by increasing or reducing the volume of nutrients available, and by speeding up or slowing down the rate at which these circulate. However, the volume and rate of circulation are so closely interrelated that a change in one will be reflected in a change in the other, in either a positive or negative direction (see Table 6.1). Further, humans have exercised an increasingly disruptive effect on the biological cycle by the *addition of synthetic, biologically non-essential and/or harmful substances*. In extreme cases, they have so disrupted the cycle as to cause a complete breakdown which may be difficult or impossible to rectify.

Some biological cycles are more susceptible to disruption than others. The gaseous cycles, for instance, are relatively stable on a global scale; local imbalance of either oxygen or carbon dioxide are most common in aquatic ecosystems, where many organisms are dependent on gaseous exchanges between the atmosphere and the water body. The more complex hydrological, nitrogen and sedimentary cycles are more susceptible to disturbance and serious disruption by human activities.

Table 6.1 Matrix with specific examples illustrating human disturbance of volume and rate of the biological cycle

	Increase in volume	Decrease in volume
Increase in rate	**1** **Addition of nitrogen fertiliser in agricultural ecosystems**	**3** **Muirburn**
Decrease in rate	**2** **Cultural eutrophication**	**4** **Deforestation**

In the following sections, the effect of humans on the biological cycle will be analysed under circumstances where the volume and rate are increased or decreased, where synthetic substances are added, and where human actions can lead to a breakdown of nutrient circulation.

B. Increase in Volume and Rate of Biological Cycling

1. Addition of fertilisers

The most important means by which humans increase the volume of nutrients and accelerate the rate of biological cycling is by the deliberate addition of elements, particularly nitrogen, phosphorus and potassium, to soils, in the form of either organic or inorganic fertilisers. Their aim is to increase the yield of primary (crops) or secondary (animals) agricultural produce; in doing so they speed up the rate of nutrient turnover.

Nitrogen, phosphorus and potassium (The Big Three) are the most important nutrients in this process because they are required in such large quantities relative to the others. Also, the readily available amount tends to be low in most soils because they are very susceptible to loss from the biological cycle by: harvesting of crops; leaching, particularly of the more soluble forms; fixation of insoluble compounds, especially those of phosphorus; and, in the case of nitrogen, by anaerobic denitrifying bacteria in the soil, which can convert nitrates to elemental gaseous nitrogen.

115

(a) Organic fertilisers

In the past, the main source of additional nutrients has been organic forms such as dung, human sewage, crop residues, seaweed and peat. There are various ecosystems which are still heavily dependent on the addition of nutrients in an organic form. These include some types of labour-intensive tropical agriculture, urban and suburban gardens (leaf mould, compost, peat, dry-manure), horticulture (peat), and farming systems where there is a combination or close juxtaposition of intensive livestock and crop production.

The progressive decay of such organic matter in the soil makes nitrogen (together with a wide range of other nutrients) available at the same time as the maximum demand by crop-growth. Rate of release is naturally regulated. The addition of nutrient-rich organic matter also has an indirect effect on the rate of nutrient turnover. Organic matter which breaks down rapidly into humus increases the water and nutrient holding properties of the soil. This is because humus, like the fine clay particles in the soil, has the ability to act as a negatively charged material and to attract and hold (i.e. adsorb) positively charged nutrient ions (i.e. cations) and thereby counteract the tendency to loss by leaching from the nutrient cycle.

Organic matter also helps to keep the soil in good physical or structural condition — in what the farmer would call 'good heart'. Soil structure is dependent on the way in which the individual mineral and/or organic particles are combined in the soil to form compound aggregates or *peds*. Figure 6.1 illustrates the main types of peds, according to size and shape, which may be found in soils. From the point of view of nutrient cycling, a good structure, that which the farmer calls a good tilth, is the crumb. This is because the combination of fine clay and humus particles forming the crumbs provides optimum nutrient and water-holding properties, while the spaces or pores between the crumbs ensure good drainage and aeration. A crumb structure, therefore, minimises nutrient loss and maximises nutrient uptake (soil structure is discussed further in Chapter 8). It is also necessary to maintain the soil base-status, (that is, the degree of acidity or alkalinity measured in terms of its pH) at the optimum level, and apply nutrients in the correct proportions, in relation to the type of crop and the purpose for which it is produced.

(b) Inorganic fertilisers

There has been, particularly since 1939, a drastic decline in the use of organic fertilisers, because of a reduction in sources (of which draught animals were one of the most important), combined with increasing availability, relative cheapness and ease of application by machinery of inorganic fertilisers. The latter are now the main direct nutrient addition to the global biological cycle, particularly in intensively managed agricultural, horticultural and silvicultural ecosystems. In the period 1954–68 phosphate fertiliser consumption doubled, nitrogen quadrupled.

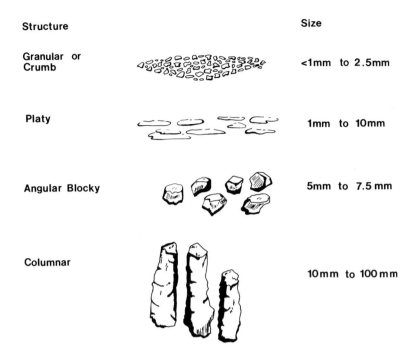

Structure		Size
Granular or Crumb		<1mm to 2.5mm
Platy		1mm to 10mm
Angular Blocky		5mm to 7.5 mm
Columnar		10mm to 100 mm

Figure 6.1   Types of soil structure

Humans have supplemented the natural nutrient input on a massive scale. For example, they have apparently already increased the global rate of nitrogen fixation by over 50 per cent as a result of industrial fixation processes. This has involved an absolute increase from 24 million to 54 million tons annually. They have also accelerated the rate of nutrient turnover because of the consequent rapid growth of high yielding annual crops. Inorganic fertilisers are applied in large volumes and in a form immediately available for uptake by the growing crop. In contrast to organic fertilisers, however, they are normally very soluble and hence susceptible to considerable losses by leaching. This is further exacerbated by the fact that the use of organic material (e.g. 'manure') has decreased. ·

ASSIGNMENT

Study Table 6.2:
(a) *Construct graphs to illustrate percentage use of inorganic fertilisers and FYM by region.*
(b) *Note variation* within *and* between *regions and discuss possible reasons for it.*
(c) *Does the figure for application per acre give any additional information about the regional variation of fertiliser and FYM use?*

Table 6.2 Overall use of inorganic fertilisers and farmyard manure (FYM) in England and Wales (1959–69): (1) tons per acre; (2) includes leys down for more than seven years; *the average dressing in units per acre, excluding fields receiving none of the components. 1 unit = 1.12 lb (After Agricultural Advisory Council, 1970)

Region	Percent acreage receiving				Average actual units per acre*			
	N	P_2O_5	K_2O	FYM	N	P_2O_5	K_2O	FYM[1]
Northern								
Arable	86	83	83	22	78	51	53	15
Permanent grass[2]	52	42	40	22	57	51	33	14
Yorks and Lancs								
Arable	82	76	74	9	76	47	56	13
Permanent grass	50	39	36	19	76	35	29	13
West Midland								
Arable	86	80	77	17	75	47	43	18
Permanent grass	62	48	47	19	76	43	34	12
Eastern								
Arable	88	79	77	10	82	53	69	17
Permanent grass	52	29	22	<1	75	52	24	10
South Eastern								
Arable	90	81	78	10	89	49	50	15
Permanent grass	56	39	35	16	67	37	29	15
South Western								
Arable	90	82	79	15	85	50	42	13
Permanent grass	58	44	41	18	66	40	31	12
Wales								
Arable	80	73	68	23	59	56	40	14
Permanent grass	48	46	40	12	63	57	34	14

C. Increase in Volume and Decrease in Rate of Biological Cycling

In the previous section it was shown how the rate of nutrient cycling in agricultural systems can be increased by increasing the input of organic or inorganic fertilisers. Increase in the rate of cycling is not, however, maintained indefinitely by a continuing increase in the quantity of inputs. As with so many biological processes, the relationship between volume of input and rate of nutrient turnover is a sigmoid rather than linear one (see Chapter 3F). Above an optimum level, increase in amount of nutrient input is accompanied by a slowing down, a levelling off and eventually a *decrease* in the rate of cycling. This relationship is particularly well-illustrated in the process of induced or *cultural eutrophication* (Hasler, 1974).

Cultural eutrophication

Eutrophication or nutrient-enrichment is a natural process. Under certain circumstances it can take place in ecosystems such as water-bodies or the soil. In the former, progressive addition of nutrients by surface and ground-water drainage, and in the latter, weathering of the soil parent material may be greater than the removal of nutrients by outflow from the aquatic system or by soil leaching. Cultural eutrophication, however, is a relatively recent occurrence having become increasingly evident and widespread only within the last 30–50 years. On the one hand, it is the result largely of the increasing use in agriculture of inorganic fertilisers rich in nitrates and, on the other, the mounting production of effluent, such as human sewage, in-dustrial and agricultural waste, rich in both nitrates and phosphates. Table 6.3 illustrates the relative importance of rural and urban sources of eutrophication in Lake Wisconsin.

Table 6.3 Summary of estimated nitrogen and phosphorus loads reaching Lake Wisconsin surface waters; *excludes industrial wastes that discharge to municipal systems (After A.D. Hasler, 1974).

| Source | N | P | N | P |
	lbs per year		(% of total)	
Municipal treatment facilities	20 000 000	7 000 000	24.5	55.7
Private sewage systems	4 800 000	280 000	5.9	2.2
Industrial wastes*	1 500 000	100 000	1.8	0.8
Rural sources				
Manured lands	8 110 000	2 700 000	9.9	21.5
Other cropland	576 000	384 000	0.7	3.1
Forest land	435 000	43 500	0.5	0.3
Pasture, woodland and				
other lands	540 000	360 000	0.7	2.9
Ground water	34 300 000	285 000	42.0	2.3
Urban run-off	4 450 000	1 250 000	5.5	10.0
Precipitation on water areas	6 950 000	155 000	8.5	1.2
Total	81 661 000	12 557 500	100.0	100.0

(a) Water eutrophication

Large and increasing inputs from these sources, indicated in Table 6.3, can cause serious disturbance of normal biological cycles, particularly in the two types of habitats already noted. The first, and most susceptible to cultural eutrophication, are relatively small, shallow and calm, sheltered water-bodies such as lakes and estuaries. Increasingly large quantities of nutrient-rich effluent draining into freshwater lakes can result in the accumulation of nutrients at a rate greater than they can be cycled by the natural process of decomposition and photosynthesis. Nutrient enrichment stimulates the growth of plant plankton, particularly the blue-green algae, near the surface of the water where light is available. These algae grow at a rate greatly in excess of that which can be consumed by the water-fleas (the staple food of all fish larvae). As a result, a green scum or 'algal bloom' tends to form over

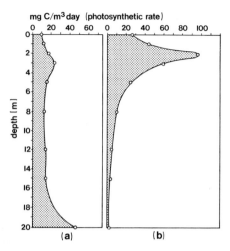

Figure 6.2   Production of carbon by photosynthesising algae in two Alpine lakes (a) Klopeiner and (b) lower part of Lake Constance (After A.D. Hasler, 1974)

part or all of the water surface. Figure 6.2 shows how primary productivity by photosynthesising algae is concentrated in the surface water of a highly eutrophic (nutrient enriched) lake compared with a less polluted one.

In the first place, this scum cuts down the penetration of oxygen, light and heat into the water below and creates conditions inimical to many forms of life. Secondly, and more significantly for the biological cycle, are a set of processes which take place during the subsequent death and decay of the algal mass. The oxygen requirement or the biological oxygen demand (BOD) of the aerobic bacteria needed to effect the decomposition of the dead plants is usually greater than the supply in the water. In still and stagnant water, oxygen replenishment from the atmosphere cannot take place. Thirdly, any dead and partially decayed vegetation accumulates on the bed of the lake, where carbon dioxide and sulphuretted hydrogen are given off and may build up to levels toxic to all organisms other than certain specialised bacteria. Hence the additional nutrients become stored in the bottom sediments; indeed, they may become permanently lost to the cycle unless released by the disturbance and up-welling of bottom water.

Cultural eutrophication has been detected and studied in a number of lakes. It is becoming a problem particularly in relatively small (Loch Leven, Loch Neagh, The Broads, Lake Windermere) and moderately sized (Lakes Zurich, Washington, Mendota, Wisconsin) lakes. It has been noted that the Zurichsee, a lake in the foothills of the Alps, changed from an oxygen-rich trout to an oxygen-poor coarse fish (bream, carp, pike) ecosystem, as a result of progressive eutrophication from domestic effluent. In Lake Zurich deep-water 'gourmet' fishes disappeared within 20 years of the sewage disposal in surrounding villages being changed from septic tanks to flush toilets (Hasler, 1974).

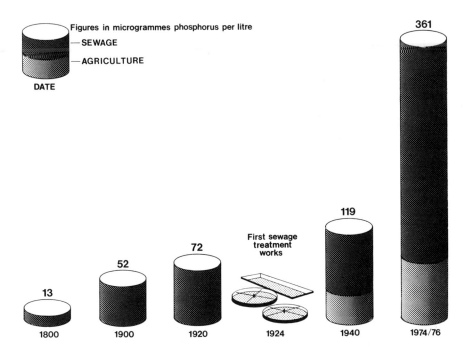

Figure 6.3   Average total phosphorus concentration in Barton Broad (After T. O'Riordan, 1979)

Cultural eutrophication is also occurring in some very large inland water-bodies such as the Lower Great Lakes (Ontario and Erie) and in urban/industrial estuarine areas, despite their large diluting and purifying (i.e. oxygen cycling) capacities. As previously suggested, the major contributor to cultural eutrophication is human sewage and industrial waste high in phosphate content (see Table 6.3). Also, as indicated in Figure 6.3., analyses of the bottom sediments in the English Broads have shown a rapid increase in phosphorus concentration from about the 1920s. This is most likely associated with an increase in urban population centres in this area, together with the establishment of major sewage works.

Eutrophication leads to a slowing down in the rate of the biological cycle. It also results in a loss from the global cycle as nutrients become immobilised in lakes and offshore bottom sediments. This is particularly serious in the case of phosphorus, given world shortages of this essential nutrient and diminishing sources from which to replenish the nutrient cycle. At present rates of population increase and phosphorus use it has been estimated that there may be as little as 90 years supply left (Cox, 1974).

(b) Soil eutrophication

The second habitat susceptible to cultural eutrophication is the soil, as a result of the expanding use of inorganic fertilisers and the application of agricultural effluent (or slurry) to farmland. These substances are in a readily soluble form and can be easily leached from the nutrient cycle. Some nutrients may be lost in soil-water draining from the land; some through conversion by denitrifying bacteria into gaseous nitrogen, particularly in wet soils deficient in aerobic bacteria.

Amounts of inorganic fertilisers in excess of the requirements for optimum crop yield can result in either loss from global cycles or decrease in the rate of nutrient cycling or turnover via the crop produced. Increasing acidity or alkalinity consequent upon increased fertiliser use reduces or increases the rate of nutrient uptake, depending on the element involved. Very high dosages of nitrates and phosphates can also depress plant growth. Finally, the application of excessive amounts of nitrogen, phosphorous and potassium can stimulate growth to an extent that the demand for other nutrients, such as calcium, magnesium and trace elements, is greater than that available in the soil; hence, crop growth and the associated nutrient cycle slows down.

More serious disturbance of the biological cycle is caused by the problems of slurry ('muck' or organic effluent from domestic animals) disposal particularly from intensive dairy, pig and poultry farms which produce large quantities of liquid waste. Application to the soil has both direct and indirect effects on nutrient cycling. Added to a soil incapable of absorbing or discharging excessive quantities of organic effluent, it can lead to 'sealing' of the soil surface. This retards infiltration of water and particularly oxygen; it tends to be more serious where soils are initially poorly drained, since it depresses further an already slow rate of organic decomposition and nutrient turnover. In addition, excess slurry can contaminate the herbage, and make it unpalatable to stock for several weeks. It can also cause toxicity in soils where nitrogen levels are already high, this is because excessive stimulation of plant growth may cause an increase in uptake of trace elements from the soil to levels which can be toxic to both plants and animals.

ASSIGNMENT

(a) *Using Table 6.3 analyse, in relative and absolute terms, sources of nitrogen and phosphorus loads entering Lake Wisconsin.*
(b) *Comment on your findings.*

D. Reduction in Volume and Increase in Rate of Biological Cycling

1. Mode of operation

Humans, as has been illustrated in the two preceding sections, tend to increase the magnitude of the biological cycle mainly by the direct addition of soluble substances to the 'active pool' of nutrients in the soil. In contrast, they reduce the volume of nutrients indirectly, primarily by cropping or re-

Plate 6.1 Well-managed grouse moor in Grampian Region, showing the patchwork pattern of heather at various stages of growth after burning. (*Dr N Picozzi*)

moving part or all of what has been called the 'utilised pool' (Chadwick and Goodman, 1975) of nutrients in the plant and animal biomass. In some cases reduction of the biomass is accompanied by an increased rate, in others by a decreased rate of nutrient cycling.

Increase in rate of nutrient turnover with decrease in volume is effected in two principal ways. The first is by the replacement of large, long-run plants (i.e. trees, shrubs and woody perennials) in which a proportion of the total nutrient capital is temporarily stored for a relatively long period of time, by short-run plants (smaller, less bulky perennial or annual plants) with a rapid growth-rate and relatively short life or harvest cycle. This is exemplified by the replacement of forest by rotation grassland, or of grassland by an annual arable crop. The second way is grazing or burning of plants whose growth, and hence nutrient uptake, is stimulated by periodic reduction in the amount of their biomass. As was noted in Chapter 3, burning of semi-natural vegetation is a long-used method of reducing the volume of organic matter in order to speed up the nutrient cycle and thereby the growth of more nutritious herbage. The practice of 'muirburn' in Scotland (see Plate 6.1) is a classic example of this process and has already been mentioned in Chapter 4B.

2. Muirburn

This is the deliberate practice of periodically burning off the above ground vegetation of heather (*Calluna vulgaris*) dominated moorland in Britain, with the aim of maintaining it in as nutritive and as productive a condition as possible.

(a) Stages in the growth of heather

Four stages in the growth of heather have been recognised (Gimingham, 1975). The *pioneer stage* is the first 6–10 years when heather seedlings are establishing themselves and the root system is growing more rapidly than the shoots; the latter, however, are at this stage characterised by a high nutrient content. The *building stage* is characterised by vigorous branched growth, prolific flowering and an increase in biomass to form a continuous ground cover; this is the most valuable and productive stage which lasts for about six years. Thereafter the heather plant becomes *mature*. The ratio of woody stems to green productive shoots increases; the plant acquires a recumbent form and the cover becomes discontinuous. At 20–25 years the shrubby heather plant will have reached its maximum height, growth slows down, the old central branches die off and large gaps form in the cover. At this *degenerate* or *senile* stage, the feeding value of the heather plant is very limited. The object of muirburn, therefore, is to maintain as much of the moorland area in the *building stage* as possible. The surface heather should, ideally, be burned off on a 10–15 year rotation dependent on site conditions.

(b) Effects of heather burning

Burning has two main effects. The first is to destroy the old, woodier plant parts in which an increasing proportion of the nutrients have become stored. They are thereby released in the ashes for uptake by the new shoots. The second effect is to stimulate the growth of new nutritious shoots. Provided the burn is not too severe these are produced by perennating (overwintering) buds situated on the root stock just below the ground surface and protected from the fire by the usually thick layer of heather litter. However, should the heather be burned in the mature to senile stages, recovery from the root stock does not take place; the whole plant is killed and re-establishment has to be effected by natural re-seeding. This is a much slower and more precarious method of reproduction, particularly in face of continuous sheep grazing.

Normally a well-managed heather moor should have little heather over 15–20 years of age. It will be composed of areas varying in age from those burnt in the current year to those of 15 years old. The extent, however, to which the nutrient balance is maintained is a matter of debate. Some analyses suggest that, while nutrient turnover is kept at the optimum rate, a nutrient balance between input and output is likewise achieved, so that the volume of nutrients is maintained throughout the whole heather ecosystem. As shown in Figure 6.4, such a thesis would argue that inputs to the heather ecosystem from rainfall, airborne dust particles, soil weathering and lateral soil-water movement equal losses from burning, grazing and stock removal, soil run-off, leaching and erosion. Other investigators, however, suggest that such a balance is not maintained and that there may well be a progressive drain on at least some nutrients from the system.

Figure 6.4 Main sources of nutrient input and loss in vegetation subject to burning and grazing (After C.H. Gimingham, 1975)

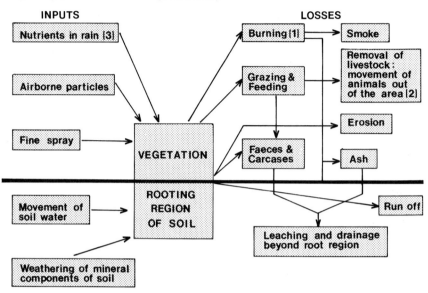

	Nitrogen	Phosphorus	Calcium	Potassium
		(kg/ha/year)		
(1) Losses due to burning heather moorland (average per year if burnt once in 10 years)	4–6	0.3–0.6	0.2–0.4	0.5–0.8
(2) Losses due to sale of ewes and lambs:				
i. Stocking rate 1.5–2 ha/ewe; less than 70% lambing; liveweight sold 10 kg/ha	0.3	0.05	0.09	0.016
ii. 0.5–1 ha/ewe; over 100% lambing; liveweight sold 40 kg/ha	1.2	0.20	0.36	0.064
iii. 0.5–1 ha/ewe, over 100% lambing; liveweight sold 80 kg/ha	2.4	0.40	0.72	0.128
(3) Inputs in rainfall:				
i. Kerloch, near Banchory, Kincardineshire	8.9	0.2	6.7	3.9
ii. Leanachan, West Inverness-shire	14.8	0.44	7.2	13.3

Study the quantitative data given with Figure 6.4:

(*a*) *What types of input and loss shown in the diagram are not covered by the list of data?*

(*b*) *What does the data itself tell you about the nutrient budget of a heather moorland?*

(*c*) *With reference to the data and the diagram, assess the probability of a nutrient balance being maintained in this system.*

E. Reduction in Volume and Rate of Biological Cycling

1. Mode of operation

In the previous section it was demonstrated how human disturbance by the reduction of the quantity of plant biomass, the 'utilised nutrient pool', could under certain circumstances result in an increase in the rate of nutrient cycling. More commonly, however, reduction in biomass is accompanied by a decline in the rate of cycling. This is the case in careless primary cropping (as in deforestation) and secondary cropping as in long-continued overgrazing of semi-natural pastures (e.g. moorland, steppe, savanna, deserts and tundra). In both instances, the effect on the biological cycle involves (a) the extraction of nutrients via the plant biomass in the former, and the animal carcase in the latter, at a rate greater than replenishment, so that the ecosystem progressively runs down in response to a volumetric loss of mineral stocks; (b) the decline in volume and change in the balance of nutrients, frequently accompanied by structural instability in the soil which can accelerate nutrient loss by leaching and/or soil erosion; (c) the replacement of the existing nutrient-rich, easily decomposed organic matter by nutrient-deficient and less easily decomposed types of secondary vegetation, which is accompanied by a slowing down in the rate of nutrient cycling. It is proposed to illustrate these processes in more detail in the following section, in relation to deforestation.

2. Deforestation

The extent of global deforestation has already been noted in Chapter 4. Clearance of such an extensive area has had a considerable impact on the nutrient cycles of the areas involved.

The depletion of the utilised nutrient pool of the forest biomass, together with the active pool of nutrients in the soil, takes place by way of three main routes. Firstly, the initial loss is via the felled trees. This can be substantial since so much nutrient material is stored in the tree biomass during the period of growth. Reduction in nutrient volume will, obviously, be relatively greater from nutrient-poor than nutrient-rich soils. It is, however, generally accepted that reduction is very much more pronounced in tropical than in temperate deciduous forests.

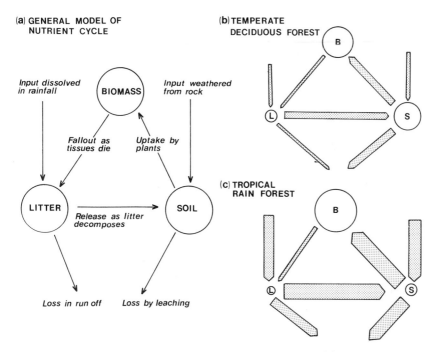

Figure 6.5 Nutrient circulation in three idealised situations: (a) general model of nutrient cycle, (b) temperate deciduous, and (c) tropical rain forest. Arrow widths indicate quantity of nutrient flow expressed as a proportion of amount stored in the source compartment (circles). Circle size denotes the amount of nutrient stored in source compartment (nutrient pool) at equilibrium (After P.J. Gersmehl, 1976)

Figure 6.5 compares the relative sizes of the biomass, soil and litter components of tropical and temperate deciduous forest. This illustrates the fact that the proportion of nutrients in the tree biomass compared to that in the litter layer and the soil is much greater in the former than in the latter. Although data about tropical forests is incomplete and inconclusive, it is widely believed that most of the nutrients are tied up or stored in the above ground vegetation. This is certainly true of carbon; in northern coniferous forests more than 50 per cent, in the tropical rain forest less than 25 per cent, of the organic carbon occurs in the litter and soil (Ricklefs, 1973). Further, in the tropical rain forest, most of the carbon is contained in the woody parts of the trees. Since the main reservoir for carbon is the atmosphere, the disturbance of its cycle is not affected in the same way as that of mineral nutrients whose reservoir is the lithosphere.

There are conflicting opinions, however, about the distribution of mineral nutrients and particularly nitrogen in the tropical rain forest ecosystem. E.P. Odum (1971) and P.J. Gersmehl (1976), for example, maintain that tropical soils are deficient in both respects. In contrast, R.E. Ricklefs (1973) has produced evidence to demonstrate that some tropical forest soils contain as high or higher levels of nutrients than temperate soils (see Table 6.4).

Secondly, as was noted in Chapter 4, deforestation disturbs the soil moisture content by reducing the water loss by evapo-transpiration; eliminating the interception of precipitation by the tree canopy (which can vary from 20–50 per cent of the total) and hence increasing the volume and rate of precipitation reaching the soil surface; this increases rainfall impact which causes surface-soil compaction and thereby accelerates surface run-off of water. It has been estimated that deforestation can augment surface run-off by two to three times its volume under forest (Kovda, 1972). This disruption of the hydrological cycle in the forest ecosystem increases nutrient loss further, as a result of enhanced soil leaching and soil erosion.

Thirdly, deforestation and the consequent exposure of the forest floor to increased sunlight and higher temperatures can accelerate the decomposition and eventual disappearance of litter and its associated nutrients; further, the drastic reduction in supply of organic matter disturbs the normal nitrogen cycle. Recent quantitative analyses of nutrient budgets in forest ecosystems have emphasised that these processes may be more important than erosion per se in causing the reduction of nutrients as a result of deforestation.

Table 6.4   The distribution of mineral nutrients in the soil and vegetation components of representative temperate and tropical forest ecosystems (After R.E. Ricklefs, 1973)

Forest (and locality)	Age (years)	Biomass (tons/ha)	Potassium	Calcium	Magnesium	Phosphorus	Nitrogen
Ash and oak (Belgium)	150	380					
Living			624	1 648	156	95	1 260
Soil			767	13 865	1 007	2 200	14 000
Soil/Living			1.2	8.4	6.5	23.1	11.1
Oak and beech (Belgium)	75	156					
Living			342	1 248	102	44	533
Soil			157	13 600	151	900	4 500
Soil/Living			0.5	10.9	1.5	20.5	8.4
Oak plantation (England)	47	130					
Living			246	257	45	35	393
Soil (70 cm)			329	424	301	36	7 474
Soil/Living			1.3	1.7	6.7	1.0	19.0
Tropical deciduous (Ghana)	50	333					
Living			808	2 477	340	124	1 794
Soil (30 cm)			649	2 573	369	13	4 587
Soil/Living			0.8	1.0	1.1	0.1	2.0

3. Hubbard Brook experimental forest

At this experimental forest situated in the mountains of central New Hampshire (USA), nutrient inputs and outputs were monitored during 1965–68 from a watershed deliberately deforested and then sprayed with herbicide to suppress growth of secondary vegetation. The results have been compared with data from adjacent undisturbed watersheds (i.e. control areas) and with the pattern of nutrient cycling analysed prior to cutting. The principal consequences of deforestation are illustrated in Figure 6.6. Although the output of water run-off from one felled site increased by about only 40 per cent (mainly due to reduction of water loss by evapo-transpiration), it resulted in the increased outflow of particulate (up 4 times) and dissolved organic and inorganic matter (up 15 times). The total export of dissolved inorganic substances from the watershed was 6 to 8 times that of the undisturbed system. The concentration of all cations (i.e. positively charged ions) greatly increased in the run-off; for instance, calcium increased 5 to 6 times, magnesium 5 times and potassium about 8 times, although some anions (negatively charged ions, e.g. $SO_4^=$) decreased. The accelerated loss of these nutrients was closely related to major modifications in the nitrogen cycle and to the interaction of this cycle with that of other nutrients following deforestation, as will now be explained.

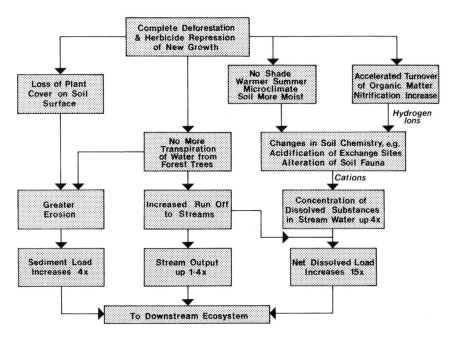

Figure 6.6   Effects of deforestation on ecosystem processes in watershed No. 2 in the Hubbard Brook Experimental Forest (After F.B. Bormann and G.E. Likens, 1970)

Under normal watershed conditions, the decomposition of organic matter releases ammonia (NH_4) which is taken up by the forest vegetation and eventually converted to nitrate within the plants. On the cleared watershed, ammonia released by accelerated organic decay was not taken up by the greatly reduced plant cover but was mostly converted by nitrifying bacteria to nitrate with, at the same time, release of hydrogen.

$$NH_4 \longrightarrow NO_2 \longrightarrow NO_3$$
(ammonia)   (nitrite)   (nitrate)

———— (nitrification) ⟶

└⟶ release of H_2 ions

As already explained, cations are normally held or adsorbed by fairly strong electrical charges to negatively charged soil colloids (clay and humus). The production of hydrogen ions during nitrification allowed these cations to be displaced and hence to be leached away in the drainage waters. The very large quantity of extremely soluble nitrate released by bacteria was also subject to strong leaching effects as was indicated by its greatly increased (30–40 times) concentration in stream water.

4. Secondary vegetation

Deforestation is accompanied, as we have seen, by a fairly drastic reduction in the amount of nutrients in the ecosystem. It can also, under certain circumstances, be accompanied by, or lead to a retardation in the rate of nutrient cycling. This tends to occur where the forest is replaced by nutrient-poor types of secondary vegetation. A classic example is that where temperate oak or birch woodland is replaced by some form of heather dominated vegetation as previously analysed in Chapter 4C. In this case, the formerly extensive, relatively large and rapid nutrient cycle characteristic of the brown earth type of soil of the original forest is replaced by a shallow, smaller and slower circulation of nutrients in the podsolised heather moorland soil.

ASSIGNMENTS

1. *Under what circumstances can the grazing of domestic animals (i) increase, (ii) decrease the rate of nutrient turnover?*
2. *On the basis of Figure 6.5, construct diagrams to illustrate the nutrient cycles of (i) a heather moorland and (ii) a coniferous plantation.*

F. Addition of Synthetic Materials to the Biological Cycle

1. Types of synthetic materials

So far we have been considering some of the effects of humans on the circulation of nutrients, and particularly those required in the greatest quantities for organic growth in the ecosystem. One of the more recent ways in which the biological cycle has been disturbed is by the addition of non-essential, synthetic and frequently harmful substances to the environment. Some are 'accidental' additions in that they are industrial waste products, among which detergents play an important role. Others are synthetic chemical compounds deliberately manufactured for a specific purpose.

Among the latter the most important are the *pesticides* and *herbicides*, poisons designed to kill specific harmful or undesirable animals and plants (i.e. *target species*). Particularly since World War II, there has been an increasing use of these substances in agricultural ecosystems. Nevertheless, despite their direct beneficial effects in the elimination of plant and animal (including human) parasites and disease, these substances can enter the biological cycle (via either plants or animals) and can be circulated or stored en route with directly or indirectly harmful consequences for the ecosystem.

2. Effects of pesticides and herbicides

Some synthetic poisons such as the *organo-phosphate pesticides* (parathion, azodrin and phosdrin) are relatively unstable; that is to say, they are fairly rapidly transformed into an innocuous chemical form either in the soil or in the tissues of organisms. Hence, they are not widely dispersed through the physical environment and do not accumulate in plant or animal tissues. However, they are among the most deadly poisons known. They attack the central nervous system of invertebrates and vertebrates alike, including humans, and kill off many organisms other than target species in areas where they are applied.

These substances, however, have much less impact on the biological cycle than the *organo-chlorine* or *chlorinated hydrocarbon* insecticides such as DDT and its derivatives DDD and DDE, aldrin, dieldrin and the benzene hexachlorides (BHCs) designed specifically to kill insects. They combine general toxicity with a number of other properties which make them particularly harmful (Ehrlich, 1977). First, they are highly soluble in fats and fatty tissue and hence tend to move rapidly from the physical environment into organisms. However, they are more toxic to insects than to mammals, mainly because they can be absorbed more easily through the insect cuticle than through the mammalian skin. Second, the organo-chlorines have great chemical stability and may persist in a toxic form for years or even decades in the ecosystem. Table 6.5 indicates that, even after 17 years, some soils may retain as much as 39 per cent of their original application of DDT.

As a consequence these substances not only accumulate in the physical environment but, more significantly, become rapidly concentrated and stored in organic tissues.

The concentration and storage of DDT and other insecticides have been investigated in a number of mainly aquatic ecosystems. Table 6.6 summarises the results of investigations into the Long Island saltmarshes and quite

Table 6.5   Persistence of organo-chlorines in the soil (After P.R. Ehrlich *et al.*, 1977)

Insecticide	Years since treatment	Percent remaining
Aldrin	14	40
Chlordane	14	40
Endrin	14	41
Heptachlor	14	16
Dilan	14	23
Isodrin	14	15
Benzene hexachloride	14	10
Toxaphene	14	45
Dieldrin	15	31
DDT	17	39

Table 6.6   Concentration of DDT, in parts per million (ppm), in Long Island saltmarsh ecosystem (After G.M. Woodwell, 1967)

Predatory birds or fish (cormorant)	(carnivore)	23– 26 ppm
Birds (green heron)	(carnivore)	3– 18 ppm
Predatory fish (fluke, billfish)	(carnivore)	1.2–2.1 ppm
Marsh insects (mud snails)	(herbivores and carnivores)	0.30 ppm
Bay shrimp	(herbivore)	0.16 ppm
Plankton algae	(primary producer)	0.04 ppm
DDT in water	—	0.05 pp thousand m

clearly demonstrates the increasingly high accumulation of DDT as it moves from water, first to primary producers and then, in turn, to herbivores, carnivores and higher carnivores.

Also, in Clear Lake (California) where DDD was used in the late 1940s and 1950s to control a large midge population, concentration ratios were about 265 times from water into plant plankton, 500 times into small fishes and up to 80 000 times into the fatty tissues of grebes and 75 000 times into that of predatory fishes. The progressive accumulation and concentration of these toxic substances tends to have more serious repercussions at the highest trophic levels at the end of the food chains. For example, high concentrations of DDD (1600 ppm) in the tissues of the Western Grebe resulted in the decimation of a colony of a thousand birds in Clear Lake.

The elimination or marked reduction of natural populations can also result from the indirect and less obvious effects of long-term exposure to lower levels of tissue contamination by pesticides. The failure of certain aquatic carnivorous birds (Osprey, Bald Eagle, Brown Pelican) and terrestrial feeders (Peregrine Falcon, European Sparrow Hawk) have been traced to residues of DDT and its derivatives. These chemicals, appear to interfere with calcium assimilation, and result in eggs with shells so thin that they are crushed by the weight of the incubating parent.

Since the organo-chlorine insecticides are very mobile they and, more particularly, DDT have attained worldwide distribution. Despite its low solubility, DDT is carried in water draining from the land into lakes and streams and eventually into the oceans. In addition, it can be volatilised and, adhering to fine dust particles, can be airbone around the globe. Some marine birds and fish off the Antarctic coast, remote from areas of direct application, have low levels of DDT and DDD in their tissues.

ASSIGNMENT

(a) *Study Table 6.6 and Figure 2.5b. Note the species shown in Table 6.6 and identify them on the energy food web shown in Figure 2.5b.*
(b) *What relationship exists between the concentration of DDT in the organism and its trophic position in the food web?*
(c) *Suggest a mechanism for this relationship.*

G. Collapse of the Biological Cycle

Humans alter the volume and rate of nutrient cycling, and contaminate the cycle with biologically non-essential substances. Ultimately, any of the disruptive actions examined so far can eventually lead to the complete breakdown of the biological cycle. This can result from the entire depletion of the active and utilised pools of nutrients, or by a break or blockage in the biological cycle. For instance, removal of all surface organic matter (as already noted in deforestation, overcropping, overgrazing and overburning) from a given ecosystem can lead to accelerated soil-erosion such that the active pool of weathered soil parent-material is removed and unweathered, bare rock is exposed.

1. Laterisation and desertification

The removal of tropical rain forest, with its continuous supply of litter to the soil, can have particularly drastic results. Under conditions of constantly high temperatures and humidity the breakdown and turnover of litter is rapid, so that organic matter quickly declines on or in the soil. In addition, intense leaching promotes progressive *laterisation*. This is the soil process whereby nutrients and silica compounds in the soil are removed, leaving a deeply weathered parent material rich in compounds of iron and aluminium. Deforestation, particularly when followed by cultivation and/or grazing, exposes the ground surface to a greater amount and intensity of precipitation and, in the case of cultivation, to higher amounts of oxygen.

These processes rapidly deplete soil organic matter. Direct exposure, particularly to high temperatures, results in the progressive hardening of the soil and the eventual formation of a thick, strongly cemented and sterile lateritic (i.e. brick-like) horizon or hardpan on or near the ground surface. Furthermore, in the semi-arid areas of Africa, overgrazing with the removal of organic matter and a breakdown of the soil structure leads to increased loss of rainfall by direct surface evaporation. This is thought to be the main reason for the rapid expansion of desert conditions or *desertification*. For example, in 1882 desert and waste land amounted to 9.4 per cent of the world's land area; by 1952 they were estimated at 23.5 per cent. Even allowing for more complete information and standardised definitions this is a considerable change. Not only do such processes result in a breakdown of the biological cycle, but they can give rise to a physical habitat which may be almost or completely biologically sterile. It may, in addition, produce a change which is either extremely difficult to reverse or is, given existing technology, irreversible.

2. Salinisation and alkalinisation

A particularly striking example of the collapse of the biological cycle as a result of the human attempt to increase nutrient cycling and agricultural productivity is *salinisation* and *alkalinisation* of irrigated soils in arid regions of the world. In many such areas rainfall is low, evapo-transpiration is high and, in the absence of leaching, the active pool of nutrients in the soil is large.

However, biological cycling is limited, indeed intermittent, due to an absolute deficiency of soil-water in desert areas. The addition of water by various methods of irrigation allows the potential fertility to be released and nutrient cycling speeded up quite spectacularly. Indeed, given the high insolation of hot deserts and an all-year-round water supply, it is possible to obtain two to four, and occasionally more, crop harvests per year.

Unfortunately, irrigation has within it the seeds of its own destruction. Continual addition of water, without adequate drainage, tends to cause a gradual raising of the general or local water-table. This causes waterlogging of much of the sub-soil; restriction in depth of the potential rooting zone; and the lifting of the zone in which water can rise by capillary action from the water-table to within reach of the ground surface. It further effects increasing salinisation of the upper soil horizons.

Desert and semi-arid soils are characteristically saline, i.e. relatively rich in the easily leached ions of sodium, magnesium and calcium. Not only are these nutrients initially present in the soil, but irrigation water dependent on its source, may also be relatively saline. As a result of high evaporation rates, excess compounds such as sodium chloride, magnesium and calcium carbonate and sulphate are precipitated in the soil pores and on the soil surface. In time this process becomes evident in a whitish 'bloom' on the surface, characteristic of 'white alkali' soils. While many irrigated crops are relatively salt-tolerant (e.g. sugar beet and alfalfa) increasing accumulation of salts above optimum levels are deleterious. High salt content tends to inhibit the absorption of water and hence the nutrient uptake by plants; to create nutrient imbalance because excess sodium and calcium, and hence alkalinity, may create conditions which make other nutrients, such as iron, phosphorus and copper, unavailable; and to destroy the soil structure, and hence soil drainage and aeration. Yields fall below economic levels and the successful cultivation of the particular salt-intolerant crops, such as citrus fruit, may be inhibited completely. Very considerable areas, literally millions of acres of irrigated land, have been affected by the human-induced 'disease' of salinisation. The Soviet soil scientist V.A. Kovda (1972) asserts that 60–80 per cent of all irrigated land (3–4 per cent of all that cultivated) is gradually being transformed into 'saline deserts'.

Salinisation may be checked or even reversed by lowering the water-table to prevent waterlogging, and by 'flushing' the soils with fresh water to wash out excessive salts, as well as ensuring adequate drainage during irrigation. Unfortunately, such attempts to rectify salinisation can cause even more difficult conditions of alkalinisation. This occurs when there is a high concentration of free sodium chloride in the soil. The addition of water and downward leaching produces compounds of sodium with either carbonates or hydroxides, both of which make the soil solution excessively alkaline, with pH levels of 9 to 10. This is beyond the limits of tolerance of all crops. It also causes the soil structure to become unstable, and fine clay particles can be washed downwards. Organic matter is dispersed and goes into solution. When the soils eventually dry out they become highly compacted and impermeable, covered with a black surface scum of very alkaline organic matter. The latter gives to such soils the name of 'black alkalis', which are practically sterile. Under these circumstances alkalinisation causes a complete collapse of the biological cycle which is extremely difficult to reverse on an extensive scale.

ASSIGNMENTS

1. *Outline the similarities and contrasts between the processes of laterisation and desertification.*
2. *Discuss the ways in which the following processes may lead to a 'collapse' of the biological cycle: overgrazing; cultural eutrophication; production of toxic wastes.*

Key ideas

A. *Human disturbance of the biological cycle*
1. Human activities disturb the biological cycle by altering the composition, volume and rate of turnover of nutrients.
2. They can also affect the cycle by the addition of synthetic non-essential substances.

B. *Increase in volume and rate of biological cycling*
1. The most important way humans increase the volume and rate of biological cycling is by the addition of organic and, more particularly, inorganic fertilisers.

2. The principal advantages of organic fertilisers are that they improve the structural and the nutrient conserving properties of the soil.
3. Inorganic fertilisers increase the volume and rate of nutrient cycle but are more susceptible to leaching.

C. *Increase in volume and decrease in rate of biological cycling*
1. Addition of nutrients from agricultural, domestic and industrial waste has resulted in cultural eutrophication (nutrient enrichment) in water bodies and soil.
2. In nutrient enriched (eutrophic) ecosystems, rapid increase of net primary productivity, followed by a rapid but incomplete decay, result in conditions which eventually decrease the rate of nutrient turnover.

D. *Reduction in volume and increase in rate of biological cycling*
1. Increase in rate of nutrient turnover with decrease in volume can be brought about either by replacement of long-run by short-run plants; or by periodic reduction in biomass by grazing or burning.
2. Muirburn accelerates the release of nutrients and maintains the vegetation at a stage when NPP, but not the biomass, is at a maximum.

E. *Reduction in volume and rate of biological cycling*
1. Extraction of nutrients, generally by grazing and cropping, at a rate greater than replacement, leads to a reduction in volume and rate of nutrient cycling.
2. Reduction is most marked in the case of deforestation because of the relative volume of nutrients stored in the living plant.
3. Deforestation also causes further, indirect reduction in nutrient volume and turnover, through leaching and soil erosion.
4. Rates of nutrient turnover may be slower in deforested areas because of the subsequent development of slow growing, nutrient-deficient secondary vegetation.

F. *Addition of synthetic materials to the biological cycle*
1. The most harmful synthetic materials which enter the biological cycle are pesticides and herbicides.
2. These either accumulate in the physical environment or are rapidly concentrated in animal tissues.
3. High solubility in organic (fatty) tissue combined with high stability and mobility in the environment make the organo-chlorine insecticides, in particular, a serious pollution threat to the biological cycle.

G. *Collapse of the biological cycle*
1. Any actions can deplete the nutrient pool and/or disrupt the nutrient cycle so as to cause an irreversible breakdown.
2. Laterisation and desertification, characteristic of wet and sub-humid tro-

pical areas respectively, result in excessive nutrient-pool depletion and, eventually, in widespread collapse of the biological cycle.
3. Salinisation and alkalinisation common to the hot desert and irrigated areas of the world cause a major disruption in the biological cycle and ultimately its collapse over extensive areas.

Additional Activities

1. Field Project A

(a) In a selected area see if you can locate two or more of the following types of farm: dairy; pig; livestock rearing and/or fattening; predominantly arable; fruit and/or vegetable.

(b) Ask the farmer to give you a list of what would be considered waste materials and how they are treated.

(c) Comment on differences between types of waste material and methods of treatment in and between selected farms.

2. Field Project B

(a) Arrange to visit the factory (or plant) of a selected manufacturing industry.

(b) Try to make a list of the waste materials (and their composition), and the methods of disposal.

(c) What, if any, are the main biological problems associated with their disposal.

3. Field Project C

(a) In a selected area locate, if possible, two small water bodies, one in a rural the other in an urban/industrial area or fringe area. For each:

(b) Record and map the surrounding land use.

(c) Find out what you can about the origin of the water-bodies and their past and present uses.

(d) Note the presence of any waterside or floating vegetation; relative transparency of water; nature of substratum (e.g. mud, stones, etc.); colour of water; presence and type of any pollutants.

(e) From near the water's edge, take samples of water (1 litre) at 10 cm and 30 cm.

(f) In the laboratory, if possible, measure: pH; dissolved oxygen content; algae concentration; suspended solids from the two water bodies.

(g) Compare the two types of water and suggest reasons for any differences or similarities.

4. (a) Refer to Table 6.4. Comment on the degree of comparability and standardisation of the data shown.
   (b) Despite the lack of comparability of the data, how can you use the table to support the hypothesis that not all tropical soils are nutrient-poor?

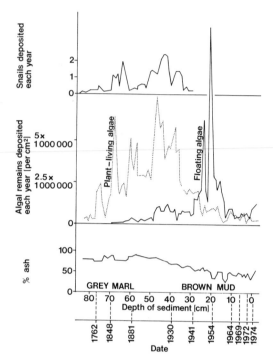

Figure 6.7   Environmental indicators in the sediments of Strumpshaw Broad. Analyses of sediments in Strumpshaw Broad chart the fortunes of aquatic life as nearby Norwich grew and added nutrients (especially phosphorus) to waterways through its wastes (After B. Moss, 1979)

5. (a) Study Figure 6.3 and Table 6.7. What do they tell us about the nutrient economy of the Broads?
   (b) With the aid of the text, comment on the likely sources of supply of the two nutrients shown.
   (c) Consult Figure 6.7 and Table 6.8. Describe the recent changes in fauna and flora which have occured in the Broads.
   (d) What changes are taking place in the type and rate of sedimentation in Strumpshaw Broad? Refer to Figure 6.7.
   (e) In what ways may alterations to the nutrient economy of the Broads be responsible for recent ecosystem change?
   (f) Analyse the trends shown in Table 6.9 which have taken place in private boating activity in the Broads in recent years.

Table 6.7 Maximum winter nitrate levels in Hickling Broad (After T. O'Riordan, 1979)

Date	Nitrate levels mg/litre
1952	0.6
1975	1.1
1976	2.1
1978	1.9
1979	2.1

Table 6.8 Water plant decline in Hickling Broad (After T. O'Riordan, 1979)

Date	Tons of water plant removed by River Commissioners
1960	2000
1965	1800
1970	800
1975	negligible

Table 6.9 The numbers of private craft registered in Broadland, 1968–78 (After T. O'Riordan, 1979)

Date	Number of Private Craft	
	Motor Craft	Yachts
1968	3000	1200
1969	2900	1300
1970	3000	1200
1971	3400	1500
1972	3500	1550
1973	4200	1600
1974	4300	1700
1975	4400	1800
1976	4300	1500
1977	4200	1300
1978	4600	1200

(g) In what ways may recent changes in tourist activity be responsible for recent ecosystem change in the Broadlands? (See B. Moss, 1979).

7 Ecosystem Stability

A. Ecosystem Regulation

A characteristic feature of the ecosystem is its ability within limits to regulate itself (see Chapter 2B). This is seen first in the process of *succession*, whereby the system develops through a series of stages each of which, as a result of habitat modification, prepares the way for, and is replaced by, a more demanding organic community which can make fuller use of the available resources. This is an example of a positive feedback mechanism (see page 8), since at each stage in the succession more energy and nutrients accumulate in the system than are degraded. The final stage is the *climax*, at which it is assumed that any further development under existing environmental conditions ceases. The second aspect of ecosystem self-regulation is the ability of the climax to maintain and perpetuate itself, by negative feedback mechanisms in a *steady* or *stable* state.

The main aim of this chapter is to analyse the principal ways in which humans can affect the self-regulating mechanisms and, more particularly, the stability of ecosystems. However, it is first necessary to consider the concepts of climax and stability in more detail.

B. The Climax Concept

The climax concept has long been, and indeed still is, central to many ecological principles. It has also been a topic of considerable and continuing debate. The climax is the final or, as it is sometimes described, the mature stage or end point of ecosystem development. This is the stage at which it is assumed that the maximum biomass possible, under prevailing environmental conditions, has been attained. The ecosystem has reached a steady state which implies a relative balance or equilibrium in respect of its biomass, species populations, inputs and outputs of energy and nutrients, and biological productivity. Also, the maximum use possible is being made of the available inorganic resources. The climax, therefore, implies that ecosystem development has reached a limit. Initially there were two schools of thought regarding the type and relative importance of the limiting factors involved.

(*i*)   *The mono-climax* school maintained that the climate was the principal limiting factor. Irrespective of the initial site conditions, all successions would eventually culminate in an ecosystem dominated by a type of vegetation whose form and function would be determined by prevailing climatic conditions. It would be dominated by those species whose height and form allowed them to compete most successfully for the available resources. For instance, tropical rain forest, monsoon forest, temperate deciduous forest are classic examples of climax vegetation. This approach, however, recognised only one type of climax vegetation — the climatic *climax*.

(*ii*)   *The poly-climax* school, in contrast, maintained that the climax vegetation could be determined by one of a number of limiting factors including climate, geological conditions, soils, microclimate and even humans. Thus, there could be as many climax types of vegetation as there are limiting factors. However, climate was still implicitly, if not explicity, regarded as the dominant limiting factor.

Both the 'mono' and 'poly' schools base the climax concept on vegetation; the form and/or composition of the dominant plants are used to identify discrete types of climax communities.

(*iii*)   A third, more recent *climax pattern* school (Whittaker, 1975) interprets the climax in terms of the relative stability of the whole ecosystem in relation to all the interacting environmental variables. The result, it is maintained, will be a continuously varying pattern of climax ecosystems in response to varying sets of habitat conditions. This concept does not, however, provide a practical basis for the classification and identification of actual climax communities because of the difficulty of determining whether or not an ecosystem is in a steady state.

The climax concept is very elusive. However interpreted, there is no unanimity as to the exact criteria by which it should be defined. Even if the dominant vegetation is used, it is difficult to assess whether or not the prerequisite condition has been achieved on the ground. The data which have been accumulating from recent detailed measurements and monitoring programmes may eventually provide an aid in the identification of the characteristics of actual or potential climax ecosystems. Identification and mapping, however, are still done largely on the basis of observation of existing vegetation communities, and the comparison of what are known to be successional or seral stages with those which seem to be more stable. Many attempts have also been made to map what the potential climax would be given the prevailing climatic conditions (Küchler, 1964).

Humans and the climax

However, there are few ecosystems in which humans are not direct or indirect factors of varying significance. The areas occupied by ecosystems, in which humans are the limiting or controlling factors are as, if not more, extensive than those occupied by undisturbed climaxes. With respect to the effect of humans two types of climax can be distinguished:

(a) The deflected or plagio-climax

In this case, the effect either of direct (e.g. fire) or indirect (e.g. domestic grazing animals) human activities is to change the direction of the natural succession and produce a regulated climax ecosystem which would not otherwise have developed. The climax vegetation, be it produced by fire or grazing, will be dominated by components resistant to, or tolerant of, these processes. Should the particular limiting factor cease to operate the ecosystem may or may not develop towards the potential climatic climax.

(b) The human-controlled climax

The human-controlled climax is that represented by agricultural and silvicultural systems which can only be maintained by energy and nutrient subsidies (see Chapter 5C).

Table 7.1 Annual energy flow in a second-growth forest in New Hampshire, USA (After J.R. Gosz et al., 1978)

Energy Component	Kcal/m²/yr
Solar radiation	480 000
Gross primary productivity	10 400
Plant respiration	5 720
Net primary productivity	4 680

Net primary productivity *entering*
  1. Grazing food web ⎱
  2. Detrital food web ⎰
	3 481

Biomass storage above ground	952
Biomass storage below ground	247
Total biomass storage (a)	1 199
Dead organic matter storage on the forest floor (b)	150
Total net production of organic matter by the ecosystem (a + b)	1 349
Net output of energy from ecosystem by stream flow	47

ASSIGNMENTS

1. *What does the data in Table 7.1 tell us about ecosystem development? (If necessary, refer back to Chapter 2.)*
2. *Compare and contrast the three main climax concepts.*

C. The Concept of Stability

As has been explained, one of the most important attributes of the climax or mature ecosystem, is that of *stability*. This is the ability of a system to maintain a relatively constant condition in terms of its species composition, biomass and productivity, with minor fluctuations around a mean value (the equilibrium point), and to return to this steady condition fairly rapidly after internal or external disturbances. The idea that stability and constancy of an ecosystem are positively correlated with diversity of species and with the complexity of community structure (see Chapter 2A) has long been accepted. It is still a widely held ecological theorem.

This idea is based on the assumption that the greater the number of species, and hence of links in the food web, the greater will be the ability of the system to resist and buffer changes in the external environment and ensuing population fluctuations. Also, it is assumed that a large number of food chains and a high degree of complexity of the food web ensure a high development of negative feedback loops whereby abnormal population increases or decreases can be controlled. Population increases or decreases may begin to fluctuate widely, for instance, if an external environmental factor (such as humans or disease) removes the only significant predator from a simple ecosystem. Then herbivore numbers, unchecked by predation, may rapidly increase to overgraze and possibly damage the primary production of the system. On the other hand, removing a similar predator from a complex and diverse ecosystem will have much less serious repercussions. In this case the increase in herbivore populations will most likely be checked by the presence of a diverse range of alternative predators, some of which will quickly fill the unoccupied niche of the eliminated species. Following this argument, diversity plus complexity should give a high degree of homeostasis (Chapter 1B), so that variations of a given ecosystem component or character will always be less than that of the external environmental factors.

However, evidence has been accumulating which casts serious doubt on this hypothesis, and which suggests that there is no *consistent* causal relationship between stability and diversity; in some cases the relationship may, in fact, be an inverse one. Ecosystem complexity may, in certain circumstances, even act to reduce stability. For instance, in a very complex and diverse system a relatively small environmental disturbance may, because of the very complexity of the trophic links, give rise to extensive and long-term repercussions throughout the ecosystem.

In simpler systems response to environmental fluctuations may be more direct, rapid and short-lived. Following this line of thought, it is argued that large disturbances caused by human activities are likely to have more drastic results in a complex than in a simple ecosystem. It has been suggested, for example, that the more complex tropical and subtropical ecosystems are less able to withstand the assaults of humans than the simpler temperate and boreal ones (Margalef, 1975).

(a) *Refer back to Figure 2.5b and analyse the possible effects of overfishing of shrimps, eels and clams.*

(b) *Compare the effect of the removal of the redwing black bird from the simple plant — herbivore — carnivore food chain and the merganser duck from the main, much more complex food web.*

(c) *Comment on the implications of these impacts for ecosystem stability.*

D. The Concept of Fragility

Another important ecosystem characteristic related to stability, is that of *fragility*; this is the ease with which an ecosystem can be disruputed. It will depend, first, on the relative resilience of the system and, second, on the type of disturbance to which it is subjected.

1. Ecosystem resilience

Resilience, sometimes referred to as 'robustness' or 'durability' (Holling, 1973), is the term used to describe the ability of an ecosystem to persist and to maintain itself in the face of disturbances due to weather or climate, chemical factors, organisms, or humans. The relative resilience of an ecosystem is dependent on: (a) its *amplitude* or how far it can deviate from the equilibrium or steady state before complete disruption and replacement by another system occurs; and (b) its *elasticity* or the rate with which it can recover from disturbances. Resilience, therefore, is an expression of how much an ecosystem can be disturbed, how drastically its condition can fluctuate in space or time before it is disrupted completely. It has been described as 'a measure of the probability of the extinction of an ecosystem' (Holling, 1973).

The relative resilience, or fragility, of an ecosystem will be related to that attribute which is most susceptible to disruption or to that environmental disturbance against which the ecosystem has the least resistance. Fragility will, therefore, be dependent on the weakest component or link which will obviously vary form one ecosystem to another. For example, if the system is a relatively stable one because of a constant environment with a small range of fluctuation, as in the case of the tropical rain forest, its resilience will be low; it will be potentially fragile in the face of environmental changes. On the other hand, an ecosystem such as the Arctic tundra, whose populations may fluctuate dramatically in response to an intensely unstable environment, will tend to be more resilient and less fragile.

2. Type of disturbance

Fragility is also dependent upon the *type of disturbance*, in terms of intensity and duration, to which the ecosystem is subjected. For example, very diverse and complex systems such as are found in the humid tropics can be resilient in the face of violent storms to which they have long been adapted On the other hand, they can be extremely vulnerable and potentially very fragile to disturbances of an apparently minor but unusual nature — such as a road or electric power line. In contrast, there are some systems which seem to require periodic disturbance in order to perpetuate themselves. This is common in the northern boreal forest where the climax vegetation may create microclimatic and soil conditions inimical to the germination of its own seed. Periodic fire would appear to be essential, in that it not only stimulates the dispersal of seed from cones, but opens up the forest and creates light conditions necessary for rapid seedling growth.

Nearly all human activities disturb 'natural' ecosystems to a lesser or greater extent. And, as has already been stressed, there are very few areas of the earth's surface entirely unaffected by direct or indirect human influence. They can, and often do, cause disturbances such as were formerly not encountered by organisms and which are beyond the limit of tolerance of the ecosystem. They subject the ecosytem to stresses greater than would otherwise occur. These, as have already been noted, can completely destroy an ecosystem. In some cases, severe stress may inhibit its re-establishment or effect an irreversible change. Nevertheless, the relative resilience of many regulated and controlled ecosystems can be surprisingly high. It has been said that the price humans have had to pay for the successful exploitation of organic resources is that of maintaining the stability and increasing the resilience of the man-made ecosystem by constant management.

In the following sections, we will analyse the factors contributing to the relative fragility or resilience of some selected ecosystems. Among the principal objectives will be that of identifying those attributes most sensitive to stress, and of illustrating how the bases of fragility or resilience vary from one type of ecosystem to another.

E. Fragile Ecosystems

Fragile ecosystems are: those with a high proportion of the energy and nutrient store in the above-ground biomass; those on youthful unstable soils; those with a limited extent as in islands of all kinds. The following sections illustrate these different types of fragility.

1. Fragile biomass

The most fragile of the world ecosystems is, undoubtedly, the tropical rain forest. Its extreme vulnerability to disturbance is related to its diversity or species richness, and the volume and vertical distribution of its biomass.

(a) Diversity

An outstanding characteristic of the forest is its richness in species, many of which are extremely rare; 40–100 species of tree per hectare is not unusual in relatively undisturbed stands. Species' populations, therefore, tend to be relatively small in comparison with temperate and boreal forests, where the dominance over considerable areas of a few species with large populations is more usual. Furthermore, the primary climax rain forest trees tend to have relatively low seed production and dispersal capabilities, small numbers of large seeds per climax tree, and seeds which exhibit very little or no dormancy. Unless they germinate almost immediately after dispersal, they are likely either to be eaten or to decompose very rapidly. The scarcity of viable primary tree seeds on or under the ground surface has been corroborated in many areas. In addition, there are very few migratory species of climax trees, so that quite limited barriers can very effectively check dispersal. In the deep shade of the dense, thick canopy of the climax forest, seedlings of the primary trees are either absent or sparse, small and extremely slow-growing. Gomez (1972) has suggested that the survival potential of these forests is dependent on species whose seeds can germinate very rapidly and whose seedlings can persist for a long time in a slow-growing condition.

Regeneration of the tropical rain forest is, therefore, precarious and complex. It is linked with relatively small clearings which occur naturally in the course of the death of primary trees, or may result from localised tropical storms or from floods. In such clearings, any seedlings of primary trees that are present will start to grow at a greatly increased rate. At the same time, secondary or colonising seedlings become established. These are the fast-growing, light demanding trees whose seeds have a high degree of dormancy, long viability in the soil and very efficient dispersal mechanisms. Thus, the seeds of secondary species, which may remain dormant in the soil for long periods of time, would appear to be the most important regenerative agents. In time, however, the secondary species will be overtopped and suppressed by the shade of the primary tree canopy. But this final re-establishment can take a very long time, at least 500 years as far as can be gathered from available evidence (Gourou, 1966).

The ability of the tropical rain forest to perpetuate itself is, as a result, somewhat delicately balanced on a knife edge. It can, in fact, be put at risk by quite minor disturbances which can have far-reaching implications for the recovery of the whole ecosystem. The intensity of human impact is dependent on the size of the area that is cleared and on the use to which it is put. The tropical rain forest appears to have adapted reasonably well, until recently, to small-scale, long-rotation, shifting agriculture by the indigenous populations. However, as cleared areas have become more extensive, (see Plate 7.1) the sources of primary tree seeds have been reduced. They become less available because of the relative scarcity of individuals of any one species, combined with a very short dispersal range. Hence, large areas beyond the dispersal range of primary trees tend to become colonised by secondary species alone or by species adapted to disturbance. The latter include species from drier areas whose seeds also have the ability to remain in a dormant condition for long periods of time. As a result, an ecosystem

Plate 7.1 Wilderness road facilitating development of Amazonia in the Trombetas area, Brazil. (*Pascal Villiers le Moy, Camera Press Ltd*)

consisting of species from drier areas mixed with secondary tropical rain forest trees becomes established. It is lower in height than the original climax vegetation, often open and savanna-like in form, as a consequence of a mass extinction of climax species and their associated organisms.

(b) Biomass

The tropical rain forest has the largest biomass of any of the world's ecosystems. It is not only the most massive and most diverse, but it is also the most structurally complex. Under optimum conditions, it may be characterised by two or three strata of trees of varying height potential and species composition. Constantly high temperature and humidity are reflected in continuous growth and an evergreen appearance. The result is a deep dense canopy, the shade of which tends to suppress understorey growth of shrub, field and ground strata such as are found in temperate forests.

Furthermore, the ratio of above to below ground biomass in the rain forest is very high indeed (see Chapter 6E). This is because the trees have characteristically shallow root systems. Also, the rate of biological decomposition is so rapid that the amount of litter on the ground and of organic matter in the soil is low. Almost the entire energy-nutrient pool is, therefore, concentrated above ground; as Gourou has described it 'the capital is large but the turnover is rapid'. Paradoxically, this large organic production is generally associated with nutrient-poor soils, the principal characteristics of which are shown in Figure 7.1. A long uninterrupted period of weathering and leaching has resulted in many tropical soils having poorly developed organic horizons (already outlined in Chapter 6G) overlying an often deep, intensely leached horizon composed largely of iron and/or aluminum compounds. The root system is completely divorced from that other potential source of nutrients, the freshly weathered bed rock. Losses of nutrients have, therefore, to be balanced by inputs from outside the system, for example in rainfall. Over all, however, the forest is 'living on itself' in so far as it is highly dependent on the rapid decomposition and nutrient return from its own litter.

(c) Effects of disturbance

Forest clearing even on a limited scale can result in extreme laterisation. In Brazil rapid laterite formation, following destruction of the tropical rain forest, has converted cultivated fields into sterile rock-pavements within the space of five years. When this happens, it is virtually impossible for the forest to recover or be re-established, and the process is at present difficult, both technologically and economically, to reverse.

The crux of the problem is that many plants and animals of the primary climax rain forest do not live in the secondary forests which have replaced it over considerable areas. They are not adapted to a disturbed environment and the plant seeds are not capable of long-distance dispersal. In parts of

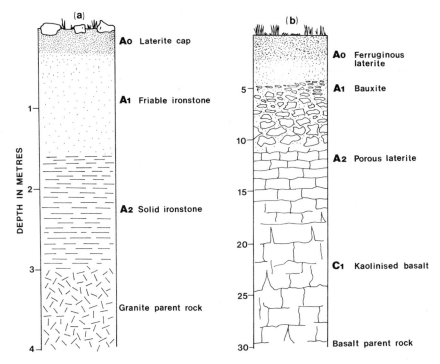

Figure 7.1 Profiles of lateritic soils as found in (a) Benin, West Africa and (b) Southern India. Letters on the right identify the principal soil horizons (After M. McNeil, 1964).

South East Asia and of Africa, the rain forest has been cleared for so long that it is doubtful whether, even if the soils were rehabilitated, it could re-establish itself because the plant genetic loss in the interim has been so great.

The nature of the rain forest's fragility has only recently been fully recognised and understood. The implications are serious, given the recent and increasingly rapid contraction of the forest in face of population growth and agricultural development. This commenced earlier in Africa and Asia than in South America. Now, however, efforts to develop the tropical lowlands, particularly in South America, have involved the recent building of great trans-continental highways, many paralleled by 16–20 km wide strips of land cleared for agriculture (see Figure 7.2 and Plate 7.2) As a result, the rate of rain forest destruction has increased alarmingly. While there are no really realistic figures available, it has been estimated that 5 per cent of the non-riverine forest in South America has been cleared during the past 20–30 years. Denevan (1973) goes so far as to say that 'within a 100 years, probably less, the Amazon rain forest will cease to exist and will be replaced by shrub savanna with some second-growth forest'. If this happens, there is a real danger that there will be a mass extinction of literally thousands of species (some as yet unrecorded) because they are incapable of recolonising large areas opened up by an extensive or intensive agriculture.

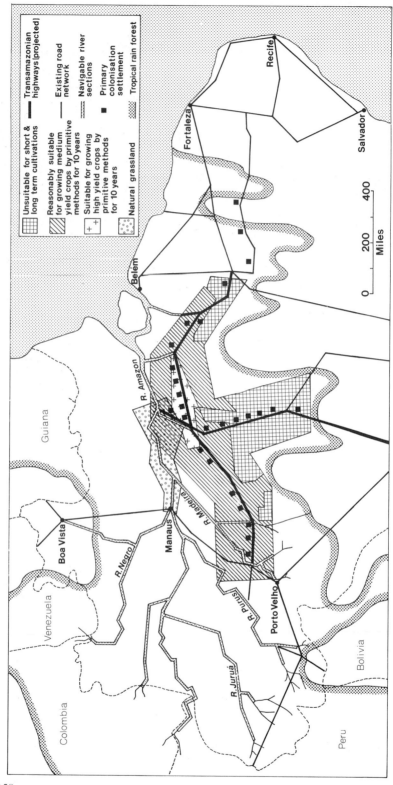

Figure 7.2 Existing roads and projected Transamazonian Highways (After J.M.G. Kleinpenning, 1971)

Plate 7.2 The Trans-Amazonia Highway under construction. After tree felling, the road surface is laid with laterite. (*Edward P Leahy/Geo, Camera Press Ltd*)

In conclusion, the tropical rain forest is in one respect a stable, constant ecosystem with high diversity and complexity because a large part of it must have evolved uninterrupted in a relatively constant climate over a very long period of time. It is, however, not adapted to natural stresses and its resilience is low because of a low density-dependent reproductive rate, the extreme habitat specialisation of many of its species, a lack of seed dormancy, a low dispersal rate, and few migrants. The number of disturbances which may have a significant impact on the rain forest are much greater than in temperate forests because they represent a more drastic departure from those with which the tropical rain forest has evolved and to which it is adapted.

2. Youthful and unstable soils

In marked contrast to the tropical rain forest, the *Arctic tundra* ecosystem is very young, having evolved to its present condition only since the last glaciation in the Pleistocene period. Also, it is a comparatively simple system. Primary biological productivity is limited by a short, cool growing season — one or two months in the High (N.73°) three to four in the Low Arctic. The vegetation is short in stature, dominated by a relatively small number of species of low shrubs, heaths, sedges, grasses, mosses and lichens; it becomes open and discontinuous in the High Arctic tundra. As in the tropics, human impact on the tundra has increased considerably within the last decade or so, particularly with the discovery of oil, natural gas and minerals, together with road building and other developments consequent on exploitation. As a result, the relative fragility or resilience of the tundra has become a matter of practical concern. It has, in fact, long been assumed by biologists that the tundra ecosystem is fragile because of a low species diversity combined with widely fluctuating, small, predatory, mammal populations, and the inherent youthfulness and physical instability of its soils. It is relevant then, to assess the extent to which these two characteristics contribute to the ecosystem's fragility.

(a) Poor and fluctuating species composition

Characteristic of the Arctic tundra is not only a small number of plant and, more particularly, animal species, but also the marked cyclic fluctuations of many of its bird and mammal populations (see Figure 3.7). The frequency of these fluctuations can vary between and even within species. Small herbivores such as voles and the notorious lemmings usually exhibit four-year population cycles; larger species such as muskrat, grouse and ptarmigan, nine to ten years. The length of these cycles, however, tends to be related to the nature of the habitat, with the short cycles more characteristic of the harsher conditions of the High Arctic.

Of these animals the Arctic lemming has received most publicity. Its biological rhythms have been studied in some detail on the coastal plain near Barren Point, Alaska. Here the tundra ecosystem is extremely simple with 100 species of higher plants, 10 of which account for 90 per cent of the total biomass. There is only one major herbivore, the brown lemming, whose diet is composed largely of three vascular species. There are only two major bird, and six minor mammal and bird predators that eat the lemming.

A popular and plausible explanation of the lemming population cycle is the nutrient-recovery hypothesis (Schultz, 1969), which involves the whole Arctic ecosytem. The surface is underlain by permanently frozen ground called permafrost, only the top few decimetres of which thaw out during the short summer. As a result, surface soils are frequently saturated in summer. Decomposition of organic matter is retarded by the cold waterlogged conditions and peat accumulates. Ninety-six per cent of all carbon in the Northern Alaskan tundra is bound up in peat and the ratio of above to below ground biomass is extremely low, in the order of 25:75. The nutrient cycle is not in a steady state because of the slow accumulation of organic matter in the form of peat, which acts as a rather stagnant nutrient pool. Nutrient input via precipitation is negligible, a consequence of clean and low snowfall. On the generally level terrain, surface run-off is retarded; loss of precipitation by evaporation is relatively high in summer, and leaching is thereby minimised. In addition, the permafrost further restricts leaching. The nutrient capital is relatively high but is held in the peat which decomposes slowly so that release and turnover is very slow. Hence, low nutrient availability limits primary biological production.

Research has revealed that during the periods when lemming populations are building up (1959–60 and 1964–65 in particular) they fertilise the soil with urine and phosphorus-rich faeces. Intensive grazing by a growing population subsequently removes much of the surface vegetation, with the result that in summer the soil thaws to a greater depth than before. Roots can, therefore, penetrate deeper into the soil where nutrient levels are lower than near the surface. Reduced uptake leads to poorer quality forage in the summer after the lemming population has reached its peak. It seems reasonable to suggest that such a reduction in the quality and quantity of the forage will have an adverse effect on the size of the lemming population together with its reproductive capacity. Falling herbivore numbers however, will allow, the 'vicious cycle' to repeat itself. During the succeeding two to three years the process is reversed; the vegetation slowly recovers and the biomass increases. The depth to which the surface soil thaws out decreases consequent upon improved insulation. The active roots are once again confined to the surface peat-rich soil horizon. The nutrient value of the forage increases, lemming breeding improves and the populations build up again. There is considerable evidence to support this hypothesis though not all the links have been satisfactorily substantiated.

It would, however, seem to complement previous theories which have suggested that population instability, such as that exhibited by lemmings, is a result of the simplicity of the Arctic ecosystem. Because of the simple trophic structure and the small number of links in the food chains, disturbance could result in the disruption and possible complete destruction of the tundra ecosystem. There are so few species, especially of predators, that it would be difficult to fill the niches if one or more were exterminated. Instead, there might well be a build-up of herbivores which could seriously overgraze the vegetation to an extent that recovery would be difficult or impossible. It is now suggested, however, that such wide fluctuations of animal numbers contributes to natural resilience rather than fragility of the ecosystem. This, however, would only appear to hold good provided the extent of the tundra is great enough to allow population migration in face of disturbances and reduction of food supply. In fact, reduction or severe fragmentation of potential grazing grounds could reduce the population's ability to recover, and have drastic, even irreversible effects on the ecosystem.

(b) Permafrost soils

The reputation of the tundra's fragility has been associated more with soil conditions than with the nature of its biomass. In the Arctic, soils and soil parent material freeze to depths which may exceed 300 m in the Canadian Arctic archipelago. All but the surface layer remain permanently frozen.

The so-called 'active' surface layer thaws out during the short summer to depths which vary from 30–50 cm in fine-textured mineral and organic soils, to 200 cm in well-drained sands and gravels. The underlying permafrost limits normal soil development, drainage and leaching are impeded and the surface soil may remain permanently saturated with a consequent accumulation of peat, or peaty humus. The alternating contraction and expansion characteristic of seasonal freeze/thaw cycles gives rise to very unstable soils. Frost-heave is typical and combined with saturated soil conditions in summer results in the gravity flow of soil on sloping ground. Furthermore, since in winter soils freeze from the surface downwards, the active layer is subjected to squeezing and disturbance between surface-ice and the underlying permafrost. Only hardy plants adapted to these very severe types of soil stress can maintain themselves. These include sedges and grasses with durable root systems, heaths and low shrubs, and a high proportion of mosses and lichens. Vegetation growth is slow, as is organic decomposition.

If this insulating vegetation cover and particularly the peaty organic horizon is reduced, compacted or destroyed, the exposed permafrost can melt very rapidly to considerable depths in summer. This results in surface subsidence (see Plate 7.3); the hollows and ditches so produced widen and deepen from year to year and eventually, if extensive, produce a deeply pitted surface described as thermokarst. Where thermokarst has developed, along river and lake banks and around coasts, it has triggered off accelerated erosion. Breaching of the protective vegetation/organic cover on slop-

Plate 7.3 Building distortion consequent on thaw of permafrost in May, 1969; Richardson Highway, Copper River Region, Alaska. (*US Geological Survey*)

ing ground will give rise to an increased rate of soil flow or solifluction. The increased instability of the exposed mineral material in the Arctic tundra makes it increasingly difficult for perennial plants with deep root systems to re-establish themselves. In fact, the very low rate of primary biological productivity and of decomposition means that ecosystem recovery rate is inevitably slow, and the resulting fragility of the system high. Although direct exploitation of the tundra has been relatively limited, physical damage increased markedly during the 1960s, particularly in the areas subjected to the impact of construction work and vehicle movements.

3. Island ecosystems

Islands comprise another type of particularly fragile ecosystem. The usual concept of an island is a small land mass (not a continent) surrounded by water. However, in biological terms an *island ecosystem* is one which is surrounded by a different habitat, in which its species can either survive with difficulty or not at all, and which is wide enough to form an effective barrier to migration.

Oceanic islands tend to be more vulnerable to human disturbance than adjacent land areas with a comparable physical environment. Their relative fragility is related to their small size (area), isolation, species poverty and ecosystem simplicity.

(a) Isolation and species poverty

The number of island species and their susceptibility to extinction depend on the size and physical environment of the island and its distance from the mainland. The relative isolation and youthful formation of many oceanic islands (e.g. volcanic islands, atolls, etc.) has resulted in impoverished flora and fauna (see Table 7.2). Because of the migration barrier of sea, many groups of plants and animals have failed to reach islands.

This is a characteristic even of larger offshore epi-continental islands. Isolation of the British Isles in the post-glacial period deprived them of species found across the Channel, and in Ireland the number of species of plants and animals is less than that in Britain. In other cases, extreme and long-established isolation has resulted in the divergent evolution of species, sub-species or varieties of plants and animals distinct from those on the neighbouring mainland, as in the case of the Galapagos Islands.

(b) Endemism

Islands usually have a high incidence of *endemism*, that is to say of species naturally exclusive to them (see Table 7.2). One of the results of species poverty is that ecological niches may be unoccupied or be occupied by species which would have been excluded from them had they been subjected to the same degree of competition as occurs on the adjacent mainland. For

Table 7.2   Number of species and endemics on islands and island-like areas compared with continental areas (After S. Carlquist, 1974)

	Number of species	% Endemics
1. *Continental areas*		
California	5529	38.0
West Virginia	2040	0
2. *Continental islands*		
British Isles	1666	0
3. *Old continental islands*		
New Caledonia	2600	90.0 ?
4. *Island-like areas*		
Afro-alpine flora	279	?
South-western Australia	3886	90.0 + ?
5. *Oceanic islands*		
Canary	826	53.3
Fernando	826	12.0
Galapagos Islands	386	40.9
Hawaiian Islands	1729	94.4
Juan Fernandez	146	66.7
St. Helena	45	88.9

instance, the absence of predatory vertebrates has permitted the evolution and existence of extremely large populations of ground-nesting sea birds and flightless land birds, and also the development of vegetation normally very sensitive to grazing, such as tussock grass formations so characteristic of southern latitude oceanic islands. Indeed, lack of competition is a very important factor which allows many island species to fluctuate widely. It has also resulted in the survival of *relict* species, particularly on some of the older tropical islands which survived the effects of Pleistocene glaciation. Conversely, plants, particularly annual plants, associated with early seral stages in vegetation development are scarce or absent. As a result, there is a paucity of species capable of colonising disturbed or bare ground.

(c) Effects of humans

Despite their isolation, islands have been early subjected to human impact. The majority of the world's tropical and sub-tropical oceanic islands have been settled, temporarily or permanently, and their flora and fauna modified some centuries ago. The number of undisturbed islands (mainly in the southern temperate and sub-Antarctic zones) are, as a result, of particular scientific interest. Human impact has involved first, the early deliberate destruction of native species of fur seals, elephant seals and penguins by temporary visitors such as whalers, sealers and explorers; second, the liberation, often accidentally, of domestic grazing and browsing stock, predatory animals and vermin, the most common being the pig, goat, deer, rabbit and rat; and third, the modification of the natural vegetation cover by cutting and burning, and the widespread introduction of exotic species.

The result has been the extinction of many native animal and plant species. Island faunas are particularly vulnerable to decimation because their populations are small, often fluctuating and confined to relatively wide but few habitats. Most significantly, however, they have often evolved without predators. Those mammals with the highest extinction rates have been the large carnivores and those with very specialised habitat requirements. The rate of species extinction on islands is potentially high and a large proportion of all those species exterminated have been island ones.

Even more catastrophic has been the introduction of grazing and browsing animals not formerly present. In some cases this has resulted in the destruction of the maritime tussock grass; in others, such as St Helena and Juan Fernandez Islands, the complete destruction of their floras by goats introduced as early as the sixteenth century. Also, the single vegetation dominant, a grass species (*Poa foliosa*) on Macquarie Island, the only plant capable of stabilising steep slopes, has been heavily grazed by rabbits. Vegetation destruction or overgrazing by introduced herbivores has resulted in accelerated soil erosion on all these islands.

Isolation, small areal extent, species poverty and consequent lack of competition, therefore, make island ecosystems particularly fragile in the face of disturbance. The endemic ecosystems, which are often only partially developed in comparison to those on the mainland, have limited powers of recovery and can easily be replaced by another completely different, often even more degraded system.

ASSIGNMENTS

1. (a) Note the salient features of the two lateritic soils shown in Figure 7.1. How do such soils differ from an acid brown forest soil and a podsol (see Fig. 4.4)?
   (b) Using this information and with the aid of the text, compare the relative stability of a cool temperate deciduous and a boreal coniferous forest with that of the tropical rain forest.
2. Refer back to Table 7.2.
   (a) Comment on the relationship between the numbers of species and isolation in each of the areas shown.
   (b) What other factors might have an effect on species number?
   (c) Discuss the relationship between the degree of isolation of the different areas and their respective degree of endemism (percentage of endemic species).
   (d) Why are oceanic islands less resilient than continental areas to forms of disturbance?

F. Resilient (Durable) Ecosystems

In contrast to fragile ecosystems, *resilient* ecosystems might be expected to be more durable and robust in the face of environmental and human-induced disturbances, to be maintained and persist longer under stressful conditions and to recover more rapidly from the effect of sub-lethal stresses. However, as in fragile systems, resilience is a function of one or a combination of attributes which vary from one system to another. It is dependent on the strongest component or link in the system. This can be (i) a wide range of tolerance and a variety of adaptations by organisms to environmental stresses as in arid deserts; and (ii) a large below to above ground biomass associated with many types of perennial herbaceous vegetation; and (iii) a high and naturally subsidised energy/nutrient pool characteristic of many estuaries.

1. Arid environments

In marked contrast to the tropical rain forest, the arid desert has the smallest biomass and the lowest biological productivity of all terrestrial ecosystems. It is, however, one of the most resilient and aggressive systems just because it is adapted to survival in a particularly difficult and stressful environment.

An absolute deficiency of water is combined with a supply so variable in time as to be unpredictable. Precipitation is extremely low and episodic; evapo-transpiration rates are high. Water therefore, is, the limiting factor in ecosystem development and productivity. Aridity is exacerbated further by extreme diurnal temperature ranges. Nevertheless the desert ecosystem is remarkably stable. It has the potential to persist in the face of often extreme, short-term, environmental variability. The latter is reflected in irregular variation in species populations, biomass amount and primary biological productivity, from place to place. The inherent resilience of the desert ecosystem is probably dependent on two basic features: the soil conditions, and the ability of plant and animal life to survive in often extreme and prolonged drought.

Table 7.3   Relationship between desert plants and soil-water stores (After I. Noy-Meir, 1973)

	Vertical extent main soil-water stores	Dominant plants
1.	0– 10 cm	algae/lichens
2.	10– 30 cm	fast-growing ephemerals; shrub seedlings
3.	30– 60 cm	established ephemerals; annuals and herbaceous perennials; shrubs with horizontal and vertical roots
4.	60–120 cm	established ephemerals (only if shrubs absent); trees/ shrubs with deep perennial root systems

(a) Soil conditions

Desert soils are, characteristically, poorly developed. Lack of moisture results in a sparse, discontinuous and often ephemeral vegetation cover, and a limited amount of litter and DOM. Soils tend to be *skeletal*, in the sense that they are formed mainly by the mechanical weathering of parent material which varies from rock outcrop to boulders and stones (hamada), shifting sand dunes (barchans) and fine silts and clays. However, the soil can, to a greater or lesser extent, act as a temporary water-store. Its efficiency in this respect is dependent on texture. Coarse-grained materials promoting rapid infiltration and percolation cut down water losses from either run-off or, more frequently, high potential evaporation from the surface. Direct evaporation of water from the soil decreases with depth and again, depending on texture, becomes ineffective below approximately 22 cm or so below the ground surface. Water below this level is stored and becomes available for plant roots and for the many burrowing animals typical of the desert ecosystem.

Furthermore, soil water may be stored with varying effectiveness, at different levels below the surface and, hence, can be tapped by plants with root systems of differing lengths. The dominant plants will be those which can compete most successfully for the largest water-store available at a particular site (see Table 7.3).

(b) Adaptation to drought

The ability of plants and animals to survive drought, however, is probably more important for the resilience of the ecosystem as a whole. Both have a wide range of adaptation to drought, the most important of which are summarised in Table 7.4.

Table 7.4 Adaptations to drought in desert organisms (After R.F. Daubenmire, 1974)

Animals	Plants
1. Increasing water intake	1. Deep, spreading roots
2. Direct water intake from atmosphere	2. Water storage tissues
3. Efficient use of water produced in metabolism	3. Reduction leaf transpiration
4. Reduction of water loss	4. Deciduous habit and/or very small leaves
5. Impermeable covering	5. Photosynthetic stems
6. Behaviour designed to reduce water loss	6. Photosynthetic modifications
	7. Tolerance of tissues to reduced water content
	8. Increased ability to extract soil-water
	9. Synchronisation of growth with periods of favourable precipitation

Such adaptations allow a number of perennial species, in particular the shallow-rooted succulents (cacti) and the deep-rooted shrubs (mesquite) which combine reduced transpiration and water content with the ability to use deep-seated sources of soil or ground water, to resist extreme drought.

However, the ways in which many desert plants synchronise their activity with rainfall, and accumulate reserves of energy, water and nutrients necessary for drought survival, are more important for ecosystem resilience. It has been pointed out by certain workers (Noy-Meir, 1973) that many biological processes in deserts occur in short bursts or pulses of activity which are triggered off by a sudden episodic rainfall of a given amount and duration. The relationship between the pulse, trigger-factor and energy/nutrient reserve is illustrated in Figure 7.3. Herbivores, carnivores and decomposers at the higher trophic levels must adapt to this primary system either by adopting a pulse-reserve pattern of activity as in the case of insects, by utilising reserves of other organisms (e.g. seed-eaters), or by adopting flexible feeding habits which may involve either water storage in their tissues, or migratory feeding patterns.

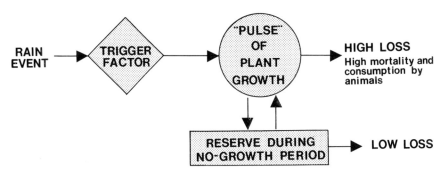

Figure 7.3 Relationship between pulse, trigger and reserve in desert ecosystems (After I. Noy-Meir, 1973)

Three types of desert plants, dependent on their water needs for growth and the nature and location of their main energy/water reserves, can be recognised:

(i) *Poikilohydrics* or plants which maintain all their structures under extreme variation of cell-water content. They can tolerate extreme drought and desiccation, and respond immediately to increased moisture from either the atmosphere or the soil. Such are the surface-living algae, lichens and a few specialised ferns and higher plants.

(ii) *Ephemerals*, the so-called drought evaders, which account for the highest proportion of desert floras. They are capable of completing their life cycle rapidly in the short-period of moisture availability in the upper 5–30 cm of the soil. They include annuals and herbaceous perennials with underground storage organs. The reserve in the annual plant is the seed, rich in nutrients and energy; seed longevity and heterogenity are distinctive characteristics of desert annuals. The former allows delayed germination; the latter, differential germination-timing in the same species. Many desert seeds have their germination very delicately and closely regulated to respond to a precise amount and duration of rainfall, as well as other factors or sequence of factors.

(iii) *Drought-resistant plants*, all of which are perennial, mainly deep-rooted shrubs which can tap sub-surface water, or succulents which can store water in their tissues.

The most important and resistant reserves on which the ability of the desert ecosystem to survive drought stress depends are the plant seed and, to a lesser extent, the underground storage organs. The nutrient cycle, particularly in desert annuals, is, very rapid; it is certainly much higher than in either forest or tundra ecosystems. Nutrient losses from the seed reserve during periods of non-growth are small in comparison to those from litter and DOM in ecosystems with a greater biomass and a slower nutrient cycle. The predominance of the seed reserve pulse explains the resilience of the desert ecosystem in spite of its very simple structure and extreme environmental variability. It would appear to be resistant to all but a complete change of environment such as is effected by irrigation or construction. Also, because of its adaptability to water stress, the more aggressive desert ecosystem has replaced other less tolerant ecosystems where indirect or direct human activities have so disrupted the hydrological cycle as to cause *desertification* of formerly more humid areas.

2. Durable biomass

One of the most widespread and resilient ecosystems is the semi-natural permanent grassland. For convenience it can be defined as 'a plant community in which the dominant species are perennial grasses, and there are few or no shrubs'. Grasses are outstanding in their ability to tolerate a wide range of ecological conditions. They can attain dominance in habitats which range from arctic/alpine to tropical and from arid to humid regions. Their persistence and relative stability of composition in many areas that might otherwise support woody growth is thought to owe much to the direct or indirect effects of humans.

The resilience of the grassland ecosystem is closely related to the durability of its plant biomass and, more particularly, to the growth-form of the grass component, and the relative contribution of the shoot, root, litter and DOM fractions to the total amount of organic matter.

Characteristic features shared by members of the grass family which make the plants exceptionally well-adapted to grazing, cutting and trampling are illustrated in Figure 7.4. The elongated, blade or needle shaped leaves are relatively resistant to physical damage. Unlike many other plants whose leaves grow from their tips, the growth (meristematic) tissues are located at the base of the shoot, very close to the soil surface. During the period of vegetation growth, before flowering, leaf formation can continue after, and

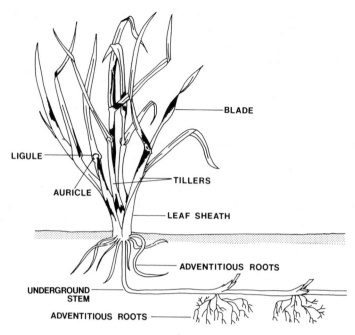

Figure 7.4   Grass growth form (After R.H. M. Langer, 1972)

indeed is stimulated by, grazing and cutting. Grasses can also grow and spread by branching or tillering; tillers are new shoots which develop from buds in the leaf-axil at the base of existing shoots. This means that the number of shoots is increased without a marked lengthening of the stem. Grass species vary in their ability to tiller, however, while the amount and rate of tillering is determined by environmental conditions such as temperature, light and nutrients. It can also be stimulated by defoliation by grazing and cutting.

Another important feature of the grass family is a complex, highly branched and complexly ramified root system. All roots, it seems, have a limited lifespan, rarely exceeding more than a year. This means that there is a continual turnover of organic material in the soil, with the death and decay of old and the production of new roots. The perennial mat-forming grasses have underground stems (rhizomes, stolons, etc.) which not only produce roots at their internodes, but can themselves branch and increase the extent of the root system. Further disturbance, damage and breakage of these stems promotes branching; this feature is particularly well-developed in such persistent weeds as couch grass, and soil stabilisers such as marram grass which colonises sand dunes.

The very high concentration of grass stems and roots, together with leaf and stem litter in the upper layers of the soil, gives rise to a dense, tough turf. This acts as a very effective insulating layer which protects the underlying soil from environmental impact, and from invasion by other plants. It undoubtedly contributes to the persistence and stability of grassland after limiting factors such as cutting and grazing have ceased.

The ratios of root to shoot in the grass plant is relatively high, from 1:3 to 3:2. In addition, the contribution of the stem base and root litter results in a high contribution of DOM in the soil and a high below to above ground ratio (about 90–95 per cent) of total organic matter. The biomass and nutrient content of the surface litter may exceed that of the shoots except after fire. The accumulation of organic matter in the soil, particularly in cool temperate climates, makes it a particularly rich and efficient nutrient store. Figure 7.5 shows the highly developed humus-rich store of the typical chernozem soil. In this case, initial rapid release of minerals in decomposition is followed by a slow release as the organic matter is gradually transformed into humus and incorporated with the mineral matter. Loss by leaching is minimised by the soil crumb structure, the development of which is promoted by the grass root system.

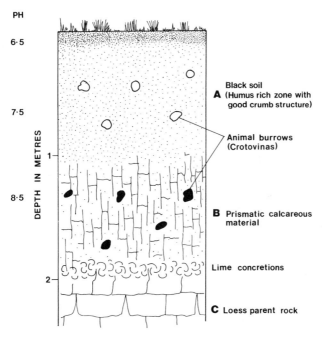

Figure 7.5   Chernozem profile (After S. G. Brade-Birks, 1962)

The grassland ecosystem is relatively simple in composition, structure and organisation compared with forests. Its stability is largely a product of direct or indirect human use by grazing, cutting and burning. Nevertheless, it is a particularly resilient ecosystem. It can absorb a high degree of physical stress or impact. This is further emphasised in the use of grass swards for recreational uses and their relatively high degree of resistance to human and animal trampling. Also, given the size of the soil's nutrient store, the grass-

Plate 7.4 Recreational and urban development on the Lymington estuary (Grid Ref. SZ/325955). (*Aerofilms Ltd*)

land's ability to recover after heavy use, even after destruction of surface biomass, is high. The most highly developed grassland soils — the black earth (chernozem) of the semi-arid prairies and steppes — have been able to withstand a long period of cultivation without a drastic decline in yields.

3. High detrital (DOM) system

One of the most environmentally variable, yet potentially very resilient ecosystems is the estuary (see Plate 7.4). This is usually described as a 'semi-enclosed body of water which has free connection with the open sea and is affected by tidal action' (Odum, 1971), or 'a passage where tides meet currents — a 'firth' where the mixing of fresh and salt water is the principal diagnostic feature' (Woodwell and Pecan, 1973). In comparison with the terrestrial or marine ecosystems which flank it, the estuarine habitat is a biologically difficult and stressful one because of its physical instability and the extreme range of variation in environmental conditions.

(a) The estuarine environment

First, it is subject to a high degree of water turbulence as a result of tidal movements, strong currents and wind-generated waves, all of which may be reinforced by relief, aspect and exposure. Second, tidal movement and turbulence, combined with the meeting of marine and fresh water, give rise to wide ranges in water level, temperature and salinity from the head to the mouth, and from the surface to the floor of the estuary. Third, estuaries tend to act as sediment traps for material brought in from either the land or seaward margins and deposited in the shallow, relatively sheltered marginal waters. Relatively few species of plants and animals can tolerate these extremely variable conditions. They are characterised by a high degree of adaptation to a particular range of environmental conditions and there is a marked zonation of communities, dominated by a few species, closely related to tidal movements.

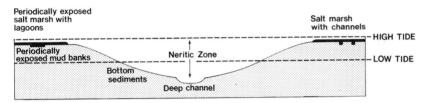

Figure 7.6   Diagrammatic cross section of micro-habitats in a wide shallow estuary

The amount of physical stress, however, varies considerably according to latitude, exposure, aspect and the physical form of the particular estuary. Those which combine shelter, moderate tidal currents, shallow water and moderate rates of sedimentation are biologically among the most productive systems in the world. High productivity is a function of a number of inter-related factors. The diversity of micro-habitats (see Figure 7.6), particularly in temperate and warm latitudes, allows photosynthesis to continue all year round. In the absence of grazing herbivores a very high proportion of the NPP becomes detrital material (DOM), either suspended in the water or accumulating as bottom sediment. As a result, the biomass of detrital feeders is very large, and the *benthic* (bottom) feeding route is comparable to, and is as important in the estuarine system as the decomposing route in terrestrial soils (see Figure 7.7). In shallow water, nutrient cycling is rapid and is effected by large-rooted plants and the often very large populations of benthic animals, which include filter feeders (such as oysters, clams), bottom-living fish and a variety of burrowing animals, as well as bacterial decomposers. Finally, and most importantly, estuaries are subject to continual nutrient enrichment or *natural eutrophication* as a result of material brought in from either the surrounding land by river flow or from offshore tidal circulation. In other words there is a large energy subsidy in detrital form from outside the system.

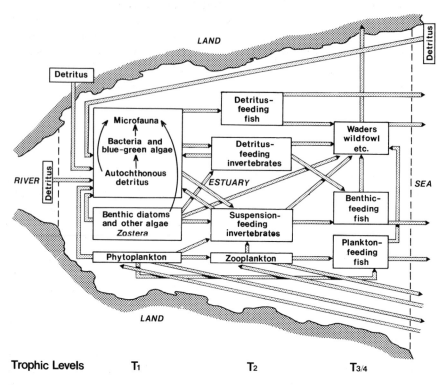

Figure 7.7   Estuarine food web (After R.S.K. Barnes, 1974)

Despite its nutrient richness, the estuarine ecosystem is relatively species poor and has a fairly simple trophic structure. As Figure 7.7 shows, there are three main trophic levels: T_1 = the largely microscopic plants; T_2 = herbivores, a high proportion of which are saprophytic (detritus feeding) invertebrates; $T_{3/4}$ = carnivorous birds and fish. The food web is composed of a relatively small number of short food chains; amongst the shortest is that from dead organic matter to detritus-eating fish such as flounders. The cross links (as represented by phytoplankton to zooplankton to either suspension feeding invertebrates or plankton feeding fish) are few. However, energy use in the system itself is inefficient and the estuary can, therefore, support large populations of migratory carnivores (fish) and predators (birds).

The estuary is also a nutrient trap, so that inputs tend to be greater than outputs. The exceptionally large detrital input results in a comparatively high biological oxygen demand (BOD). This could not be satisfied and a balance achieved between biological production and degradation without constant oxygen renewal. This is effected in estuaries by the continuous 'flushing' with fresh water from rivers and the vigorous turbulent tidal circulation. Both contribute to an efficient recycling of nutrients from bottom to surface waters. Obviously some estuaries are more efficient in this respect than others. Those with silty/clayey (i.e. muddy) bottom sediments are more susceptible to anaerobic conditions than are those with coarse grained materials. Similarly, glacially overdeepened estuaries, with a marked lip or sill at their mouths, may result in the accumulation of a layer of deep, cold, stagnant anaerobic bottom water in which nutrients become trapped.

(b) Degree of resilience

These features are characteristic of an incompletely developed, youthful and hence inherently unstable ecosystem. And this lack of stability in terms of biomass, population numbers and productivity is reinforced by an extremely unstable physical environment. Some ecologists would maintain that because estuaries are so inherently unstable, they are easily disturbed, fragile systems. On the other hand, there are those who argue that the estuarine ecosystem has a high inherent resilience to disturbance (Barnes, 1974) precisely because its organisms are adapted to, and can persist in face of, extreme fluctuations of habitat character and populations.

Estuaries tend to be major foci of human activity. Of the world's largest cities, 22 are situated on estuaries, including four of the largest, Tokyo, London, Shanghai and New York. Ever mounting loads of waste material, the introduction of new and persistent chemical effluents and increased oil pollution are putting more and more stress on estuaries; hence the need to assess their degree of resilience has become urgent. Recently, estuaries have become centres of intensive study and research, as at Sullom Voe, the site of a recently established oil-terminal in Shetland. Monitoring programmes designed to measure natural variation and hence detect abnormal changes due to human disturbance of the ecosystem have been established. This problem, however, is considerable because of the number and complexity of the environmental variables involved, and because of the continual changes in the range of natural variation in both time and space in the estuarine ecosystem.

ASSIGNMENTS

1. *Refer back to Table 7.4.*
   (a) *Compare the number of morphological (physical form) and physiological (metabolic) adaptations to drought in desert animals and plants respectively.*
   (b) *Would you expect animals to have greater homeostatic control over external variations in moisture supply than plants? (See Chapter 1B)*
2. *With reference to Figure 7.5 and the text, analyse the characteristics of the chernozem soil which make it particularly resilient to the impact of cultivation.*

3. (a) *Compare the relative resilience of grassland and forest to human impact.*
   (b) *Comment on the stability of the grassland ecosystem in the absence of human activity.*

Key Ideas

A. Ecosystem regulation
1. Successional development towards a steady state (or climax stage) is a fundamental characteristic of eco-regulation.

B. The climax concept
1. A steady state implies that an equilibrium has been reached in ecosystem biomass, populations, energy and nutrient budgets and NPP.
2. There are three main interpretations of the climax concept based on the type and relative importance of the factor(s) limiting ecosystem development.
3. The mono-climax concept emphasises the role of climate; the poly-climax, the role of climate together with other individual factors such as geology, soils and humans; the climax-pattern concept underlines the role of a complex interactionary set of many environmental factors at work.
4. There are few ecosystems that have not, in some way, been deflected or controlled by humans.

C. The concept of stability
1. Ecosystem stability is its ability to maintain a relatively constant condition in the face of disturbance.
2. The commonly assumed close relationship between the degree of stability (homeostasis) and the diversity and complexity of the ecosystem does not always hold good.

D. The concept of fragility
1. Fragility is the susceptibility to disruption of ecosystem stability.
2. Fragility of an ecosystem depends on its relative resilience or durability, and the type of disturbance involved.

E. Fragile ecosystems
1. The three most important bases of ecosystem fragility are: a large above ground biomass, youthful unstable soils, or a limited areal extent.
2. The fragility of an ecosystem with a large above ground biomass, such as the tropical rain forest, is a function of species diversity and biomass size and complexity.
3. The fragility of an ecosystem with youthful soils as exemplified by the tundra, is related more to the inherent instability of its soils than to the simplicity of its biomass.

4. Physical or biological islands are fragile because of their relative isolation, small areal extent and ecosystem simplicity.

F. Resilient ecosystems
1. Ecosystem resilience is a function of one or a combination of attributes such as a wide range of tolerance, organic adaption to environmental stress, a large below ground biomass and natural energy subsidisation.
2. The most successful organic adaptation to environmental stress found in desert and grassland areas is a short life-cycle and a durable regenerating system.
3. A high below to above ground ratio in total organic matter, characteristic of grasslands and desert areas, provides an energy and nutrient reserve which buffers the ecosystem in the face of external impact.
4. Continual input of energy and nutrients into an ecosystem, such as that produced by natural forces in the estuary, also contributes to a high degree of homeostasis.

Additional Activities

1. *Field Project A*

    (a) In a selected area identify what might be considered a 'biological island'.
    (b) Record its size (area); degree of isolation; number of plant and, if possible, bird and mammal species; and ecosystem structure.
    (c) Would you consider this a fragile ecosystem or not, and why?

2. *Field Project B*

Select an area in a well-managed long-established lawn: (a) using six, randomly placed, half-metre square quadrats record the following information: the total number of species; number of different mosses, grasses and other species; abundance or dominance of grasses; depth of litter horizon (A_o); depth of organic horizon (A); maximum depth of root penetration; root density in top and bottom A horizon; (b) draw an annotated profile to summarise your findings; (c) decide whether you think it is a relatively fragile or durable type of ecosystem, and why.

3. Categorise the environmental and man-made 'stresses' to which ecosystems can be subjected in terms of magnitude, frequency and duration.

4. Assess the relative fragility or durability of coastal habitats to oil pollution. See and play 'The Ecology Game' by M. Tribe and D. Peacock (1975).
    Another useful text is *'Torrey Canyon' Pollution and Marine Life*, edited by J.E. Smith (1968).

Resource Values and the Ecosystem

So far we have illustrated the ways in which humans, as distinct from other animals, have exploited and thereby disturbed ecosystem components and functions. They have made and continue to make an increasingly greater use of the ecosystem than any other organism. This, as has already been noted, is because their needs are not only greater and different from those of other animals but because the means by which they can satisfy these needs are so much more powerful and varied. In other words, the *value of the ecosystem* as a resource base is greater for humans than for any other animal. This, however, immediately begs the question as to what is meant by a *resource*?

A. What is a Resource?

The long-accepted meaning of the word resource is a 'stock of some material of use or value to humans'. The traditional and still used economic distinc-

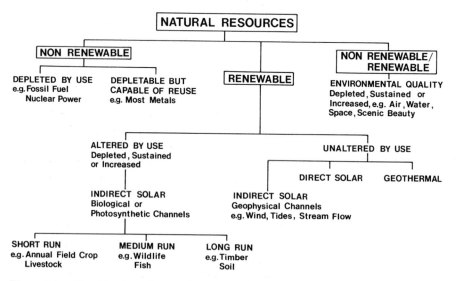

Figure 8.1   Classification of natural resources (After P. Haggett, 1979)

tion is that between *natural resources* (unchanged materials) available from the lithosphere, atmosphere, hydrosphere and biosphere, and others (such as labour, capital, etc.) which are used in the exploitation and utilisation of natural resources to create wealth. It has been customary to divide natural resources into *organic* and *inorganic* materials. Figure 8.1 highlights the basic distinction between the former which are *renewable* resources, capable of self-perpetuation, and the latter which are *non-renewable* resources, available only in fixed, finite quantities.

1. Resource classification

All resources are, strictly speaking, renewable in the sense that they are part of natural cycles (e.g. geological, sedimentary, hydrological, oceanic, atmospheric and biological) of varying duration. However, only resources which are based on short cycles can renew themselves within a time span relevant to humans (see Table 8.1).

Table 8.1 Approximate duration of selected short-cycle renewable and long-cycle non-renewable resources (After Open University Press, 1973)

Cycles of Renewable Resources		Duration
Solar energy	....	days
Hydrological	....	days and years
Nitrogen	....	decades
Plant and animal	....	c. 1–100 years (max. 4000)
Soil	....	c. 200–8000+
Cycles of Non-Renewable Resources		
Erosion cycle	....	millions of years*
Sedimentary cycles	....	millions of years*
Orogenic cycle	....	tens of millions of years

* may be accelerated by humans to years or even days

All biological resources, together with several physical ones, such as water and solar energy, may be included in the renewable category. In contrast, some resources such as fossil fuels and metals form so slowly that from the human point of view the limits of supply may be regarded as fixed.

However, this simple two-fold division fails to demonstrate adequately the complex interchange which takes place between the renewable and non-renewable components, or to emphasise the fact that there are also limits to the amount of renewable resources that can be produced. Renewable resources can be modified and may, as indicated in Figure 8.1, be depleted, sustained or increased by human actions. Since the earth is a closed system, except for incoming solar and cosmic radiation, increase in renewable resources may be at the expense of other essentially non-renewable ones. Food crops, for instance, which constitute short-run renewable resources, are increased at the cost of greater inputs of finite non-renewable fertilizers, fossil energy and land. As a corollary, any serious depletion of physical resources may have disturbing consequences for the continued production of renewable resources such as food and even humans themselves (see Figure 3.10). Finally, in the process of exploiting non-renewable resources humans interfere with the shorter-term cycles of renewable resources such as water and air on which all biological resources depend; such actions can pollute ecosystems and result in alterations to species distribution.

2. Resource evaluation

By definition the existence of a resource depends, basically, on its value to humans. *Resource evaluation*, however, is particularly difficult because it is dependent upon an ever-changing set of interacting variables which are illustrated in Figure 8.2. To create resources, therefore, humans employ technological and organisational skills along the pathways of opportunity. However, their actions may be further restricted by ecological resistances and negative feedback loops (see Chapter 1) The actual realisation and utilisation of a resource depends on supply and demand as determined by the prevailing socio-economic climate. As a result, the relationship between a stock of material and a resource is, as Haggett (1979) points out, reversible. With increasing knowledge, combined with scientific and technical skills, a stock can gradually or suddenly become a valuable resource, and what was once a resource may revert to a stock. Also, as human perception and appraisal of the environment has changed, so the concept of resource eval-

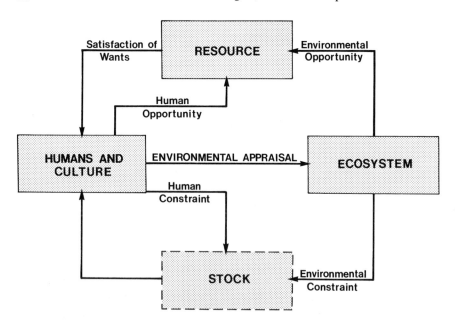

Figure 8.2   Model of elements and interactions involved in resource evaluation (Modified from E.W. Zimmermann, 1951).

uation has widened. With the rise in demand for services, more leisure time and increasing mobility, there has been a concomitant growth in public concern for environmental quality. Hence, greater emphasis is now being placed on the more intangible, qualitative and less easily measured resource values, in contrast to an exclusive preoccupation with those more amenable to traditional methods of economic costing.

3. Varying resource values

It is obvious, therefore, that resource values are relative and variable. Three types of variation can be identified in relation to any resource: (i) according to the opportunities afforded by a given resource or multiple resource value; (ii) in resource value with time, and (iii) in the appraisal of relative resource values.

In the following sections it is intended to illustrate, with particular reference to organic or renewable resources, these three types of resource variation.

ASSIGNMENTS

1. *Study Table 8.1. Does length of cycling time rather than physical form (ie. organic or inorganic) determine the renewability or non-renewability of a natural resource?*
2. *Refer to Figure 8.2. Can you think of any organic resources that have reverted from a resource to a stock, or from a stock to a resource within the last 200 years?*
3. *Study Figure 8.2 carefully. For one or more selected resources construct a diagram based on this model.*

B. Multiple Resource Values

First, any given type of organic material can and often does have more than one type of use or value for humans. Their evaluation is dependent on which of a number of attributes are considered to be most important or for which there is the greatest demand at a particular time. For instance, the resource value of the common heather (*Calluna vulgaris*), one of the most important components of British heath and moorland vegetation, is compounded of a range of values.

1. Biological values

The *biological* value of heather is dependent on the quantity of primary (plant) and/or secondary (animal) biological production expressed in yields of all or some part of the plant matter per unit area, or in stocking rates, i.e. animal units per unit area per unit time. Biological value, however, may be a function as much of the nutritive levels or palatibility as of the quantity of the organic material. In this case value is dependent on qualitative attributes which are less easy to express quantitatively. The biological value of heather varies, as one might expect, with latitude and altitude in Britain. In upland Scotland it is comparable to less productive temperate grasslands and the richer desert shrubs. It also varies with age, the nutritive values of young (1–3 years) heather shoots are high but their productivity is low at this stage of growth.

2. Economic values

Organic resources of any kind, however, are normally valued or costed in traditional *economic* terms. Unless the known quantitative or qualitative biological value is sufficient to make exploitation profitable, the material will have little or no economic or commercial value. Indeed, formerly, it might have been said that under these circumstances the material had no resource value as such. The commercial value of heather itself is practically nil; it is related more to its secondary production of animals. However, even in this case there is no direct relationship between biological and economic values, since the latter are dependent on demand as well as supply. The commercial value of grouse and deer is very much higher, while their biological value is very much lower than that of sheep. The commercial value of grouse, in particular, is dependent not so much on its food as on game values which are expressed in terms of the amount of money people are prepared to pay to pursue the sport of shooting. On many a well-managed heather moorland at present, income from grouse shooting will be greater than from the maximum sheep crop it can produce. Indeed, the spatial limits of organic resource exploitation tend to be determined by economic or commercial, rather than biological factors except where the resource may have, for want of a better term, a political or strategic value. This may be to promote the exploitation of what might otherwise be considered a resource with an uneconomic value. Hill sheep and cattle subsidies in marginal and upland farms provide a case in point.

3. Ecological values

In addition to these more commonly accepted values, heather has acquired others less easy to measure, on which it is often difficult if not impossible to put a 'price tag'. These are values not susceptible to quantitative, cost-benefit analyses. They are also more difficult to define simply. The *ecological* value, for instance, of an organic resource such as heather is dependent upon its contribution to or its effect on the particular ecosystem of which it is a component. On Scottish uplands muirburn, as we have already seen, is the main type of management used to maintain as high a sustained yield (or biological value) of new heather shoots as possible. In so far as the heather dominated vegetation results in a progressive decline in potential biological value, and in species diversity, its ecological value might be rated low in comparison with other types of vegetation growing under similar environmental conditions.

In this respect, the contrast between the resource values of heather and bracken are illuminating. Bracken (*Pteridium aquilinum*) has no commercial value. Indeed, its status is that of the most virulent and widespread weed of upland grazings in Britain. In marked contrast to heather, however, it could be argued that bracken's ecological value is relatively high. It has already been noted (Chapter 4) that bracken can reverse the soil degradation resulting from heather. In addition, by virtue of its rhizome system, bracken has a greater ability than any other plant to colonise and stabilise screes which may have resulted from overburning and overgrazing of former moorland.

4. Scientific value

The *scientific* value of an organic resource is dependent on such factors as rarity of particular species and/or communities, or on its value for scientific experiments whose results may have implications more far-reaching than for the resource itself. It could be said that the scientific value of Scottish heather moorlands is related to the opportunity that presently managed animals, such as grouse and red deer, afford for the study of the scientific basis of game management in general.

5. Cultural value

Finally, heather has a certain weak (in comparison to the sacred cow in India) *cultural* or what might be termed sentimental value. It has acquired the status of a Scottish emblem, or symbol, which, particularly in the case of the white variety, has given it a direct, though limited, economic value for tourists. Cultural and *aesthetic* values are so closely interrelated, however, that it is impossible to understand the latter without the context of the former. This is often easier to see in other, more traditional cultures than our own. In Scotland, however, the popular reaction on aesthetic grounds against the replacement of the uniform monoculture of the heather moorland by a uniform monoculture of coniferous trees is a very telling example of aesthetic being conditioned by cultural values!

ASSIGNMENT

Select another organic resource (e.g. corn (maize), hardwood, cows, horses) and with reference to Section B on heather, analyse its multiple resource value.

C. Varying Resource Values in Time

1. Vegetation

The second characteristic of resource values is that they are neither absolute, as has already been implied, nor constant, since they are a function of an ever-changing set of interacting variables.

In the case of heather, its resource value has in fact declined as its former range of uses (as a source of tannin, vegetable dye and honey nectar, as a roofing and bedding material, as well as a forage plant) has dwindled (Mitchell, 1973). Its resource value as a forage plant has fluctuated markedly over the past two hundred years with the changing economic and other values of hill sheep, grouse and red deer. It has not, however, like bracken lost its former resource value as bedding and thatching material completely and reverted to a stock.

On the other hand, resource values can, dependent on the nature of their exploitation or what perhaps is better referred to as their level of management, be increased or decreased. The amount of appreciation or depreciation of an organic resource will be determined by the extent to which it is profitable, desirable and, in the ultimate circumstance, possible to modify the ecosystem. For instance, it has already been demonstrated that the value of heather as a forage plant can be considerably upgraded by good burning management (Chapter 4). However, overburning has often resulted in the removal of heather shoots and the destruction of its roots at a rate faster than they can be renewed by natural processes; this has led to the replacement of heather by plants with lower forage values such as the moor mat grass (*Nardus stricta*) and bracken. In extreme cases, the organic layer in the soil may be destroyed, and the underlying mineral material exposed to accelerated erosion and ultimately to complete destruction of the resource.

2. Soil

Soil is an important, if not the most important, human resource. It is first and foremost the essential store or reservoir of water and nutrients on which primary productivity depends. Second, it is a renewable resource whose value is primarily dependent on its agricultural productivity (or yield). However, its resource value has varied, and continues to vary, in time and space according to what humans choose to do with it, their scientific knowledge about its nature, and their technical ability to exploit it. Very broadly we can recognise three stages in the increase in soil value through time consequent upon increasing human knowledge and skill.

(a) Exploitive or robber stage

The simplest and earliest forms of agriculture were characterised by the limited use of inputs and a high dependence on the natural or inherent value or fertility of the soil. This is exemplified in the shifting agriculture still practised in tropical areas and which was probably used by Neolithic farmers in Britain. Medieval farming systems represented only a slight variation on this basic method — the alternation of cropping and fallow and the folding of animals (allowing them to graze on stubble) in the autumn on the arable

176

land. There are areas in Europe where this system still persists in a modified form. Also, initial New World farming was based on continuous cropping until yields began to fall, after which fresh land would be ploughed. In this case, soil robbing was encouraged either by an initial abundance of land and a demand for high value but very nutrient demanding products such as tobacco and cotton, or by an abundance of land combined with soils of high natural fertility such as the prairie and chernozem. In all cases, however, the result was a rapid or gradual decrease in the agricultural value of the soil; in extreme cases accelerated erosion or laterisation led to resource destruction.

(b) Conservative stage

Some areas of the earth's surface naturally lend themselves to a form of exploitation that maintained the natural or enriched soil fertility. Annual silt renewal in the great flood plains of the Far East has supported centuries of rice production. In other countries, particularly China, the concentration of all available organic debris on crop land or in fish ponds ensured continuously high yields.

The most important changes in soil value were effected during that period in Britain known as the Agricultural Revolution. During the period from the end of the sixteenth to the mid-nineteenth century in particular, scientific discoveries, allied to the development of agricultural management techniques, promoted a spectacular increase in soil value. They culminated in the establishment of the system of ley-farming which was to be the basis of modern methods of agriculture until relatively recently. Ley-farming depends on the rotation of arable crops of varying use and effects on soil fertility, with a break or ley crop of grass or a grass-legume mixture. Nutrient-demanding grain crops were traditionally followed after two or three years by a root crop (normally the turnip) which played an important role in providing winter feed and as a soil-cleaning crop. The latter property was related to the amount of tillage required in its cultivation and its dense horizontal leaf cover, both of which helped to suppress weeds inherited from the preceding grain crop. The ley grass sown down for a period, which varied from three to as much as fifteen years, was the principal method of restoring and maintaining soil fertility.

It did so in two ways: by the addition of nutrients, particularly nitrogen from nitrogen fixing clovers; and by the addition of organic matter which, with the grass root mat, helped to build up the soil crumb structure upon which the regulation of fertility depended (see Chapter 6). However, crop rotations alone would not have been sufficient to maintain soil fertility, since agricultural exploitation inevitably extracts more than it returns to the ecosystem. Other methods of returning nutrients included the application of a variety of organic waste material such as farmyard manure, urban waste, fish and bone meal, seaweed and phosphate-rich guano. It was, however, not until the mid nineteenth century that the role of nutrients in the agricultural fertility of soils was properly understood. Organic fertilisers began

Plate 8.1 Burning wheat stubble, Harold Wood, Essex (Grid Ref. TL/565965). (*Aerofilms Ltd*)

to be supplemented and eventually replaced by inorganic compounds of, particularly, potassium, phosphorous and nitrogen. The ley system, however, was the key to the maintenance and the conservation of the human-enriched soil values, as expressed in high yields of crops or animal products.

(c) *Intensive stage*

The third stage in the increase in the agricultural value of the soil has sometimes been ascribed to what is known as the Biological Revolution. It was initiated primarily by: the introduction of exceptionally high yielding, often hybrid varieties of crops (e.g. corn, cotton, soya bean, wheat, rice); the increased use of chemical compounds to reduce competition from weeds and pests; and a greatly increased input of inorganic, particularly nitrogen, fertiliser to satisfy the demands and realise the full potential of the new high-yielding crop breeds. This energy intensive farming has escalated since 1939, particularly in the highly developed western countries. It has been accompanied in Britain by the gradual breakdown of the traditional rotation system and its replacement by intensive grassland management and arable monoculture. The labour intensive soil cleaning turnip crop has all but disappeared.

However, it has already been noted in Chapter 5 that attainment of ever higher crop yields has been at the expense of the mechanical fabric or structure of the soil. There is evidence that, without the renewal of soil organic matter and under the increasing impact of heavy machinery, the structure of some intensively exploited soils is deteriorating, if it has not already been destroyed completely (see Plate 8.1). Figure 8.3 illustrates the harmful effects of ploughing on two heavy textured soils, a clay loam and a silt respectively. Structural deterioration of these soils can cause impeded drainage and waterlogging. In contrast, on sandier light-textured soils, lack of organic matter and breakdown of former structural aggregates renders the soil susceptible to drying out and severe wind erosion.

In addition, renewed weed infestation has resulted from the increase in weeds resistant to herbicides and which can be stimulated and spread by modern continuous grain cultivation. It is perhaps not surprising that two of the most rapidly spreading weeds of agricultural land are the weed grasses, wild oats and couch grass. Both soil structural deterioration and weed infestation can lead to either a decrease in yields or the need to expend even more energy to maintain output. Both are indicative of a decline in soil value and more particularly a decline in the value of that attribute, soil structure, on which the efficiency of the water and nutrient cycle depend.

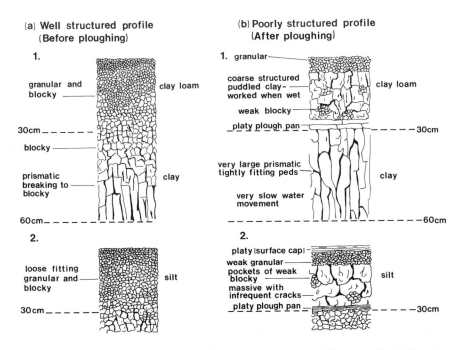

Figure 8.3   Harmful effects of ploughing on the structure of 'heavy' soils (After Agricultural Advisory Council, 1970)

1. *Comment on the multiple resource values of two or three contrasting habitats with which you are familiar.*
2. *Refer back to Figure 8.3.*
   (a) *Analyse and describe the effects of ploughing on the structure of the clay loam and the silt soil.*
   (b) *Discuss the implications of such changes for plant growth.*
3. *Select examples of particular organic resources whose value has changed as a result primarily of (a) economic factors; (b) social conditions; or (c) management techniques respectively. Comment on the nature of and reasons for the change.*

D. Varying Appraisal of Resource Values

1. Changing perceptions

Finally, the third aspect of change in resource values is exemplified by the more recent, marked shift in emphasis in many developed and over-developed parts of the world, from a concern for the economic to the non-economic values, and more particularly towards the ecological/aesthetic values of organic resources. This trend has been partly engendered by modern developments in farming and forestry. The consequent decrease in uncultivated semi-wild habitats such as hedges and copses, amenity woodlands, marshes and bogs has created tension and conflict between the biological/economic and the ecological/aesthetic values of the organic resources involved. This has been further exacerbated by increasing urban-industrial impact on the countryside. The problems of reconciling economic with non-economic values have perhaps become most acute with respect to the rapid post-war growth of outdoor countryside or resource-oriented recreation.

2. Outdoor recreation

The aesthetic, ecological and closely associated amenity values of organic resources probably attain their greatest significance with respect to this type of land use. Recreation differs markedly from other more traditional methods of exploiting organic resources in two principal ways. First, unlike agriculture or forestry it is a biologically non-productive activity; second, it is, in itself, a non-economic activity in that the benefit obtained from its pursuit is the level or degree of satisfaction experienced by the person(s) involved. Since one of the most important objectives for the majority of outdoor recreationists is viewing scenery, the aesthetic value of the vegetation cover and the associated wildlife habitats have become important resources. The recreational value of organic resources is also related to the contribution they make to peoples' physical enjoyment or comfort in providing shelter, protection and privacy, and, not least, to the capability of the resource to accommodate different types of outdoor pursuit.

In contrast to other values the problems of maintaining aesthetic and ecological values are particularly difficult. By its very nature much resource-oriented outdoor recreation is uncontrolled and relatively unmanaged. It is an exploitive activity and it tends to reduce the very values on which it depends; the danger of resource destruction is very great. This is because the physical impact generated is high and is further highly concentrated in localised areas and frequently in fragile habitats.

(a) Recreational impacts

Physical impacts common to all types of outdoor recreational activity are trampling by human feet and the rolling of vehicle wheels; a secondary type of impact is the abrasive, scouring action effected by boat launching and beaching on waterside sites lacking proper facilities.

Observation and measurement of the effect of trampling accompanied by experimental simulation of the type of impact, confirm that areas subjected to recreational use eventually show signs of resource deterioration. These include: (i) a reduction of the plant biomass and ground cover; a decrease in the density of herbs, shrubs and tree seedlings; and the replacement of species less tolerant by those more tolerant to the impact of trampling; and (ii) associated soil changes which are often less obvious but none the less important, since in time they can lead to a decline in plant vigour and a reduction in the soil animal biomass. Such changes involve increased soil compaction, a reduction in organic matter content, a decrease in water infiltration rates

Table 8.2 Plant species arranged in order of decreasing degree of tolerance to trampling on neutral grassland (After A.K. Crawford and M.D. Liddle, 1977)

*Poa annua	(Annual meadow grass)
Plantago major	(Large plantain)
*Poa pratense	(Meadow grass)
*Lolium perenne	(Perennial rye grass)
Bellis perennis	(Daisy)
Taraxacum officinialis	(Dandelion)
Carex flacca	(Flaccid sedge)
*Cynosurus cristatus	(Crested dog's tail)
Ranunculus acris	(Creeping buttercup)
*Deschampsia caespitosa	(Tufted hair grass)
Prunella vulgaris	(Self-heal)
*Festuca rubra	(Red fescue)
Trifolium pratense	(Clover)
*Hordeum secalinum	(Wild barley)
*Phleum bertolionii	(Timothy)
*Agrostis stolonifera	(Creeping bent)
*Holcus lanatus	(Yorkshire fog)

* Grass species

and an increase in surface run-off and, particularly on sloping ground, soil erosion.

Stages in the deterioration of vegetation as a result of trampling which are common to a wide range of habitats have now been identified. Low levels of use can, at first, actually result in increased species diversity because of reduction in shading by formerly taller plants and in the stimulation of the growth of some species of grass, since trampling has an effect on grasses not unlike that of cutting or grazing. Intermediate or moderate use normally results in a decrease in height and biomass of the field vegetation and an increase in the more trample-resistant species (see Table 8.2). These include those with tough leaves (sedges and the needle-leaved grasses), flattened leaf-rosettes (daisy, plantain, dandelion), persistent underground rhizomes and stolons (creeping buttercup) and a few species which, like the grass *Poa annua*, flower outside the main trampling period. The actual species, however, on moderate to heavily used recreation sites will vary with the habitat and its particular physical condition and original species composition.

Figure 8.4 shows the relationship between numbers of people on footpaths and variations in selected vegetation and soil characteristics on the used and unused parts of the site. It illustrates firstly that with increased path use there is a general tendency, indicated by a decrease in soil depth

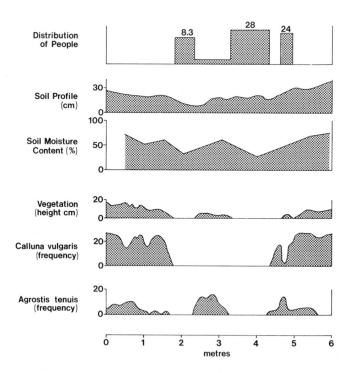

Figure 8.4   Transect taken on Tresco showing frequency of plant species in relation to topography and other environmental factors (After Goldsmith *et al.*, 1970)

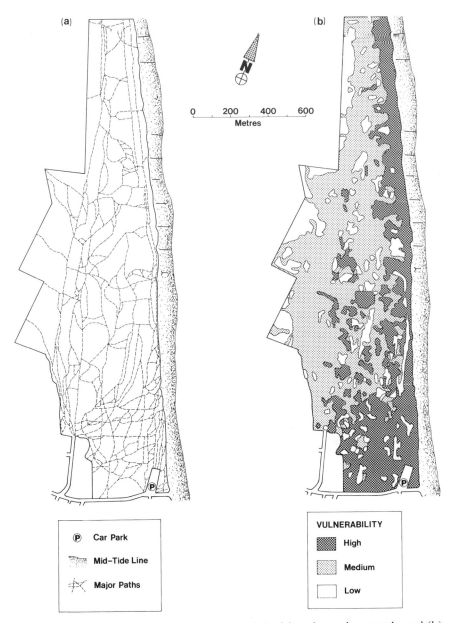

(a) (b)

N

0   200   400   600
Metres

VULNERABILITY

☒ High

▒ Medium

☐ Low

Ⓟ Car Park

Mid–Tide Line

Major Paths

Figure 8.5   The sand dunes at Winterton, Norfolk: (a) major path network, and (b) relative vulnerability to damage by trampling of dune vegetation (After L.A. Boorman and R.M. Fuller, 1977)

and percentage moisture content, for soil compaction to increase. Secondly, vegetation declines in rough proportion to trampling pressure both in terms of its structure (height) and frequency of species occurrence. However, it should be noted that heather (*Calluna vulgaris*) shows more marked reductions in frequency and tends to become absent over a wider path area than the common bent grass (*Agrostis tenuis*).

Heavy recreational pressure will finally eliminate all but the most trample-resistant plants. Among the most persistent species are *Poa pratensis* and *Poa annua* which are common in heavily used garden lawns and well-worn footpaths across heather moorland. The final stage in resource deterioration is marked by an increase in the amount of bare ground and eventually the initiation of accelerated soil erosion.

A recent study of a heavily used sand-dune area on the Norfolk coast has demonstrated the relative vulnerability to damage by trampling of the vegetation. The high density of footpaths across the area shown in Figure 8.5a is indicative of its degree of recreational use. By comparing the percentage of paths which were worn bare with the percentage of paths on each type of vegetation, three grades of vulnerability were defined (see Table 8.3) and mapped. Figure 8.5b shows the marked decrease in vulnerability with distance landwards from the dune edge, which is closely related to the change from open marram grass to rough grass, heather, scrub and woodland vegetation types.

Table 8.3   The vulnerability of different areas to human pressure and their proportion at Winterton, Norfolk. The data excludes all bare sand, the car park and the pond. The total area is thus 96.4 hectares (After L.A. Boorman and R.M. Fuller, 1977)

Vulnerability	% of paths worn bare	Vegetation formation	Area (ha)	% of total area
High	over 50%	Marram grass	21.0	21.8
Medium	10–50%	Rough grass Heather	57.6	59.7
Low	less 10%	Short grass Scrub Rhododendron Woodland	17.8	18.5

Another type of physical impact common to many habitats used for informal (i.e. unorganised) recreation is that of the picnic fire. The persistent lighting of fires on the same piece of ground will eventually destroy the surface vegetation and underlying organic matter and leave a permanent scar. This may be sufficient to initiate accelerated erosion. More serious, however, is the effect of fires set, as is so frequently the case in exposed sites, at the base of tree trunks (see Plate 8.2). Continued use of the same 'fireplace' results in initial charring of the bark, followed by distinctive deep triangular scars and the eventual hollowing of the bole. Once all the growth tissues (cambium) under the bark have been destroyed the tree will eventually die. A contributory factor to this destructive process is the breaking of branches and the use of the exposed lateral root-mat to provide firewood.

Plate 8.2 Oak tree with funnel-shaped scar and charred and broken lateral roots caused by picnic fires, East Loch Lomondside (Grid Ref. NS/409926). (*Joy Tivy*)

The destruction of trees has a marked impact on the aesthetic value of the landscape and, particularly on river and lake banks or coastal sites, can trigger serious erosion and rapid cliff or bank retreat (Tivy, 1979).

(b) Recreation habitats

Habitats most vulnerable to recreational impact are those which are inherently unstable and where the concentration of recreationists tends to be particularly high. They include *sandy dune or link coasts*, which became established as the national holiday sites in Britain in the latter part of the nineteenth century. Direct impact, in many heavily used dune areas, has caused the destruction of those grasses such as marram (*Ammophila arenaria*) and lyme (*Elymus arenarius*) which were in the process of trapping and forming dunes, or those such as the peat-forming fescues and mosses which had already formed a protective cover over the highly mobile material. The delicate balance between aggradation and erosion is disrupted, and if impact continues unabated the whole dune ecosystem can be destroyed.

The post-war increase in affluence has been accompanied by ever-growing numbers of people participating in skiing. This has resulted in an exceptionally high concentration in those limited areas where the sport is possible in Scotland. These all occur in *montane* (or what used to be called arctic-alpine) habitats, above the tree line. Inherent soil instability is a function of a number of closely interrelated factors: severe climatic conditions; a low-

Plate 8.3 Cairngorm ski area, Aviemore (Grid Ref. NH/896130); reseeding has been carried out in part of this area since the photograph was taken in June, 1969. (*Aerofilms Ltd*)

growing and frequently incomplète vegetation cover; shallow, skeletal soils subjected to seasonal and daily fluctuations of freezing and thawing. As in the coastal habitat, the rather precarious relationship between soil and vegetation is very susceptible to disruption, particularly where it is unprotected by a complete snow cover. The most severe impact results during the installation of ski-lifts and access roads (see Plate 8.3). However, the increasing concentration of summer visitors on the mountain tops as a result of improved accessibility has a greater impact than skiing itself. The depreciation of organic resources in Scotland, however, is limited compared with that which has already occurred on mountain top areas subject to even greater summer visitor pressures, as on Snowdonia and in the Lake and Peak Districts (O'Hare, 1978).

More recently the growth of car-based recreation and tourism has seen increasing use of the *loch or lakeside*, one of the most characteristic of recreation sites in Scotland (Tivy, 1979, 1981). It differs from the coast in extent. Loch levels vary but are not subject to the regular, periodic, tidal range which along gently shelving seashores can, at low tide in the summer, make extensive areas of beach available for recreational use. The comparable lochside zone is much more restricted both lochward and landward. Also the lochshore is subjected to a greater degree than the seashore to impact from both land-based and water-based activities. Impact, concentrated on a narrower zone than on the seashore, is often more intense. The depletion of the vegetation fringe either by impact from peoples' feet, cars and/or boats and by picnic fires results in accelerated wave erosion. This is particularly serious around large heavily used lochs such as Loch Lomond (Countryside Commission for Scotland, 1979). Here accelerated erosion and consequent rapid bank retreat (which can be in excess of 1 m/annum) is leading to the reduction in area of already limited sites as well as a deterioration in aesthetic value.

(c) Recreational carrying capacity

Consideration of recreation re-introduces the concept of carrying capacity in relation to the value of organic resources (Tivy, 1973a). Uncontrolled outdoor recreation tends by its very nature to be exploitive and, as has been demonstrated, the aesthetic value of the resources on which it often depends, depreciates very rapidly; indeed the danger of resource destruction is high. However, unlike agricultural carrying capacity, which is related to the biological values of the particular resources, recreational carrying capacity is more related to ecological and what have been called perceptual values. In the former instance, carrying capacity can be defined as the intensity of impact the resource can withstand before an acceptable degree of ecological change is exceeded; in the latter, it is the intensity of use that the resource can sustain before the quality of the experience (i.e. the user's enjoyment) decreases. In both instances the value is not absolute, indeed it is probably impossible to measure as it is dependent not only on the resource but on human evaluation of it — on the sum of each person's 'sense of values' using it.

In conclusion, two major problems emerge from this consideration of resource values. The first is the extent to which organic resources can be exploited to meet increasing demands before acceptable thresholds or levels of use are crossed and their values deteriorate to a point beyond which it is either difficult or impossible to restore them. The second is the degree to which ecological/aesthetic values can be reconciled with biological/ecological values in a world where the need for food is increasing so rapidly. These problems have assumed a high degree of relevance in a world where resource values are constantly and rapidly changing in response to accelerating technological, social and cultural change.

ASSIGNMENTS

1. *Explain the conflict between ecological and economic values with reference to (a) hedgerows and (b) marshes.*

2. *What factors might affect the recreational carrying capacity of an urban park; a safari park; a nature reserve; and a coastal sand-dune area respectively?*

Key Ideas

A. What is a resource?
1. A resource is a stock of some material of use or value to humans.
2. The basic division of resources is between renewable biological and non-renewable inorganic materials.
3. Resource evaluation is dependent on a complex set of interacting economic, technical and social factors.
4. Resources values are relative and variable.

B. Multiple resource values
1. Organic resources may have one or more of the following values: biological, economic, ecological, scientific, cultural and aesthetic.
2. Some of these resource values are more clearly defined and easier to measure than others.

C. Varying resource values in time
1. Resource values are subject to change through time.
2. Some organic resource values depreciate, others appreciate, with changing demand.
3. Some organic resource values decrease or increase with management.

D. Varying appraisal of resource values
1. Human appreciation of non-economic values has developed with increasing resource exploitation.
2. Non-economic values have attained their greatest significance in relation to the recreational use of organic resources.
3. Recreational carrying capacity of organic resources is related to ecological and perceptual rather than biological or economic values.

Additional Activities

1. *Field Project A*

   In an area used for informal outdoor recreation, map the footpaths and assess the vulnerability of the vegetation using the method illustrated in Table 8.3.

2. *Field Project B*

   Select a semi-wild habitat which is not, or has not recently been used for recreational purposes. Using the experimental trampling methods described in Tivy and Rees (1977) assess the vulnerability of the main types of vegetation and/or plants.

3. *Field Project C*

   With reference to the heather-bracken example in Section B, compare the ecological value of two contrasted ecosystems.

4. Discuss the extent to which the soil may be regarded as a renewable resource.

5. The spatial limits of resource use are determined by economic, social and political rather than by physical or biological factors. Discuss this statement with regard to the following examples:
   a) agricultural land on the urban fringe;
   b) forestry land in the UK;
   c) marginal hill farming land;
   d) grouse shooting reserves.

9 Resource Conservation

Introduction

So far we have considered the ways in which humans have deliberately or inadvertently exploited the biosphere for their ever-growing and increasingly varied needs. We have already emphasised that there are now few areas of the world that have not been subjected to either the direct or indirect effect of their actions. They have, also, become uncomfortably aware that they can trigger off a chain of reactions which may extend over a considerably larger area or persist for a much longer period of time than they may have initially realised. Unfortunately, knowledge of the full implications of present and possible future human impacts on the biosphere is still incomplete. Humans cannot always predict the effect of their actions or rectify all their mistakes. Nevertheless, awareness of these problems and of the urgent need to conserve and manage the remaining available organic resources more carefully, has been heightened, particularly during the last century, by the rapidly increasing rate of resource use and of environment degradation. Both of these trends are a direct consequence of the spiralling human population growth.

A. What is Meant by Conservation?

The word *conservation*, like pollution, has become an integral part of our everyday vocabulary, yet it is a particularly difficult term to define precisely because it can cover such a wide range of concepts. Strictly speaking it means 'to preserve', 'to retain intact or unchanged'; in a wider context it can imply wise use or management. Conservation in either sense can be applied to a great variety of phenomena including man-made objects such as paintings, historic buildings and natural features be they plants, animals, nature in general, landscape resources and even the whole environment. In relation to natural resources, conservation can involve the protection of plant and animal species from any form of exploitation at one end of the spectrum, to sustaining food production while maintaining or even improving the cleanliness and appearance of the whole environment at the other.

Development of conservation

The concept of conservation is not new. Some would maintain it is as old as the human race itself and that primitive peoples' methods of obtaining food are, largely because of limited techniques, more conservative of the organic resource than those of modern technically advanced societies. There is evidence that as early as the third century BC in China, population growth and resource use had resulted in widespread deforestation and severe soil erosion in upland and mountain areas of China. Literary sources record the existence of official forest and watershed conservators whose responsibility was to regulate timber extraction and ensure the maintainance of the last remaining stands of mountain forests respectively. Also, from the Middle Ages onwards, the land owning aristocracy in Europe set aside areas in which hunting and the exploitation of forest products were strictly conserved for their exclusive use. Medieval game laws (many of which persist up to the present), in particular, were designed to ensure the successful breeding of the animals that they hunted for food and sport.

The modern Conservation Movement, however, was a much later development which started in the early nineteenth century in the USA as a result of public concern about the rapid depletion particularly of the remaining stands of virgin forest in the western part of the continent. The setting up of State and Federal Forest Preserves was the first step in the eventual establishment of National and State Forests and Parks. Drought and agricultural depression in the 1930s, together with the impact of the 'Dust Bowl' revealed the extent and degree of accelerated soil erosion, consequent upon over cultivation in the USA and other parts of the world. Soil erosion, which is still the most widespread of what has been called 'human-induced diseases', was as emotive an expression as pollution is today. The establishment of the US Soil Conservation Service in 1934 was one of the major landmarks in the development and spread of modern conservation thinking.

Until 1945 conservation policies and technologies were concerned mainly with forest and soil use, and had developed more rapidly in the US than elsewhere. Since then, however, concern has become worldwide as expressed in the post-war establishment of the International Union for Nature Conservation. In addition, the range of issues involved and consequently the complexities of what and how to conserve have increased greatly.

Conservation in its broadest sense, is now concerned not just with the protection of discrete phenomena, but with maintaining and, if possible, enhancing the value of the whole biosphere. This inevitably raises the problem of reconciling and optimising the diverse range of values discussed in the preceding chapter. What and how to conserve then varies with the particular resource value—be it ecological, scientific, biological, economic or aesthetic—in question. In the following sections the problems of conserving and of reconciling these values will be discussed in more detail.

B. Conservation of Ecological and Scientific Values

1. Wildlife conservation

The result of human use of organic resources has inevitably been a concomitant decrease in the ecological value of the biosphere. Overall the effect of humans has been to speed up the evolution of the species they favour, at the expense of others. They have been directly or indirectly instrumental in the extinction of a considerable number of animal and plant species. As a result wildlife continues to give way to human-managed ecosystems. Reduction in wildlife has resulted from the deliberate extermination of predatory animals, pests and weeds; the overexploitation of game animals and fish; and from the decrease and/or pollution of wildlife habitats. The number of endangered species whose populations have been reduced to critical levels, and of habitats whose extent is dwindling continues to increase. An inventory (The Red Book) published in 1968, records the global loss of 36 species of mammal with a further 124 severely endangered; the comparable number of birds is listed as 94 and 187. Furthermore, the rapid development of the Third World, particularly in the species-rich tropical rain forest, may well be accompanied by the disappearance of species as yet unidentified or unrecorded. The significance of this deterioration in ecological value is the loss of genetic stock and, with it, potential resources.

Protection strategies

Wildlife (or nature) conservation is probably the most important aspect of conservation and that activity with which the term is most usually equated. Apart from its scientific and possible future economic implications, conservation of our remaining stock of wildlife in the interests of future generations is now regarded as a moral obligation.

Problems of wildlife conservation include those of the identification of rare and endangered species and habitats at local, national and international scales, and those of implementing conservation management. Among the earliest methods used were the passage of laws designed to protect wild species. One of the first to be democratically constituted was probably that passed by the Assembly in Bermuda in 1848, controlling the taking of turtles; while the earliest piece of conservation legislation in Britain was the Protection of Sea Birds Acts passed in 1869. Complementary to the protection of particular species is the conservation of habitats of ecological value as breeding or feeding sites for animals, as sites of rare plants, or because of their particular plant communities. To this end Nature or Wildlife Reserves have been set up within which habitats can be managed in the interests of nature preservation.

The degree and type of management will obviously depend on the extent to which the body or bodies responsible for conservation have statutory control, and on the former use and ecological status of the area. Few areas are

Plate 9.1 Stabilisation and management of sand dunes, Gullane, East Lothian (Grid Ref. NT/484827); cut buckthorn in the foreground plugs a wind tunnel, slab fence traps and planted marram grass stabilises drifting sand. (*Lothian District Council, Department of Physical Planning*)

so natural or wild that they have not been influenced in some way by human activities. They must, therefore, be managed to conserve the particular ecological value involved. This frequently requires the scientific culling of animal populations such as deer, rabbit and fox whose numbers would formerly have been controlled in the interests of human economic activities; if not checked, their increasing populations could endanger the balance of other plant and animal species. The conservation of heather moorland, for instance, requires the maintenance of burning after the removal of sheep stock. Similarly, careful management is essential if fragile sand-dune habitats are to survive in face of increasing recreational pressures (see Plate 9.1).

2. The wilderness concept

The concept of *wilderness* as an area of land worthy of protection and preservation has been most fully expressed in the USA. Indeed as already mentioned, the rapid disappearance of the remaining primaeval forests in the west and, with them, the last remnants of wild unexploited unsettled areas, sparked off the Conservation Movement in that country. The first nature reserves to be established were Forest Preserves which it was intended would remain 'for ever wild'. However, up to 1939 the conservation philosophy of 'wise use for the greatest good and enjoyment by the people' prevailed over that which advocated a more stringent preservationist attitude. It was not until major irrigation and hydro-power developments, followed by a spectacular increase in tourism, had made a major impact on the western landscape that the preservation of the now dwindling remnants of wilderness re-emerged as a major conservation issue. A wilderness preservation system was proposed and eventually the Wilderness Act of 1964 was passed. Wilderness was given statutory recognition and a legal definition as 'an area of undeveloped Federal land retaining its primaeval character and influence, without permanent improvements or human habitation which is protected and so managed as to preserve its natural conditions'. The Act also provided for the establishment of Wilderness Areas in already established National Forests and National Parks.

The 'vanishing wilderness' has since then received increasing publicity throughout the world, not least in Britain. There is, however, no accepted definition of wilderness in this country; nevertheless the idea that certain areas should be safeguarded as wilderness has frequently been advocated. Although there is no wilderness in the American sense left in Britain, it has been suggested that there are areas *remote* and *wild* enough in terms of terrain, climate and use to justify designation as wilderness. It has been suggested that they should be protected from the intrusion of man-made phenomena, particularly the motor-vehicle, that use should be only for those prepared to carry their requirements on their backs, and that they should be areas where self-reliance could be tested.

There are many problems attendant on the conservation of wilderness areas. The first is that wilderness is a relative concept in so far as peoples' ideas vary as to what constitutes wild land. Figures 9.1a and b demonstrate the way in which different types of tourists (resort guests) and recreationists perceive the limits of the wilderness in the Quetico National Park in the USA. Second, the concept of wilderness is closely linked to that of its conservation for the benefit of people, and the recognition of types of wilderness-recreation. Third, the statutory recognition of wilderness areas may sow the seeds of their destruction rather than their preservation. Wilderness recreational carrying capacity, that is to say the level of use beyond which the quality of the wilderness experience is reduced, is very low indeed. Increasing interest in wilderness has created greater use. Overcrowding and the destruction of values dependent on isolation and solitude are already a serious problem in many of the early designated wilderness areas in the USA. As a result, rigidly controlled access and management have had to be introduced in order to protect the wilderness from, rather than for, people.

ASSIGNMENTS

1. (a) *Find out what species of plants and animals are protected by statute in Britain.*

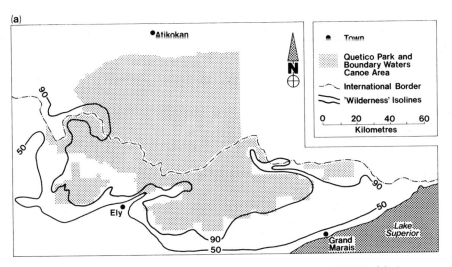

Figure 9.1 Perception of wilderness in Quetico National Park, USA. (a) Area considered wilderness by resort guests. The isoline values (50 and 90) are the percentage of parties visiting each area which described that area as being 'in the wilderness'. (b) Area considered wilderness by at least 50 per cent of each of the following four major user-types: (i) paddling canoeists, (ii) auto-campers, (iii) boat campers and (iv) resort guests (After J. Tivy, 1974)

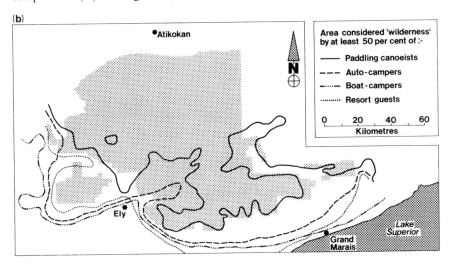

(b) *Take one example of each and discuss the problems you think might be involved in their conservation.*

2. (a) *What attributes do you consider would (i) contribute to and (ii) detract from the wilderness value of an area?*

(b) *What types of recreational activity do you consider (i) compatible and (ii) incompatible with a wilderness area?*

C. Conservation of Biological Values

1. Sustained yield

The biological value or productive capacity of the biosphere is obviously one of primary and increasing concern in a world where the rate of food production is barely keeping pace with that of population increase. There are those who would maintain that, in the long-run, all other values will have to be subordinated to increasing food output.

Conservation is concerned not just with protection and preservation but with the use and more particularly the wise use of resources. Indeed, in the early days of the Conservation Movement in the USA, the case for preserving forests 'for ever in their wild state' was rejected in favour of their exploitation on the basis of *sustained yield*. This involves the management of a particular resource for maximum continuing production, consistent with the maintenance of a constantly renewable stock (or capital). The application of the concept of sustained yield can be demonstrated in relation to three types of organic production: forestry, fishing and agriculture.

2. Forestry

In the production of wood, sustained yield is achieved by ensuring that the rate of felling equals the replacement rate over a given area. In uneven-aged stands of trees this is usually accomplished by selective felling of individual trees when they reach maturity for a particular purpose, be it pulp or timber. Obviously, no trees are retained beyond this stage, but productivity will be higher than in an unmanaged stand. Sustained yield, however, is difficult to attain on this basis since it depends on natural regeneration which will be more precarious and variable than tree extraction.

In modern forestry, clear-felling and replanting of even-aged stands which can be managed for maximum productivity is the usual practice. However, although a high proportion of the nutrients are recycled by the short-run leaves, a certain proportion becomes locked up in the wood; in fact, for calcium in hardwoods this may be equivalent to that extracted by crops over an equivalent growth period. This entails a nutrient drain on the soil which, particularly in originally nutrient deficient sites, may not be made good by natural inputs. Sustained yield can, in fact, only be maintained by initial fertilisation on replanting.

Management for wood production on a sustained or increasing yield (if land is available) basis, is the policy adopted by most of the more developed countries. The main constraints tend to be disease and wind-blow which can distort the extraction/replacement equation. On a world scale, however, and particularly in view of rapid developments in the Third World, it would seem that replacement is not keeping pace with clearance, and forest yields are, therefore, not being sustained.

3. Fishing

Fishing is still an exploitive or robber activity in so far as it continuously crops the higher levels of the food chains in the oceans without returning anything to the ecosystem. Its impact has been greatest on certain fish stock whose biological value has been seriously depleted by *overfishing*. This occurs when the catch is at a rate greater than can be replaced by natural reproduction. It is revealed in a decrease in average size of fish caught; in the average weight of total catch; and, finally, when an increasing amount of effort (energy) has to be used simply to maintain the size of the catch.

Overfishing has become a serious problem in those species most sought after. These include whales and seals whose reproductive rate is slow and among which some, including the Blue Whale, have been reduced to near extinction levels. Demersal bottom-living fish, like plaice and mackerel, and bottom-breeding species, such as herring, are susceptible to overkill because of the unselective and often destructive nature of bottom trawling. Overfishing has affected particular areas, not least those fishing banks off North West Europe which are easily accessible to a large number of fishing fleets. More recently, the use of large 'factory ships' with particularly efficient but unselective extractive techniques has exacerbated the problem in areas such as the North Sea.

If the biological productivity of the oceans is to be maintained, fishing must be at a rate such that the stock of a given species does not decrease and a sustained yield is maintained. In fact, *maximum sustained yield* can be achieved when the species is fished at a rate which keeps its stock about a third to two-thirds below its natural size. In this condition the average size of the individuals will be smaller and the age younger than in the unfished population, but the rate of growth and hence of biological productivity will be at a maximum.

The dimensions of the problem of overfishing are reflected in the number of International Commissions and Councils concerned with the difficulties of the conservation of marine resources that have been set up since the beginning of the century and more particularly in the post World War II period. Methods of conservative fishing include closed seasons to protect breeding stocks and regulations pertaining to size of fish caught or, conversely, to mesh-size of net that should be used. Extension of the limits of national territorial waters is another expression of individual countries' concern. However, the problems of marine conservation are more difficult than in any other part of the biosphere largely because the oceans are an 'open-pool' or 'common' resource and mobile fish stocks are no respecters of man-made boundaries. Successful conservation, therefore, depends on a very high degree of international co-operation.

4. Agriculture

In contrast to forestry and fishing, agriculture has been characterised by increasing productivity in terms of the yield per unit area of plant or animal food. The economic cost of increasing food production is high, dependent as it is on continuing and increasing energy subsidies in the form of direct fuel and machinery, seeds, fertilisers, pesticides and herbicides. As we have already noted (see Chapter 5), increasing agricultural yields have been accompanied by decreasing efficiency in terms of energy output:input ratios. There is already evidence in some types of highly developed agriculture in western countries that the point of diminishing returns has been reached — that returns on energy used are decreasing.

Higher yields, however, have incurred high ecological costs with an associated decrease in the ecological value of organic resources, particularly of the soil. Modern, capital-intensive farming has been accompanied by an increase in field size and the reduction of many small wildlife habitats such as hedges, copses, woods and wetland; increasing specialisation and mono-culture; a heavy dependence on inorganic fertilisers and chemicals to combat weeds and pests; and a high degree of mechanisation. The latter has involved frequent use of heavy machines on the same land because the number of cultivation processes have increased. The lack of organic material and the impact of heavy machinery has begun to take its toll in terms of a serious deterioration in soil structure (see Chapter 8).

In view of the increasing energy and ecological costs (and the future prospect of energy shortages), interest in what has been called *conservation farming* has recently been attracting considerable attention. The basic aim of conservation farming is to increase the biological value of the soil so that maximum sustained yields can be achieved with the minimum and most efficient use of energy subsidies. It depends on restoring and maintaining as efficient and as stable a soil structure as is possible given the textural properties, and on building up an energy nutrient store in the soil by the use of organic matter. This could be achieved by various means. First, a return to more traditional methods of rotation cultivation (alternating nutrient-draining crops (cereals) and nutrient-building grass/legume pastures), together with a greater application of organic material to the soil. Second, in areas less suited to cereal production, the use of managed permanent grassland to provide as much fodder as possible. Third, what Odum (1978) has called 'detritus agriculture'. The production of silage involving the fermentation of low-grade fodder, and the cultivation of detritus eating fish in the Far East are examples of this type of agriculture already being practised. Odum further points out that, at present, agriculture is based on the selection of crops for rapid growth, high yields and palatability, which makes them particularly vulnerable to disease and pests. The process could possibly be reversed if less demanding crops were selected and their biological production converted into edible products by microbial and chemical enrichment processing plants. Inevitably, however, conservation farming would necessitate lower short-term but, hopefully, sustained long-term yields.

Table 9.1   Comparison of the effects of fishing at two different intensities on (a) fish stock and (b) fish weights. The data relates to a 'static' fish stock in the sense that no allowance is made for natural gains or losses (After Sir A. Hardy, 1959)

(a)	Age class (years)	80% Rate of Fishing		50% Rate of Fishing	
		Stock (nos) (fish-years)	Annual withdrawals (nos)	Stock (nos) (fish-years)	Annual withdrawals (nos)
	1	1000	—	1000	—
	2	200	800	500	500
	3	40	160	250	250
	4	8	32	125	125
	5	2	6	62	62
	6	—	2	31	31
	7	—	—	16	16
	8	—	—	8	8
	9	—	—	4	4
	10	—	—	2	2
	11	—	—	1	1
	Totals	1250	1000	2000	1000

(b)	Age class (years)	Weight at end of year (grams per fish)	Average weight/ year class	Weight of yield (grams) 80% reduction	Weight of yield (grams) 50% reduction
	1	40	—		
	2	124	82	65000	41000
	3	227	175	28000	43750
	4	339	283	9056	35375
	5	460	400	2400	24800
	6	586	523	1046	16213
	Totals			106102	161213

ASSIGNMENTS

1. *What does Table 9.1 tell us about the effects of heavy (80 per cent rate) as compared with light (50 per cent rate) fishing on the size and age distribution of a fish stock?*
2. *With reference to Table 9.1, calculate the gain in weight per fish per year in each of the given years. Does this information indicate an optimum age at which fish should be cropped?*
3. *Which rate of fishing is able to 'sustain' yields more effectively over the period? Why are yields not sustained indefinitely by either fishing rate?*

D. Conservation of Aesthetic Values

As was noted in the previous chapter, concern about the aesthetic value of the landscape has been increasing in recent decades because of the location of certain types of large-scale urban/industrial development (power-stations, oil-terminals, chemical plants, military installations and airports) in more remote and open countryside. The decrease in the diversity of habitats and of natural elements, consequent on widespread monocultures in agriculture and forestry, has resulted in a trend towards uniformity and monotony of landscapes. In addition, the increase in resource-oriented outdoor recreation has, as already explained, reduced the ecological and closely related aesthetic value of the countryside.

The problems of conserving aesthetic values are probably more difficult than in the case of the preceding ecological and biological values. This is because, firstly, scenic evaluation is so subjective, being dependent on human perception of what is beautiful, which in turn is conditioned by peoples' cultural environment; and secondly, because of the problem of reconciling the conflicting demands for recreation with the increase in the biological/economic values of the land. The latter problem is particularly severe in small highly populated countries such as Britain. It is less severe in those where land:people ratios are high and where there is a high proportion of public land which can be managed to conserve its scenic value free of competition, as in the USA and Canada.

The conservation of aesthetic (or scenic) values of the landscape for the enjoyment and pleasure of people is inextricably tied up with recreational land use. Recreational resource values are dependent on scenic values, and the conservation of areas of high scenic value was initiated by the Conservation Movement. The original concept of the National Park (an idea which has now become universal) was based on the principle of conserving beautiful or naturally interesting areas for the enjoyment by people for all time. It should be noted that the success of means directed towards protection of scenic values varies according to the amount of statutory control that can be exercised within areas so designated.

Protected areas

In all areas, however, conservation of aesthetic/scenic values depends on the identification and designation of areas deemed worthy of protection. In Britain, National Parks on the American model were established under the terms of the Countryside Act 1949, with the aim of conserving landscape and providing for recreation in England and Wales. Little land within these boundaries is publicly owned and not used for either agriculture, forestry or some other purpose; National Park land was initially under the jurisdiction of a large number of pre-existing private and public, local and national bodies. Protection of scenic values has become increasingly difficult in face of competing demands from agriculture, forestry, urban and industrial development, as well as extreme recreational pressures.

Awareness of the increasing pressures on the countryside, both within and beyond the National Parks, culminated in the setting up, in 1968, of the Countryside Commission (with a separate body in Scotland). These bodies have a general responsibility to protect aesthetic and recreational values of the countryside, to encourage the designation of additional areas worthy of protection such as the Heritage Coasts, Areas of Outstanding Natural Beauty in England and Wales and Scenic Areas in Scotland; to assist in the setting up of Country Parks which would provide more opportunities for local outdoor recreation and, hopefully, take some of the pressures off the National Parks and other sensitive areas.

Britain's protected or as it has been called 'Cherished Land' is quite extensive. The dilemma, as elsewhere in the world, is that the methods used to protect may inadvertently detract from and ultimately destroy aesthetic values. This is because the very process of identification and designation of areas worthy of protection attracts use. In the end, conservation of landscape values may be achieved only through stricter control and management of people rather than of the resource.

ASSIGNMENT

What in your opinion are the attributes of 'beautiful' scenery? Compare your list with those of the other members of a group and discuss the reasons for any differences of opinion.

E. Conservation of Environmental Quality

More recently, and particularly during the last decade, the scope of conservation has widened to cover, in the words of the late J.F. Kennedy, 'the prevention of waste and despoilment, while preserving, improving and renewing the quality and usefulness of our resources'. Modern conservation thinking is currently concerned not merely with the protection of resource values of ecosystem components but with the quality of the whole environment as a clean, healthy medium for all forms of lie. The term *environmentalism* has become synonymous with this aspect of conservation, the main focus of which is the problem of pollution.

1. Problems of pollution control

Pollution is not a recent phenomenon. As we have already seen (see Chapters 3 and 6), it has, however, increased exponentially during the last 100–150 years consequent on increasing urbanisation and industrialisation, and the concomitant production of waste materials. Many of these wastes either cannot be recycled or are not recycled rapidly enough by the ecosystem to maintain the environment in a constant, unmodified condition. Their long or short-term accumulation in the environment causes pollution. Concern about the immediate and known harmful (as well as unknown long-term) effects on humans and other living organisms is now universal.

Table 9.2 River quality standards in relationship to aquatic life. Standards established by the UK Department of the Environment, 1970 (After D.B. James, 1978).

Class	Biota found in river
A	Rivers with widely diverse invertebrate fauna, including caddisfly larvae, mayfly and stonefly nymphs, and freshwater shrimps. Salmon, trout and grayling if ecologically favoured, or a good coarse fishing with a variety of species.
B	Stonefly and mayfly nymphs not common. Caddisfly and shrimp present. Varied invertebrate population. Good mixed coarse fisheries, trout may be present but not dominant.
C	Rivers in which invertebrate population is restricted, dominated by the water louse. Some shrimps, caddis and mayfly rare. Fisheries moderate to poor, restricted to roach and gudgeon.
D	Invertebrate fauna absent or restricted to worms and chironimids (bloodworms). Incapable of supporting fish life.

Table 9.3 Water quality standards in relation to types of use. Standards for recreational and industrial use recommended by the US Government; drinking water standards set by the World Health Organization, 1971 (After D.B. James, 1978)

Type of use	Substance	Water quality standard	
		Average or highest desirable level	Maximum permissible level
1. *Recreational*			
a) Swimming, diving, water skiing	*E.coliform* (bacteria)	200/100 ml	400/100 ml
b) Walking, boating camping	*E.coliform*	1000/100 ml	
2. *Industrial*			
a) Cooling	Dissolved solids	> 1000 mg/1	
b) Food processing		Public water standards	
3. *Public water supplies*	total solids	500 mg/1	1500 mg/1
	pH	7.0–8.5	6.5–9.2
	total hardness	100 mg/1	500 mg/1
	chloride	200 mg/1	600 mg/1
	phenols	0.001 mg/1	0.002 mg/1
	copper	0.05 mg/1	1.5 mg/1
	iron	0.1 mg/1	1.0 mg/1
	fluorides	0.6 mg 1	1.7 mg/1
	arsenic		0.05 mg/1
	cadmium		0.01 mg/1
	lead		0.1 mg/1
	mercury		0.001 mg/1
	E.coliform	0	0

Conservation of environmental quality raises two as yet incompletely solved problems. The first is how to decide what are the acceptable levels of natural or manufactured materials compatible with a high-quality environment. This involves establishing the thresholds at which pollution may be offensive, unsightly, harmful or toxic. The definition of desirable environmental standards for air and water, is made all the more difficult because there are no absolute standards which will provide optimum environmental quality for all organisms (Table 9.2) and in all situations (Table 9.3). Ironically enough, in order to provide drinking water of acceptable content and appearance, chemicals have to be added which reduce its quality for other forms of life.

The second problem is how to control pollution, both in the sense of rectifying existing, and curbing future, contamination of the environment. The earliest and still the most widely used method is legislation reinforced by financial penalities aimed at curbing pollution. The earliest legislation in Britain was influenced by health hazards arising from insanitary housing conditions and dirty factories in the mid-nineteenth century. The appointment of a Public Health Inspector in 1848, followed in 1868 by the Alkali Act, initiated clean air and water legislation in England and Wales. It was, however, not until relatively recently—and more particularly in the post-World War II period—that public concern about increasing pollution associated with aerosols, waste energy, oil and toxic chemicals was expressed in government action. The Royal Commission on Environmental Pollution was set up in 1968, and this was followed by the creation of the Central Unit on Environmental Pollution, the Clean Air Council and the Advisory Council on Noise. Such developments were paralleled in many other developed countries—as in the establishment of a Council on Environmental Quality and an Environmental Protection Agency in 1970 in the USA.

2. Externality effects and residuals

The real problem is how to impose legislation particularly in relation to private industry for whom financial penalities are not always restrictive enough. It has been suggested that industry should pay for the environmental costs of their 'spill-over' or *externality effects*, imposed on others not involved in the particular economic activity. The costs may be in terms of a deterioration in social and economic health, and amenity of the environment. Increasingly, pressure is being brought to bear on public and private industry to carry the cost of either preventing pollution or disposing of their waste material in such a way as to reduce its external effects.

Figure 9.2 illustrates the nature of environmental pollution in terms of the flow of materials through an entire (but closed) economic system, and the sources and range of the residuals or waste materials. It has been calculated that, in the USA, of the active inputs into the economy—basically fossil fuels which serve a whole range of energy needs, together with agricultural

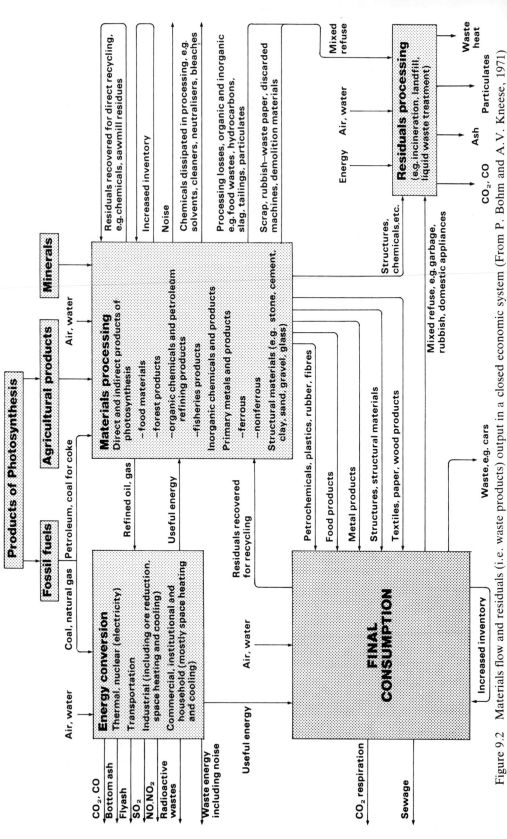

Figure 9.2 Materials flow and residuals (i.e. waste products) output in a closed economic system (From P. Bohm and A.V. Kneese, 1971)

and mineral products — about three-quarters of the overall weight is discharged into the atmosphere as carbon and hydrogen resulting from the combustion of fossil fuels and animal respiration. The remaining residuals are potentially harmful gases, e.g. sulphur dioxide, nitrogen oxides; effluent, e.g. sewage; and solid wastes, e.g. ash, particulates and mixed garbage. With the appropriate equipment and energy most undesirable substances can, in principle, be removed from air and water; what remains must be disposed of in solid form, transferred or re-used. The reduction of polluting waste and the conservation of environmental quality could be maintained if more residuals were recycled, the use-life of durable goods were extended and renewable were substituted for non-renewable resources wherever possible.

Finally, Figure 9.2 highlights the fact that the conservation of resources and of environmental quality are very closely interdependent. It has been suggested by Coddington (1974) that, with respect to the whole problem of curbing resource depletion and pollution, humans do not lack the technical know-how. The main difficulty is that they have not yet learnt to cope with the national and international economic, political and social implications of ecosystem conservation.

ASSIGNMENTS

1. *Refer to Tables 9.2 and 9.3:*
   (a) *Comment on the general value for environmental conservation of the water-quality standards shown (see Chapter 10A).*
   (b) *Analyse the possible practical and experimental problems of determining pertinent water-quality standards.*
   (c) *What part does economics play in the establishment of practical standards?*
   (d) *How 'accurate' are the water-quality zones shown in Table 9.2, and how 'safe' do you feel are the water-quality standards indicated in Table 9.3?*
   (See the two informative articles by Edward Goldsmith 'Can we control pollution?', Parts I and II in the Ecologist, 1979)
2. *Identify the final residuals in the model given in Figure 9.2; discuss how these might be further reduced.*

Key Ideas

A. *What is meant by conservation?*
1. The meaning of conservation can vary from the preservation of individual phenomena to wise use of the environment.
2. The modern conservation movement was initiated by a concern about forest depletion and soil erosion in the USA in the nineteenth century.
3. Since then conservation thinking has widened to include a greater range of phenomena and complexity of techniques.

B. *Conservation of ecological and scientific values*
1. Wildlife or nature conservation is basic to the maintenance of the scientific and ecological value of organic resources.
2. Problems of wildlife conservation include the identification and management of endangered resources.
3. Closely related to wildlife conservation is that of wilderness preservation.

C. *Conservation of biological values*
1. Central to the conservation of biological values is the concept of sustained yield.
2. Sustained yield implies the maintenance of optimal production under a given level of use.
3. Sustained yield in forestry, fishing and agriculture alike require that the rate of 'cropping' does not exceed that of resource renewal.

D. *Conservation of aesthetic values*
1. Modern intensification of land use and expansion of outdoor recreation has stimulated increasing concern for the aesthetic value of organic resources.
2. The problem basic to the conservation of aesthetic values is that of the perception of 'beauty'.
3. Conservation of aesthetic qualities tends to conflict with that of biological/economic values.

E. *Conservation of environmental quality*
1. Modern conservation has now become synonymous with the maintenance of environmental quality.
2. Pollution control is crucial to the maintenance of environmental quality.
3. The main problems of pollution control are the establishment and maintenance of environmental standards.

Additional Activities

1. *Field Project A*

   (a) Locate the nearest nature reserve in your local area.
   (b) Supplement available literature with an officially guided visit: establish the land use history, reasons for designation, present habitat characteristics and type of management.
   (c) Comment on the management problems in relation to conservation aims.

2. *Field Project B*

   For one or more of the following land uses in your local or other area, establish the extent of the problems associated with multiple use: a Forestry Commission plantation; public reservoir; privately owned upland moor; public country or regional park.

3. In what ways could primitive methods of fishing and farming be considered more resource-conservative than modern intensive methods?

4. Choose a National Park in England or Wales and analyse the major conflicts of interest within it. It is suggested that three (or more) groups of students in a class each select a different Park. Analyse and suggest reasons for any differences that may emerge. (See *Land and Leisure* by J.A. Patmore (1972); and especially the excellent series of monthly articles covering each of the ten National Parks in the *Geographical Magazine,* June 1973 to April 1974 inclusive. There is also an article on the Dartmoor National Park in *Resources for Britain's Future* edited by M. Chisholm (1972).)

5. In relation to a particular type of farm with which you are familiar (or which you may visit), consider the implications of adjusting energy-subsidies in the interests of conservation of non-renewable resources. (See the series of articles entitled 'Whither Farming' in *New Ecologist* . 1979, **2:** 46–58)

# Environmental Measurement

A. Information Demand and Use

Every species needs, for continued survival, 'information' about the habitat in which it lives. Humans, in this respect, are no exception. However, they differ from other species with regard to the sort of environmental information they require in at least three respects. First, they demand an amount and range of information necessary for their survival greatly in excess of that required by other species. Second, a good deal of the environmental data required by humans though useful is, strictly speaking, not essential for their continued existence. Third, they can collect, store, process and recall information by methods, techniques and in forms additional to that achieved by the brain, eye and other sensory organs of the living organism. Humans measure and monitor environmental data for four main reasons: scientific inquiry, stocktaking, the establishment of data base lines and environmental standards.

1. Scientific inquiry

Humans have considerable curiosity about their surroundings be it at the micro-level of the individual atom, or at the macro-scale of the universe. As a general rule, it is probably true to say that human understanding of environmental systems becomes less with their increasing size and complexity. The only way they can attain a greater understanding of very complex ecosystems is by measuring their components and monitoring the way they function. Measurement is essential to the scientific method of study; it is essential to the formulation and testing of hypotheses about ecosystems.

2. Stocktaking

The production of lists, maps and inventories of environmental information is another reason for environmental survey and surveillance. Although there tends to be a considerable amount of data acquisition for its own sake, the compilation of information inventories ('data banks'), relevant for particular purposes, can serve as the basis for both scientific inquiry and better and wiser use of organic resources. In view of present trends in population increase and the accelerating rate of resource consumption, it is clearly necessary to take stock as rapidly as possible of the distribution, amount and quality of the earth's available resources. The rational allocation of scarce resources among competing uses and efficient resource use can only be effected on the basis of knowledge about what already exists.

3. Base line data

A third and very important reason for environmental measurement is that it provides base line data necessary for comparative studies and for the analysis of change through time. Most, if not all scientific inquiry relies to a greater or lesser extent on data gained from previous work. For instance, the nature and rate of environmental (and organic) evolution can only be established from a known base line measurement. Also, it is difficult to make any satisfactory predictions about the probable reaction of ecosystems to human stresses unless their pre-impact condition is known.

4. Environmental standards

Finally, data measurement and monitoring allow the establishment of environmental standards of various kinds. Scientific measurement of the earth's surface has revealed a number of standards which are fairly precisely fixed by natural physical/chemical laws, for instance, the freezing point of water, the latent heat of evaporation, optimal thermal and moisture requirements for particular crop performances.

Precise information is also necessary for an assessment of environmental quality. This entails the quantitative definition of base lines or thresholds which define environmental conditions (air/water, etc.) of varying degrees of acceptability for particular organisms and particular purposes. Such standards provide the basis for the improvement and/or conservation of environmental quality.

B. Methods of Environmental Measurement

There is now an imposing collection of techniques of varying sophistication, used in every aspect of environmental measurement. Common to all, however, are three main types of methods which can be distinguished on the basis of whether they involve one or more of the following types of measurement: (i) qualitative or quantitative; (ii) direct or indirect; and (iii) discontinuous or continuous recording.

1. Qualitative versus quantitative methods of measurement

Environmental phenomena can be recorded with different degrees of precision and accuracy. Many types of environmental measurement can be carried out, often fairly precisely, with a degree of freedom from human bias. This is the case when specific attributes such as size, weight, volume or number need to be recorded. There is a wide variety of instruments which facilitate objective, quantitative measurement of such environmental parameters as soil texture, crop yield, atmospheric humidity and air temperature.

Although an increasing amount of data is being recorded by private individuals and public organisations on an objective, quantitative basis, it should be remembered that not all environmental attributes are amenable to this type of measurement. Nor is a mass of unco-ordinated, unrelated information any better for a particular purpose than careful, subjective description based on observation. Recordings may be subjective in that they are dependent on human value judgements and personal points of view. Human bias and perception is always present, of course, but it is particularly pronounced when *qualitative* estimates of the type, nature or character of an environmental parameter are made. For example, the ability to distinguish different types of land use, soil or rock from conventional panchromatic air photographs (see Plate 10.1) depends on the perception of visual contrasts on the film. These contrasts are a function of both the geometric attributes such as size, shape and pattern of the images (e.g. differences between roads, buildings and fields), and of other properties such as resolution (detail) texture (grain) and tone (variation in shades of grey). On Plate 10.1 tonal differences allow pasture and meadow land (dark shades) to be differentiated from arable cultivation and market gardening (lighter shades).

2. Direct and indirect methods of measurement

Quantitative or qualitative environmental data can also be acquired in two other quite different ways. The first is by *direct* measurement of the attribute; the second is by *indirect* measurement. The latter involves the use of some parameter so closely correlated with the attribute to be measured that it can be used as a surrogate for it. In the previous section the quantitative measurements were examples of the direct, the qualitative interpretation of an air photograph an illustration of the indirect method. The indirect method is frequently used where qualitative values are involved or where information about a quantitatively measurable attribute is required before sufficient direct data is available. The measurement of soil compaction by water infilteration rate or the recording of air pollution using pollution sensitive plants (O'Hare, 1973, 1975) are cases in point.

3. Discontinuous and continuous measurement

Finally, some environmental data are, or have been, recorded at discontinuous, some at continuous and regular time intervals. Discontinuous measurement is generally associated with environmental parameters whose condition does not vary much in terms of human lifespan. Geological conditions are a classic example. The type and nature of rock in a given area may be recorded on a one-off basis, and updating of information only occurs after a long period, either because of loss of records (as occurred during the Second World War) or the establishment of new methods of data measurement and classification.

Continuous measurement at regular time intervals is often referred to as 'monitoring'. This is necessary where the environmental attribute in question is highly variable in time — as in the case of atmospheric conditions; where there is a need to assess long-term change; or where the effect of a real or experimental impact on the environment needs to be recorded. Time intervals in environmental monitoring can vary from decades or years to virtually continuous automatic recording.

ASSIGNMENTS

1.(a) *Refer back to the three possible double element approaches to environmental measurement outlined in Section B. Combine one element from each of the three main approaches into a triple element association, e.g. qualitative, direct, continuous; quantitative, direct, continuous; complete the series of all possible combinations.*

(b) *Give an example of a type of environmental measurement which would involve each of the eight possible triple-approach combinations, e.g. the use of a series of regular time-lapse air photographs to measure an area under cloud cover involves a combination of indirect (air photograph), quantitative (area) and continuous (regular time intervals) approaches.*

2. (a) *Comparing Plate 10.1. with Plates 10.2–10.4, deduce what other types of map could be compiled from the data given on Plate 10.1.*

(b) *What are the problems involved in constructing maps from air photographs?*

C. Problems of Environmental Measurement

1. Sampling

Some environmental phenomena are composed of discrete units, such as plants, animals, fields and rock type distinguished by variously defined boundaries (discontinuities); others, (such as the atmosphere) are continuous media. Even on a micro-scale the number of units or size of area involved would be such as to make a completely comprehensive set of measurements so time consuming and expensive as to be impractical.

The most usual way of solving this problem is by the use of some type of sampling technique. Sampling involves the choice of a number of units, or density of locations, as the case may be, which are assumed, statistically, to be representative of the whole population of units or area. Dependent on the nature of the attribute and the use to which the data are to be put, samples can be chosen randomly, systematically, or randomly within a systematic grid (stratified sampling). Unfortunately, many measurements have been and still are taken on the basis of an arbitrarily chosen number of units or locations.

Drawing conclusions about the nature of an environmental attribute (such as the mean temperature or range of temperatures in a given area) from a sample of measurements is often difficult. Before it can be done, the degree of error between the sample and the whole population or area should be known. It is not the object of this section to calculate how much error is likely to occur by the adoption of sampling designs and techniques of various kinds. It may be useful, however, to illustrate some general problems which attend the sampling of environmental phenomena in terms of both space and time.

2. Area sampling

The construction of maps illustrating the spatial distribution of any environmental parameter raises particular sampling problems. The quality of the data will be related to the type and intensity (density) of sampling used. Recording land use (Plate 10.2), for instance, from ground survey or from air photographs (Plate 10.1) presents relatively few problems, since the fairly discrete and homogeneous units (fields or other land use boundaries) allow complete cover of a given area to be achieved.

However, data collection for maps of a continuously variable phenomenon (such as soil or air pollution levels) is usually based on *point sampling*, whereby only a minute fraction of the total available information is recorded. Mapping of this type of data necessitates a considerable amount of generalisation and simplification, dependent on the scale and density of sampling. It also gives rise to problems of (a) data interpolation and (b) intra-unit variability.

(a) Interpolation of data

Generalisations about many types of continuously variable phenomena are frequently made by joining sample points of equal value (isolines), and interpolating isolines of assumed value between those established from known data. The construction of air pollution or rainfall maps serves to illustrate some of the problems involved. For instance, the construction of isolines of equal pollution or rainfall value is particularly difficult because the density of point values is usually very low due to the cost and time involved in establishing and maintaining recording stations. This uncertainty is caused by a lack of information in certain areas, and the fact that the available point values may be too far apart to provide conclusive evidence. As a result, a number of alternative distributional interpretations can be made, based on the same set of control points.

212

(b) Intra-unit variability

Boundaries and isolines, interpolated from a spatial network of point samples, not only maximise inter-unit contrast, they also minimise intra-unit variability. This obviously tends to suggest a greater degree of intra-unit homogeneity than exists in reality; such a data generalisation inevitably masks a considerable amount of internal variability. For instance, homogeneous soil mapping units (series), such as those shown in Plate 10.3, actually contain a high degree of intra-unit variation. Beckett and Webster (1971) have provided a detailed review of soil variability based on work drawn from a variety of sources from different but mostly temperate countries. They conclude that the 'purity' of the soil series mapped or the percentage of the area that actually belongs to the series indicated on the map is often as low as 50 per cent; formerly it was assumed to be as high as 85 per cent.

Some published soil maps now include a numerical assessment of the intra-variability of the soil mapping units. These may consist of an estimation of the proportion of other soil series within any one soil mapping unit. More simply, however, an indication of the dominance/subdominance of those soil series included in each mapping unit may be given.

3. Problems of scale

Recording and mapping of environmental data, as has already been implied, is markedly influenced by the scale at which sampling is carried out. The

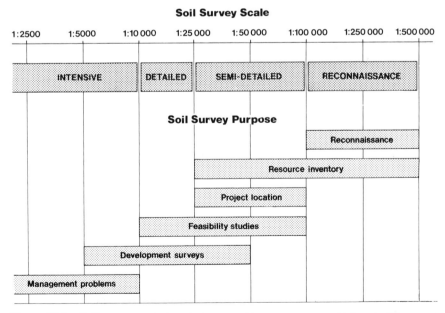

Figure 10.1   Soil survey scale in relation to soil survey purpose (After A. Young, 1973)

scale and, hence the type and detail of information, is usually determined by the purpose for which it is required. The relationship between the scale and purpose of soil surveys is shown in Figure 10.1. Reconnaissance soil surveys on scales of 1:100 000 and smaller necessarily cover whole countries or other large regions; they are intended as national resource inventories and as a guide to areas possessing development potential. They are normally surveys not only of soil itself, but of land units based on terrain, vegetation and soil. Considerable use is made of air photograph interpretation in their compilation. At the other extreme, management problem surveys are usually at an intensive scale. They are often special purpose in nature, concerned with specific management problems such as irrigation-water application or precise planting locations for high-capital crops. Since the aims are narrowly defined by scale, the information collected during survey may be clearly specified, for example, effective soil depth, pH or salinity.

Although the quality of mapped data improves with an increase of scale, it is not always possible to survey at the larger scales. Both the cost and the time needed to carry out surveys tends to increase exponentially with increase in scale — as expected from the two spatial dimensions involved — and this may set constraints on the scale of investigation.

4. Time sampling

The environment is of its nature a dynamic system. Measurements of environmental attributes are often only 'snapshots' in a constantly changing pattern of information. The value of measurements of environmental phenomena taken over a single or short time period are obviously and severely limited by considerations of time. Maps and air photographs, for instance, soon become historical documents since they freeze in one instant of time an ever changing spatial pattern. This problem is not so significant with slowly evolving attributes such as geology; time-lapse differences become more critical with regard to rapidly altering spatial patterns, such as maps of land use.

Monitoring environmental data is, therefore, important for two reasons. Not only does it put the present environmental patterns in perspective with regard to their past development, but it also, by establishing data trends, provides a basis for the prediction of future events.

Assessments of environmental change can be made only if surveys are carried out over meaningful time periods. Indeed, the quality of data and the generalisations made about data are functions of the intensity of sampling and the time period over which recordings are made. Phenomena display different generalised trends depending on whether they have been observed, intermittently or continuously, over a very short period, a few days, a season or over a number of years. As illustrated in Figure 10.2, records of the variation in the solute concentration of river water obtained over a short time period by continuous monitoring and monthly sampling reveal quite different trends. Moreover, long-term change in river solute concentration

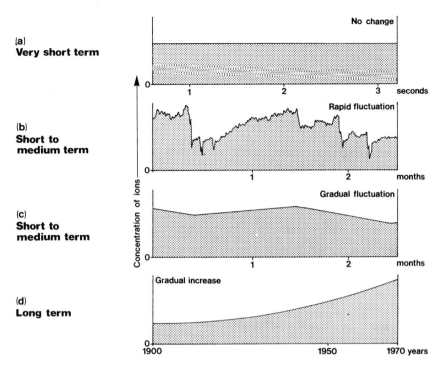

Figure 10.2 Trends in the solute concentration of river water in relation to time and intensity of sampling ((b) and (c) after D.E. Walling, 1975)

may display an altogether different pattern to that of short-term variation since different processes might be at work.

It is relatively easy to design experiments for the study and analysis of short-term continuous change and some types of long-term (but not too long!) regular fluctuation. Nevertheless, certain events are difficult if not impractical to monitor over time. Irregular, infrequent and extreme events have proved among the most difficult to measure and interpret. Records depicting the occurrence of natural hazards (e.g. flood, drought, earthquake) are usually too short for statistical patterns to emerge, and the link to physical theory is too tenuous to provide a reliable base for forecasting.

In addition, the analysis and interpretation of environmental change which occurred in the past is a problematic area of inquiry. A variety of data sources has been of value in reconstructing the nature of past environmental change. Table 10.1 illustrates some of these different sources, together with the time over which they are most representative and useful. In general terms, the further back in time one goes, the more substantially the variety of methods and the accuracy of results decreases.

5. Aesthetic values

In addition to problems generated by time and space, certain environmental attributes have not proved amenable to objective quantitative measurement

Table 10.1　Data sources and their use in the analysis of environmental change (After P. Haggett, 1979)

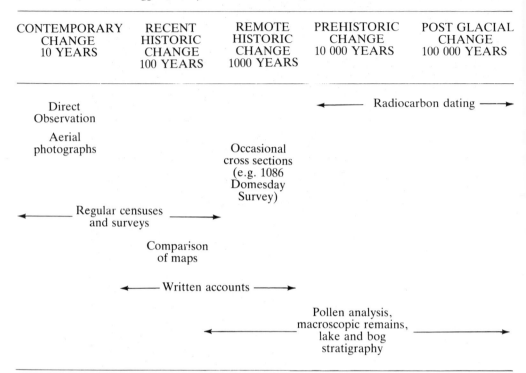

CONTEMPORARY CHANGE 10 YEARS	RECENT HISTORIC CHANGE 100 YEARS	REMOTE HISTORIC CHANGE 1000 YEARS	PREHISTORIC CHANGE 10 000 YEARS	POST GLACIAL CHANGE 100 000 YEARS

Direct Observation

← —————— Radiocarbon dating —————— →

Aerial photographs

Occasional cross sections (e.g. 1086 Domesday Survey)

← —————— Regular censuses and surveys —————— →

Comparison of maps

← —————— Written accounts —————— →

Pollen analysis, macroscopic remains, lake and bog stratigraphy

← ———————————————————————————————— →

and analysis due to their intangible nature. For example, the measurement and assessment of the aesthetic quality of landscape has defied precise analysis, since scenic quality is a nebulous, intangible and highly subjective attribute. Nevertheless, it is generally accepted that there is a need for the development of techniques of land classification so that appropriate planning action may be taken on future management and use of land (Section D3). In this respect the identification of land of high scenic quality is particularly important in view of the increasing use and demands made of open spaces for resource-oriented outdoor recreation.

The assessment of the aesthetic quality of different landscapes for the purpose of protection and/or enhancement has been a statutory duty of both local and central government since the 1947 Town and Country Planning Act came into force. The result has been the establishment of a patchwork of National Parks, Areas of Outstanding Natural Beauty and Areas of Great Landscape Value. However, although there is general agreement on the need to protect such landscapes, there is considerable disagreement about their precise definition and delimitation. The designation of such areas has proved difficult because landscape evaluation depends on a set of elusive and highly subjective attributes. As a result, each local authority and planning office has tended to adopt different systems of landscape evaluation at

Plate 10.1 Land use in a selected area north-west of Deal, Kent (scale 1:25 000), (*Based on the Ordnance Survey aerial photograph with the permission of the Controller of Her Majesty's Stationery Office. Crown copyright reserved.*)

Plate 10.2 Land use map of a selected area north-west of Deal, Kent (scale 1:25 000). (*Second Land Utilization Survey of Britain*)

Plate 10.3 Soil series map of a selected area north-west of Deal, Kent (scale 1:25 000); soil phase in rounded brackets, soil group in square brackets. (*Soil Survey of England and Wales*)

Plate 10.4 Land use capability map of a selected area north-west of Deal, Kent (scale 1:25 000). (*Soil Survey of England and Wales*)

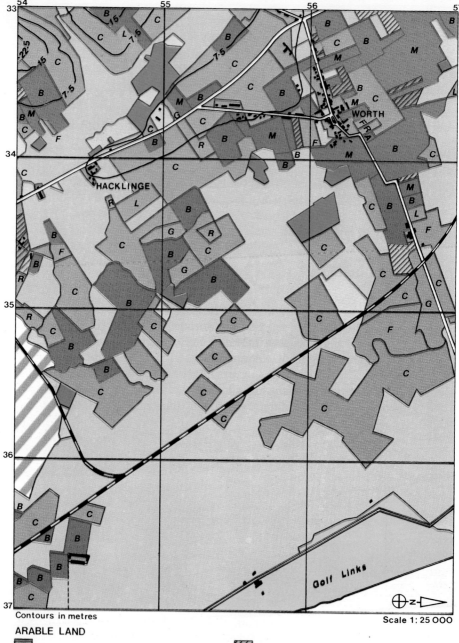

Contours in metres

Scale 1:25 000

ARABLE LAND

C	Cereals
L	Ley Legumes
R	Roots
G	Green Fodder
F	Fallow

MARKET GARDENING

B	Field food crops
M	Mixed Market Gardening
A	Allotment Gardens

Orchards with grass

Orchards with arable land

Grassland

Woodland

Rough Land

Freshwater marsh

Commercial and Residential

Open space

Spoil Heap

Plate 10.2

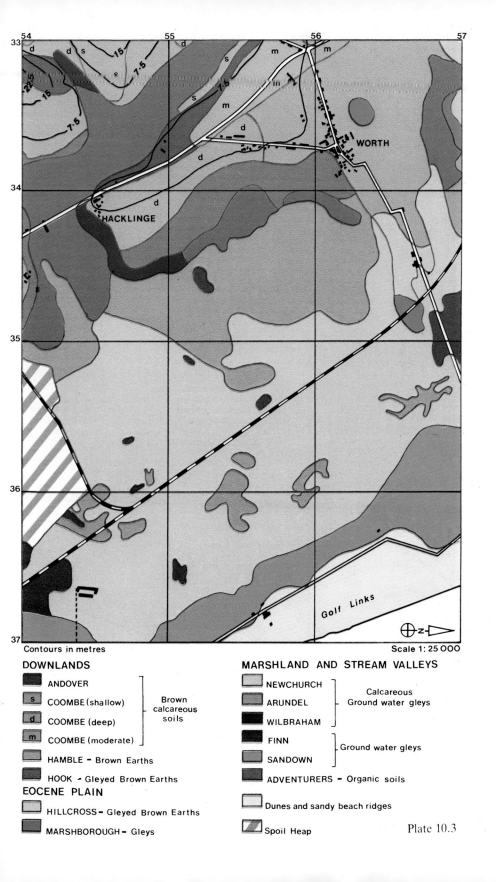

Contours in metres

Scale 1: 25 000

DOWNLANDS

- ANDOVER
- s COOMBE (shallow)
- d COOMBE (deep)
- m COOMBE (moderate)

Brown calcareous soils

- HAMBLE — Brown Earths
- HOOK — Gleyed Brown Earths

EOCENE PLAIN

- HILLCROSS — Gleyed Brown Earths
- MARSHBOROUGH — Gleys

MARSHLAND AND STREAM VALLEYS

- NEWCHURCH
- ARUNDEL
- WILBRAHAM

Calcareous Ground water gleys

- FINN
- SANDOWN

Ground water gleys

- ADVENTURERS — Organic soils

- Dunes and sandy beach ridges
- Spoil Heap

Plate 10.3

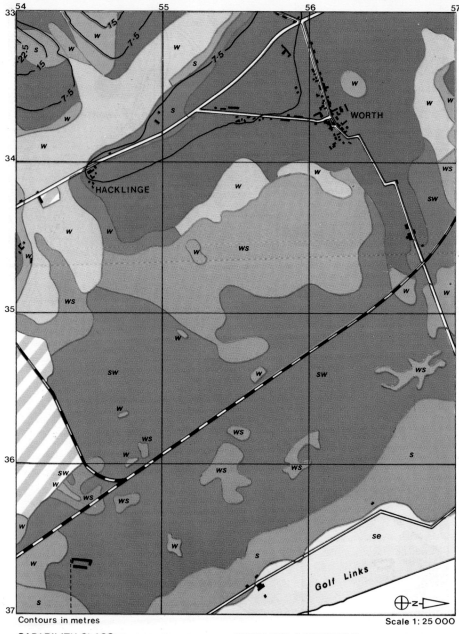

CAPABILITY CLASS
(Degree of Limitation)

	1	Very minor
	2	Minor
	3	Moderate
	4	Moderately severe
	5	Severe
	7	Extremely severe

SUBCLASS LIMITATIONS
Where two letters are used, the first
letter indicates the major limitation

w	Wetness
s	Soil
e	Erosion

Unclassified

Plate 10.4

Contours in metres

Scale 1: 25 000

different times. For instance, the designation of the National Parks and the early AONBs has been assessed by consensus techniques, that is, taking the intuitive opinion of local authority and planning department committees. The designation of more recent AONBs and other areas of landscape value has been based on more systematic semi-objective analysis; but there has still been considerable variation in methods employed. There is, as yet, no generally and universally accepted technique of analysis.

The variety of available methods for landscape evaluation, however, conforms to either 'preference' or 'parametric' techniques. *Preference* techniques, which also involve consensus methods, attempt to assess the response of individuals and groups to attributes of the general landscape usually in quantitative terms. The *parametric* approach to landscape evaluation attempts to reduce the intangible and subjective nature of landscape assessment by employing quasi-objective measurement and testing procedures. Such techniques may rely on data derived solely from maps and air photographs though field survey may also be involved.

The parametric approach rests on the assumption that the scenic quality of a piece of landscape can be calculated by adding the individual attractiveness ratings for a selection of components, e.g. types of relief, land use and water bodies, of which the landscape is composed. However, the selection of components is obviously a highly subjective and questionable process. The disposition, interaction, association and compatability of components may be more crucial than the combined effects of their individual and separate importance. Feelings such as harmony, surprise and even a sense of remoteness generated in the viewer by landscape are intangible reflections of the disposition and arrangement of components, and this cannot be satisfactorily allowed for by separate component analysis. Though there may be agreement on the relative ranking of components, the translation of ranked values into specific weightings or qualitative scores gives a dubious impression of accuracy. The weightings assigned, for instance, by Linton (1968) in his two-fold component scheme of 'landscape landforms' and 'landscape land use' is based solely on the author's own personal field experience of the Scottish landscape.

Further problems are introduced by the fact that the appearance of any landscape is affected by transient conditions of weather, lighting, daily and seasonal changes, presence of people, animals and vehicles. Though a number of techniques have attempted to include such transient features in their analysis, they have generally proved difficult to include and measure in studies of scenic quality.

Also, the scenic value of landscape is a function of a multiplicity of overlapping subjective views, and the measurement of a representative number of views would be an enormous data generating and handling task. One of the most pertinent problems of scenic evaluation is that the whole process, no matter how 'dressed up' it is in terms of science and objectivity, is highly subjective. One of the chief problems and objections directed at almost any method of scenic assessment is that such methods are generally unrepresentative of general public opinion, even though it is for their future well-being that landscapes will either be conserved or developed.

ASSIGNMENTS

1. *Using the model given in Figure 10.1 suggest what aspects of vegetation and/or flora might be recorded and mapped at varying scales for the purpose of (i) nature conservation, and (ii) commercial forestry.*
2. (a) *What methods can be used to monitor river flow and wind speeds?*
   (b) *What sort of published data is available for river flow and wind speeds respectively? Comment on the value and shortcomings of this type of data.*
3. *From a comparison of Plate 10.1 and Plate 10.2 comment on problems of recording changes in land use over time and the value of air photographs for this purpose.*
4. (a) *With reference to Figure 10.3, calculate the* average *return period of a maximal annual flood of 0.5, 1.5, and 2.0 times the magnitude of the mean maximal annual flood for the given stream system.*
   (b) *What is to stop a flood twice the mean maximal annual occuring next year (or tomorrow!) rather than in 20 or 50 years time?*

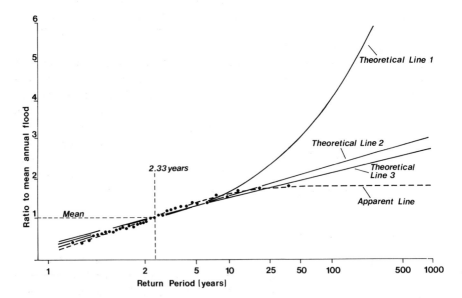

Figure 10.3 Different types of mathematical plot (prediction) of the average return periods for the maximal flood in any one year for Sugar Creek, Pennsylvania, USA. Maximum annual flood data covers a 36 year period and the return period can be calculated as follows:

$$RP = \frac{(n + 1)}{r}$$

where n = total number of years, and r = rank order of flood
(After R. Ward, 1978)

218

(c) *With reference to the text, comment on:*
  (i) *the size of the flood data record, and*
  (ii) *the variety of physical theory (types of statistical plot) used to forecast the magnitude and occurrence of future floods.*

D. Trends in Environmental Measurement

The need for environmental information has benefited from recent technical and methodological advance. Various technical improvements have facilitated not only the measurement and collection of information, but also its storage, analyses and presentation.

1. The role of remote sensing

The collection and interpretation of field data from conventional ground survey has been increasingly improved, complemented and on occasion displaced by a whole range of remote sensing techniques. Environmental remote sensing depends on the fact that all bodies at or near the surface of the earth generate and emit energy in radiant form. Each type of surface emits a characteristic array or spectrum of radiation waves identifiable in terms of their wavelengths and intensities. Devices carried in aircraft and spacecraft are able to intercept these signals and are thus able to detect or remotely sense the earth's surface features.

Various remote sensing techniques can be employed for a whole range of purposes, including those associated with photogrammetry, i.e. the production of very accurate maps showing selected features of relief and topography, and air photograph interpretation, i.e. the analysis and interpretation of earth surface phenomena. Table 10.2 summarises the advantages and disadvantages, together with the general applications of the main techniques. The particular advantages of using infra-red and near infra-red imagery should be noted. Such imagery is largely unaffected by atmospheric absorption and can be more readily received and identified by sensing devices.

2. The information explosion

The increasing need for data about the earth, and the promotion of this demand by scientific and technical advance, has produced what has been termed the 'information explosion'. There is good evidence from general surveys of the growth of scientific information to show that information expands at an exponential rate, i.e. the greater the amount of data that exists, the faster it grows. Reliable estimates suggest that the amount of environmental information tends to double within a time span of about 10–15 years or even less. Haggett (1979) considers that the current generation of scientists have about 1000 times more data at their disposal than that available to environmental scientists in the early part of the nineteenth century.

Table 10.2 The advantages, disadvantages and selected applications of the main remote sensing systems

Type of system	Sensing technique	Wave length	Advantages	Disadvantages	Selected uses
Passive Direct	*Photographic* Black and white True colour False colour Black and white False colour	Visible 0.3–0.7 μm Near infra-red 0.7–0.9 μm	Good ground or object resolution from aircraft	Day recording only Affected by haze and bad weather Expensive	Mapping vegetation and agricultural land use Rock outcrops, shoreline charting
Passive Indirect	*Photographic* Infra-red Linescan	0.9 μm– 0.1 mm (thermal)	Less influenced by smoke haze Use of radiation 'windows'	Affected by heavy rain Technical and interpretive limitations	Delimitation of forest fires, thermal effects or windbreaks, sea ice, ocean currents, drainage patterns
Active Indirect	*Non-photographic* SLAR Sideways Looking Airborne Radar	Radar 5.00 mm– 10 m	Day and night survey 'All weather' recording Long range capability	Technical problems Image distortion Shadowing effects Poor object resolution	Cheap reconnaissance Survey of large areas, especially relief and drainage patterns Preparation and revision of small scale topographic and systematic maps

Despite a consistent, ever-increasing expansion in the availability of information, the need for environmental data has accelerated at an even faster rate. This is a reflection, firstly, of the search for a more realistic and satisfactory way of explaining the environment. Traditional components of environmental survey are being analysed in new ways. In addition, a shift in emphasis to different environmental aspects such as to studies of pollution and questions of resource depletion have opened up new fields of inquiry as well as revealing areas of critical information deficiency. The desire for more information about the earth is also closely associated with a recent shift in geographic interest to tropical and arctic regions where little previous investigation has been carried out. This is testified by the rapid expansion now taking place in primary resource surveys in tropical lands (Young, 1978).

3. Practical value of environmental measurement

Together with changing demands for environmental information, and more advanced techniques for obtaining data, there has been a growing emphasis on the acquisition of data of immediate practical value in measurement programmes.

The ease with which individual features of the earth's suface can be measured and mapped has made the *single parameter* approach to environmental survey a particularly popular one, and it is still dominated by the recording and mapping of what can best be termed conventional environmental indices (e.g. relief, geology, temperature, rainfall, vegetation). There has, however, been a more recent move towards more 'valuable' and practical information. Hence, data on relief has been supplemented by slope maps, since angle of slope has a direct bearing on the limits to safety in the use of agricultural implements as well as on the rate and degree of soil erosion. Similarly, the character and economic significance of climate has been increasingly represented by such indices as length of growing season, day-degrees of accumulated temperatures, potential evapo-transpiration and irrigation-water need (see Table 10.3). In addition, measurement of the extreme values rather than the average condition, together with those that emphasise process rather than pattern, are now seen as being of increasing value in environmental studies.

Though single parameter methods still tend to dominate environmental investigation, they have always been complemented by techniques which attempt to express the complex interacting character of the total bio-physical environment in some way. Such methods, termed *multi-parameter*, often merely combine, manually or by computer, data from single parameter surveys on multi-attribute maps. Though such schemes are methodologically attractive, they have a number of drawbacks. Single parameter data cannot easily be combined to produce new multi-parameter indices (e.g. temperature + humidity + wind speed = oceanicity). This is because of incompatibilities in the different data sets resulting from the different purposes for which they were originally collected, over different periods and at different scales (see Section C).

The most successful type of multi-parameter approach is the *integrated survey*. These surveys depend on the recognition that certain environmental features (e.g. soil, vegetation, landform type) are so closely correlated that they can either singly or in combination be used as an index of environmental conditions. Integrated land surveys of this type are still basic to many methods of land evaluation. Land evaluation aims at assessing the relative value of land resources for one or a combination of particular purposes such as rural and urban, agricultural, aesthetic (Section C5), hydrological, military

Table 10.3   Examples of single thematic indices used to present spatial variations in the physical environment. (After V. Gardiner and K.J. Gregory, 1977)

Type of index	Topographic character	Climatic elements	Landscape feature or process Soil	Rock type	Vegetation/land use	Processes
Conventional	Relief representation techniques Genetic landform types	Averages of climatic elements precipitation temperature Synoptic types	Major soil groups Soil thickness	Lithology Genetic rock types	Plant types Vegetation formations	Average rate mean river discharge
Relevant	Relative relief Slope and aspect Drainage pattern density or distance from water Texture or depth of dissection River sinuosity Terrain ruggedness or roughness	Growing season Day degrees Comfort indices Radiation index of dryness Potential evapo-transpiration	pH Water content Infiltration properties Soil erodibility Bulk density	Depth to bedrock Permeability/ porosity Rippability	Habitat Productivity Periodicity	Peak discharge Low flow discharge Process components/ water balance components
Extreme value	Areas susceptible to earthquakes, mass movements, floods	Rainfall intensity Drought liability Risk of hail, frost	Shear strength Liquid limit Plastic limit	Shear strength Bearing capacity	Wilting point	Probability of extreme rates Flood risk
Comprehensive schemes	Geomorphological maps Parametric terrain mapping Basin morphometry methods Drainage types Erosion maps	Numerical classifications of climates Topoclimates	Soil mapping units	Stratigraphic units	Plant associations	Hydrological regimes

Note: The range of examples cannot be fully comprehensive and some indices could feature in more than one category.

and engineering. Interest in integrated surveys developed with the need to assess the potential of undeveloped land resources. It was given considerable impetus with the increasing availability and use of air photographs, during and after World War II, by which extensive areas of terrain could be surveyed. A system of identifying land systems and land units, which were defined on the basis of land form and associated soils and vegetation types, was developed by the Land Division Research Branch of the Commonwealth Scientific and Industrial Research Organisation (CSIRO) in Australia and subsequently used in many less developed countries.

The integrated survey was the forerunner of attempts to measure, more specifically, the capability or suitability of land for particular purposes, not least, intially, for agriculture. Many land capability schemes have been derived from the American classification by the Soil Conservation Service, United States Department of Agriculture (Klingebiel and Montgomery, 1961). This involved the technique of identifying land areas (units) on the basis mainly of the potentialities and limitations of their soil to sustain agricultural production.

The most recent land capability classification in Britain is that developed by the Soil Survey (Bibby and Mackney, 1969). This aims to assess the capability of land for agriculture on the basis of the number and severity of physical, and particularly soil, limitations to the attainment of maximum production in a given climatic regime and assuming a uniformly high level of management. Land is classified into seven capability classes, six of which are shown in Plate 10.4, on the basis of the number of limitations; and into sub-classes on that of the degree (none, moderate, severe, excessive) of limitation imposed by selected agriculturally significant parameters which include slope, exposure (climate), surface drainage (wetness), soil depth, stoniness, soil wetness and dryness. Obviously the severity of a limiting factor is related to the difficulty and hence the cost of reducing it in order to achieve the potential maximum production of agriculture crops. As with all land evaluation schemes, the Soil Survey Land Use Capability Scheme has its drawbacks. It is based on a combination of indirect quantitative and qualitative data. The assumptions on which it is based and the type of decisions that need to be made in deciding classes have to be explained and guidelines established (Bibby and Mackney, 1969). Also, there has been some controversy over the dependence of the scheme's mapping units on those of the Soil Survey itself (see Plates 10.3 and 10.4). However, the justification for this procedure is that physical units, such as those delimited by soil or terrain, provide a fairly permanent basis for an agricultural land classification, and allow the map to be revised relatively easily with change in capability. For instance, much of Class 3 and 4 land on Plate 10.4 could be improved by one class division, and Class 5 land by as many as four divisions to Class 1 with the operation of pumped drainage schemes. However, as previously discussed, soil mapping units are not uniform even in their visible morphological characteristics, quite apart from chemical properties. The Soil Survey units, like the soil series on Plate 10.3, are defined on a generic basis (i.e. on soil development) which need not, and indeed in some investigated cases has been proved does not, have a close relationship with agricultural production.

More recently the concept of land capability assessment has been developed and extended to uses other than agricultural. In North America the US Soil Conservation Service, and more particularly, the Canadian Land Division have produced schemes for the grazing, forestry and recreation capability of land. Methods of land classification for a variety of purposes are currently being studied by a number of individuals and organisations in Britain (Coppock and Thomas, 1980).

4. Co-ordinated surveys

Finally, the number of large co-ordinated environmental programmes which are now being carried out reflect the continuing need not only for greater but for more applicable data about the environment. These are a recognition that, because of the complexity of the ecosystem, the approach to environmental measurement and monitoring requires the co-ordinated efforts of a team of specialists. The International Biological Programme initiated in 1960 and the Institute of Terrestrial Ecology in Britain are examples of co-ordinated surveys at international and national levels respectively.

ASSIGNMENTS

1. *Turn back to Table 10.2 and explain why particular remote-sensing systems have been chosen for the purposes indicated.*
2. *Comment on the problems of measuring and mapping slope either from existing relief maps or on the basis of field measurement.*
3. *For each of the following environmental components select* one *index of practical value for a particular purpose: solid geology; drift geology; soil; climate; land form. Comment on the problems of measuring and mapping at an appropriate scale:*
4. *Study Plates 10.2, 10.3 and 10.4 and comment on (a) the relative value of Plates 10.3 and 10.4 to an understanding of land use distribution, and (b) their practical value for a farmer or planner in the area.*

Key Ideas

A. Information demand and use
1. Humans differ from other organisms in their demands for and use of enviromnental information.
2. They measure the environment for four main reasons: scientific inquiry, stocktaking, establishment of data base lines and environmental standards.

B. *Methods of environmental measurement*
1. There are three main approaches common to all methods of data collection (a) qualitative versus quantitative; (b) direct versus indirect; and (c) continuous versus discontinuous.

C. *Problems of environmental measurement*
1. Sampling is essential to all types of environmental measurement.
2. The type and design of sampling techniques are related to the nature and scale of the phenomena and proposed data use.
3. Point sampling of continuously variable phenomena gives rise to problems of interpolation and intra-unit variability.
4. The quality and use of environmental data are dependent on the scale of investigation.
5. The quality and use of data are also a function of the intensity and time-frequency of recording.
6. Some environmental attributes, particularly such as aesthetic value, are not amenable to objective quantitative analysis.
7. Aesthetic evaluations of land may be carried out by preference or parametric techniques.

D. *Trends in environmental measurement*
1. Recent trends have been characterised by the development of methods and techniques which have facilitated collection, storage, analysis and presentation of data.
2. Remote-sensing techniques are among the most effective methods of data collection and analysis.
3. Increased need combined with new techniques have accelerated the rate of data collection.
4. Recent trends have also been characterised by a growing emphasis on the collection of data of immediate practical value.
5. A major problem is the selection of individual environmental indices and their combination to satisfy practical needs.
6. Land measurement and classification have become the focus of many recent developments in the integration of environmental data for specific practical purposes.

Additional Activities

1. (a) From the publications of the Meteorological Office, find out what type of data are recorded about air temperature and sunshine.
   (b) For a selected area (one with at least 10 stations) construct isoline maps from both sets of the above parameters.
   (c) What particular interpolation problems do these pose?

2. For a selected river basin (at a regional scale) locate stations at which river flow and wind speeds are recorded. Construct diagrams to illustrate the spatial and temporal variations of the two parameters. Comment on the value of the two types of data for the analysis of spatial variation.

3. *Field Project A*

   (a) Select an area of varied relief for which a Soil Survey map is available. Using the method outlined in Bibby and Mackney (1969) and the Soil Survey series (England and Wales) or associations (Scotland) as major land units, construct a map (scale 1:50 000 or 1:25 000) of land capability.
   (b) Comment on the practical problems involved and their relevance for the practical value of land capability maps.

4. *Field Project B*

   (a) Select an area of relatively uniform uncultivated vegetation (but excluding permanent pasture) about the size of two tennis courts.
   (b) Record the number of different species using (i) 10 metre square quadrats and (ii) 100 point samples, located randomly, systematically and subjectively in each case.
   (c) In the light of the results of your analyses, comment on the advantages and disadvantages of the sampling methods employed.

Reading

Chapter 1

EYRE, S.R., *Vegetation and Soils*: A World Picture, Edward Arnold, London, 1975.
PEARS, N., *Basic Biogeography*, Longman, London, 1977.
SIMMONS, I.G., *Ecology of Natural Resources*, Edward Arnold, London, 1974.
SIMMONS, I.G., *Biogeography: Natural and Cultural*, Edward Arnold, London, 1979.
STODDART, D.R., 'Geography and the ecological approach: the ecosystem as a geographic principle and model', *Geography* 50: 242–51, 1965.
SUTTON, D.B. and HARMON, N.P., *Ecology: Selected Concepts*, Wiley, Chichester and New York, 1973.
TIVY, J., *Biogeography: A Study of Plants in the Ecosphere*, Oliver & Boyd, Edinburgh, 1977.
WATTS, D., *Principles of Biogeography*, McGraw-Hill, New York and Maidenhead, 1971.
WATTS, D., 'The new biogeography and its niche in physical geography', *Geography*, 63(4): 324–337, 1978.

Chapter 2

BORMANN, F.H. and LIKENS, G.E., *Pattern and Process in a Forested Ecosystem*, Springer-Verlag, New York and Heidelberg, 1979.
CLAPHAM, W.B., *Natural Ecosystems*, Collier Macmillan, West Drayton, 1973.
CLOUD, P. and GIBOR, A., 'The oxygen cycle', *Scientific American*, 223(3): 111–123, 1970.
COOPER, J.P. (Ed.), *Photosynthesis and Productivity in Different Environments* (Chapter 27), International Biological Programme 3, Cambridge University Press, 1975.
DEEVEY, E.S., 'Mineral cycles', *Scientific American*, 223(3): 149–158, 1970.
EYRE, S.R., *The Real Wealth of Nations*, Edward Arnold, London, 1978.
GOSZ, J.R., *et al.*, 'The flow of energy in a forest ecosystem', *Scientific American*, 238(3): 93–102, 1978.
LEITH, H., 'Primary productivity in ecosystems: comparative analysis of global patterns', in VAN DOBBEN, W.H., and LOWE McCONNELL, R.H., (Eds.), *Unifying Concepts in Ecology*, Dr. W. Junk, The Hague, 1975.
ODUM, E.P., *Fundamentals of Ecology*, Holt-Saunders, New York and Eastbourne, 1977.
Open University Press, *Energy Flow Through Ecosystems: Producers and Consumers*, Units 1–3, S323, OUP, Milton Keynes, 1974.

PHILLIPSON, J., *Ecological Energetics*, Studies in Biology 1, Edward Arnold, London, 1966.

Scientific American, *Man and the Ecosphere*, W.H. Freeman, San Francisco and Reading, 1971.

Scientific American, *The Biosphere*, W.H. Freeman, San Francisco and Reading, 1971.

SOLOMON, M.E., *Population Dynamics*, Studies in Biology 18, Edward Arnold, London, 1976.

SMITH, R.L., *The Ecology of Man: An Ecosystem Approach*, Harper & Row, London and New York, 1976.

STODDART, D.R., *op. cit.* (Chapter 1)

STODDART, D.R., 'Organism and ecosystem as geographical models', Chapter 13 in CHORLEY, R.J. and HAGGETT, P. (Eds.), *Models in Geography*, Methuen, London, 1967.

SUTTON, D.B. and HARMON, N.P., *op.cit.* (Chapter 1)

TIVY, J., *op.cit.* (Chapter 1)

WHITTAKER, R.H., *Communities and Ecosystems*, Collier Macmillan, West Drayton, 1975.

WHITTAKER, R.H., *et al.*, 'The Hubbard Brook ecosystem study: forest biomass and production', *Ecological Monographs*, 44: 223—254, 1974.

WOODWELL, G.M., 'Toxic substances and ecological cycles', *Scientific American*, 216(3): 23—31, 1967.

Chapter 3

BAKER, H.G., *Plants and Civilization*, Macmillan, London, 1964.

BATES, M., *Man in Nature*, Foundations of Modern Biology, Prentice-Hall, New York and Hemel Hempstead, 1964.

BOWMAN, J.C., *Animals for Man*, Studies in Biology 78, Edward Arnold, London, 1977.

COALE, A.J., *The Human Population*, Scientific American, W.H. Freeman, San Francisco and Reading, 1975.

DAUBENMIRE, R.F., *Plants and Environment*, Wiley, Chichester and New York, 1974.

DETWYLER, T.R., *Man's Impact on Environment*, McGraw-Hill, New York and Maidenhead, 1971.

DOUGHTY, R.W., 'The human predator: a survey', in MANNERS, I.R., (Ed.), *Perspectives on Environment*, Association of American Geographers, 1974.

EHRLICH, P.R., *et al.*, *Ecoscience: Population, Resources, Environment*, W.H. Freeman, San Francisco and Reading, 1978.

GOLDSMITH, E., *Blueprint for Survival*, Penguin, London, 1972.

HARLAN, J., 'The plants and animals that nourish man', in *Food and Agriculture*, Scientific American, W.H. Freeman, San Francisco and Reading, 1976.

HYNES. H.B.N., *The Biology of Polluted Waters*, Liverpool University Press, 1974.

LENIHAN, J.M.A. and FLETCHER, W.W., *The Biological Environment*, Environment and Man 9, Blackie, Glasgow, 1979.

MANGLESDORF, P.C., 'Wheat', *Scientific American*, 189(1): 50—59, 1953.

MASON, C.F., *Decomposition*, Studies in Biology 74, Edward Arnold, London, 1976.

MATTHEWS, W.H. (Ed.), *Man's Impact on the Climate*, MIT Press, 1971.

MEADOWS, D.H., *et al.*, *The Limits to Growth*, A report for the Club of Rome's project on the predicament of mankind, Universe, New York, 1972.

MELLANBY, K., *The biology of pollution*, Studies in Biology 38, Edward Arnold, London, 1972.

Open University Press, *Implications: Limits to Growth*, S26 Block 6, OUP, Milton Keynes, 1974.

SAUER, C.O., *Agricultural Origins and Dispersals*, MIT Press, 1969.
SIMMONS, I.G., *op cit* (Chapter 1)
TREWARTHA, G.T., *A Geography of Populations. World Patterns*, Wiley, Chichester and New York, 1969.
WHITTAKER, R.H., *op.cit.* (Chapter 2)
ZUBAKOV, V.A.L., 'On the content and the tásks of historical geography', *Soviet Geography*, XIX(3): 170—180, 1978.

Chapter 4

BAKER, H.G., *op.cit.* (Chapter 3)
CABORN, J.M., *Shelter Belts and Microclimate*, HMSO, London (Forestry Commission Bulletin), 1957.
COOPER, C.F., 'The ecology of fire', *Scientific American*, 204(4): 150—160, 1961.
DELUCCHI, V.L. (Ed.), *Studies in Biological Control*, International Biological Programme 9, Cambridge University Press, 1976.
DUCHAUFOUR, P., *Précis de Pédologie,* Masson et Cie, Paris, 1965.
ELTON, C.S., *The Ecology of Invasions by Animals and Plants*, Chapman & Hall, London, 1972.
EISELEY, L.C., 'Man the Fire-maker', *Scientific American* 191(3): 52—57, 1954.
GEIGER, R., *Climate Near the Ground*, Harvard University Press, 1965.
GIMINGHAM, C.H., *Ecology of Heathlands*, Chapman & Hall, London, 1976.
GRIGG, D., *The Harsh Lands: a study in agricultural development*, Macmillan, London, 1970.
HARRIS, D., 'The ecology of agricultural systems', in COOKE, R.U., and JOHNSTONE, J.H., (Eds.), *Trends in Geography*, Pergamon, Oxford, 1969.
HILL, T.A., *The Biology of Weeds*, Studies in Biology 79, Edward Arnold, London, 1977.
KOZLOWSKI, T.T. and AHLGREN, R.C. (Eds.), *Fire and Ecosystems*, Academic Press, New York and London, 1975.
MITCHELL, J., 'The bracken problem', Chapter 8 in TIVY, J., (Ed.), *The Organic Resources of Scotland*, Oliver and Boyd, Edinburgh, 1973.
MUNN, R.F., *Descriptive Micrometeorology*, Academic Press, New York and London, 1966.
MURDOCH, W.W. (Ed.), *Environment: Resources Pollution and Society*, Sinauer Association, Stamford, Connecticut, 1975.
PEREIRA, H.C., *Land Use and Water Resources*, Cambridge University Press, 1973.
PERRING, F.H., and MELLANBY, K. (Eds.), *Ecological Effects of Pesticides*, Linnean Society Symposium 5, Academic Press, New York and London, 1977.
RIEHL, H., *Introduction to the Atmosphere*, McGraw-Hill, New York and Maidenhead, 1978.
SALISBURY, Sir E.J., *Weeds and Aliens*, Collins, London, 1961.
TIVY, J., 'Britain's one-third wasteland', *Geographical Magazine*, XLVII(5): 314—317, 1975.
VAN DEN BOSCH, R. and MESSENGER, P.S., *Biological Control*, International Textbook Company, London, 1973.
VAN EMDEN, H.F., *Pest Control and its Ecology*, Studies in Biology 50, Edward Arnold, London, 1974.
WHITTAKER, R.H., *et. al., op.cit.* (Chapter 2)

Chapter 5

ALLABY, M., *World Food Resources: actual and potential*, Applied Science Publishers, Barking, 1977.

AYRES, R.U., 'Food', *Science Journal* 10: 100—106, 1967.

BLACK, J.N., 'Energy relations in crop production — a preliminary survey', *Annals of Applied Biology* 67: 272—277, 1971.

BLAXTER, K.L., 'The energetics of British Agriculture,' *Biologist* 22,(1): 14—18, 1975.

BORGSTROM, G., *The Hungry Planet*, Collier Macmillan, West Drayton, 1972.

BORGSTROM, G., *The Food and People Dilemma*, Duxbury Press, Belmont, California, 1973.

COOPER, J.P., *op.cit.* (Chapter 2)

COUSENS, J., *An Introduction to Woodland Ecology*, Oliver & Boyd, Edinburgh, 1974.

DUCKHAM, A.N., and MASEFIELD, G.B., *Farming Systems of the World*, Chapman & Hall, London, 1970.

EYRE, S.R., *op.cit.* (Chapter 2)

HILL, T.A, *op.cit.* (Chapter 4)

HOPPER, D.W., 'The development of agriculture in developing countries', in *Food and Agriculture*, Scientific American, W.H. Freeman, San Francisco and Reading, 1976.

JANICK, J., *et al.*, 'The cycles of plant and animal nutrition', in *Food and Agriculture*, Scientific American, W.H. Freeman, San Francisco and Reading, 1976.

.LEACH, G., *Energy and Food Production*, IPC Science and Technology Press, Guildford, 1976.

LEITH, H., *op.cit.* (Chapter 2)

ODUM, E.P., *op.cit.* (Chapter 2)

Open University Press, *Energy Flow Through Ecosystems: Producers and Consumers*, Units 1 — 3, S323, *Decomposers: Whole Ecosystems*, Units 4 and 5, S323, 1974.

PHILLIPSON, J., *op.cit.,* (Chapter 2)

PIMENTAL, D. and PIMENTAL, M., *Food, Energy and Society*, Edward Arnold, London, 1979.

SLESSER, M., 'Energy requirements of agriculture' in LENIHAN, J. and FLETCHER, W.W., (Eds.), *Food, Agriculture and the Environment*, Environment and Man 2, Blackie, Glasgow, 1975.

STEELE, F. and BOURNE, A., *The Man/Food Equation*, Academic Press, New York and London, 1973.

STEINHART, S.S. and STEINHART, C.E., 'Energy use in the US food system', *Science* 184: 307—316, 1974.

Chapter 6

Agricultural Advisory Council, *Modern Farming and the Soil*, Ministry of Agriculture, Fisheries and Food, HMSO, London, 1970.

BORMANN, F.G. and LIKENS, G.E., 'The nutrient cycles of an ecosystem', *Scientific American*, 223(4): 92—101, 1970.

BOWEN, H.J.M., 'Natural cycles of the elements and their perturbation by man', in LENIHAN, J., and FLETCHER, W.W., (Eds.), *The Chemical Environment*, Environment and Man 6, Blackie, Glasgow, 1977.

CHADWICK, M.J. and GOODMAN, G.T. (Eds.), *Ecology of Resource Degradation and Renewal*, Blackwell Scientific Publications, Oxford, 1975.

COX, G.W., *Dynamic Ecology*, Prentice-Hall, New York and Hemel Hempstead, 1974.

COX, G.W. (Ed.), *Readings in Conservation Ecology*, Prentice-Hall, New York and Hemel Hempstead, 1974.

EHRLICH, P.R., *et.al., op.cit.* (Chapter 3)

GERSMEHL, P.J., 'An alternative biogeography', *Annals of the Association of American Geographers* 66(2): 223—241, 1976.

GIMINGHAM, C.H., *An Introduction to Heathland Ecology*, Oliver & Boyd, Edinburgh, 1975.

HASLER, A.D., 'Cultural eutrophication is reversible', in Cox, G.W. (Ed.), *Readings in Conservation Ecology*, Prentice-Hall, New York and Hemel Hempstead, 1974.

KOVDA, V.A., 'Soil preservation', in POLUNIN, N. (Ed.), *The Environmental Future*, Macmillan, London, 1972.

LIKENS, G.E., *et.al.*, 'Effects of forest cutting and herbicide treatment on nutrient budgets in the Hubbard Brook Watershed ecosystem', *Ecological Monographs* 40: 23—47, 1970.

MCNEIL, M., 'Lateritic soils', in *Man and the Ecosphere*, Readings from Scientific American, W.H. Freeman, San Francisco and Reading, 1971.

MELLANBY, K., *op.cit.* (Chapter 3)

MOSS, B., 'Conservation problems in the Norfolk Broads and rivers of East Anglia, England — phytoplankton, boats and the causes of turbidity', *Biological Conservation* 12(2): 95—114, 1977.

MOSS, B., 'Alarm call for the Broads: an ecosystem out of phase', *Geographical Magazine* L11(1): 47—50, 1979.

NYE, P.H. and GREENLAND, D.J., *The Soil under Shifting Agriculture*, Technical Communication No. 51, Commonwealth Agricultural Bureaux, Slough, 1960.

ODUM, E.P., *op.cit.* (Chapter 2)

O'RIORDAN, T., 'Alarm call for the Broads: signs of disaster and a policy for survival', *Geographical Magazine* L11(1): 50—56, 1979.

PATON, T.R. and WILLIAMS, M.A.J., 'The concept of laterite', *Annals of the Association of American Geographers* 62: 42—56, 1972.

PEREIRA, H.C., *op.cit.* (Chapter 4)

PRATT, C.J., 'Chemical fertilisers', *Scientific American* 212(6): 62—72, 1965.

RATCLIFFE, D.A., 'Changes attributable to pesticides in egg breakage frequency and eggshell thickness in some British birds', *Journal of Applied Ecology* 7: 67—115, 1970.

RENNIE, P.J., 'The uptake of nutrients by mature forest growth', *Plant and Soil* 7: 49—95, 1956.

RICKLEFS, R.E., *Ecology*, Nelson, Sunbury-on-Thames, 1973.

SMITH, F., *et. al.*, 'Cycles of elements' in Cox G.W. (Ed.), *Readings in Conservation Ecology*, Prentice-Hall, New York and Reading, 1974.

WHITTAKER, R.H., *op.cit.* (Chapter 2)

WOODWELL, G.M., *op.cit.* (Chapter 2).

YOUNG, A., 'Some aspects of tropical soils', *Geography* 59(3): 233–239, 1974.

Chapter 7

BABB, J.A. and BLISS, L.C., 'Effects of physical disturbance on arctic vegetation in the Queen Elizabeth Islands', *Journal of Applied Ecology* 11: 549–562, 1974.

BARNES, R.S.K., *Estuarine Biology*, Studies in Biology 49, Edward Arnold, London, 1972.

BEYNON, L.R., *The 'Torrey Canyon' Incident: a review of events*, The British Petroleum Company, London, 1967.

BLISS, L.C., 'Arctic tundra ecosystems', *Annual Review of Ecology and Systematics* 4: 359—399, 1973.

BRADE-BIRKS, S.G., *Good Soil*, Teach Yourself Books, The English Universities Press, 1962.

BRETSKY, P.W., *et al.*, 'Fragile ecosystems', *Science* 179 (4078): 1147, 1973.

CARLQUIST, S., *Island Biology*, Columbia University Press, 1974.

CLAPHAM, W.B., *op.cit.* (Chapter 3)

COWELL, E.B. (Ed.), *The Ecological Effects of Oil Pollution on Littoral Communities*, Institute of Petroleum, London, 1971.

DAUBENMIRE, R.F., *op.cit.* (Chapter 3)

DENEVAN, W.H., Development and the imminent demise of the Amazon River Rain Forest, *Professional Geography* 25: 130—135, 1973.

DETWYLER, T.R., *op.cit.* (Chapter 3)

DUNBAR, M.J., 'Stability and fragility in Arctic ecosystems', *Arctic* 26(3): 179–185, 1973.

Ecologist, 'A plan to save the tropical forests', *Ecologist* 1(2), 1980.

GERSMEHL, P.J., *op.cit.* (Chapter 6)

GOMEZ-POMPA, A., *et al.*, 'The tropical rain forest: a non-renewable resource', *Science* 177 (4051): 762–765, 1973.

GORMAN, M., *Island Ecology*, Outline Studies in Ecology, Chapman & Hall, London, 1979.

GOUROU, P., *The Tropical World*, Longman, London, 1966.

HARRIS, D.R., 'The invasion of oceanic islands by alien plants: an example of the Leeward Islands, West Indies', *Transactions and Papers of the Institute of British Geographers*: 67—82, 1962.

HARRIS, D.R., 'Tropical vegetation — an outline and some misconceptions', *Geography* 59(3): 240—250, 1974.

HILL, A.R., 'Ecosystem stability in relation to stresses caused by human activities', *Canadian Geographer* XIX (3): 206—219, 1975.

HOLDGATE, M.W. and MACE, N.W., 'The influence of man on the floras and faunas of southern islands', in DETWYLER, T.R. (Ed.), *Man's Impact on the Environment*, McGraw-Hill, New York and Maidenhead, 1971.

HOLLING, C.S., 'Resilience and stability of ecological systems', *Annual Review of Ecology and Systematics*, 4: 1–23, 1973.

NOY-MEIR, I., 'Desert ecosystems: environment and producers', *Annual Review Ecology and Systematics* 4: 25–51, 1973.

ODUM, E.P., *op.cit.* (Chapter 2)

PAINE, R.T., 'A note on trophic complexity and community stability', *American Naturalist* 103: 91—93, 1969.

RICHARDS, P.W., 'Tropical rain forest', *Scientific American* 229(6): 58–67, 1973.

RICKLEFS, R.E., *op. cit.* (Chapter 6)

SCHULTZ, A.M., 'A study of an ecosystem: the Arctic tundra', in VAN DYNE, G. (Ed.), *The Ecosystem Concept in Natural Resource Management*, Academic Press, London and New York, 1969.

SMITH, J.E. (Ed.), *'Torrey Canyon' Pollution and Marine Life*, Cambridge University Press, 1968.

STOTT, P.A., 'Tropical rain forest in recent ecological thought: the reassessment of a non-renewable resource', *Progress in Physical Geography* 2(1): 90–98, 1978.

TRIBE, M. and PEACOCK, D., *The Ecology game: A simulated research exercise in ecology involving oil pollution damage on the littoral zone*, Cambridge University Press, 1975.

WHITTAKER, R.H. *op. cit.* (Chapter 2)

WOODWELL, G.M. and PECAN, F.V., *Carbon and the Biosphere*, Technical Information Centre, US Atomic Energy Commission, Springfield, Virginia, 1973.

YOUNG, A., *op. cit.* (Chapter 6)

Chapter 8

Agricultural Advisory Council, *op. cit.* (Chapter 6)

BAYFIELD, N.G., 'Some effects of walking and skiing on vegetation at Cairngorm', in DUFFY, E. and WATT, A.S. (Eds.), *The Scientific Management of Animal and Plant Communities for Conservation*, Blackwell Scientific Publications, Oxford, 1971.

BAYFIELD, N.G., 'Recovery of four montane heath communities on Cairngorm, Scotland from disturbance by trampling', *Biological Conservation* 15(3): 165—179, 1979.

BOORMAN, L.A. and FULLER, R.M., 'Studies on the impact of paths on the dune vegetation at Winterton, Norfolk, England', *Biological Conservation* 12: 203—216, 1977.

BURDEN, R.F. and RANDERSON, P.F., 'Quantitative studies of the effects of human trampling on vegetation as an aid to the management of semi-natural areas', *Journal of Applied Ecology* 9: 439—458, 1972.

Countryside Commission for Scotland, *Shore Erosion around Loch Lomond*, CCS, Perth, 1979.

CRAWFORD, A.K. and LIDDLE, M.D., 'The effect of trampling on neutral grassland', *Biological Conservation* 12: 135–142, 1977.

CRUICKSHANK, J.G., *Soil Geography*, David & Charles, Newton Abbot, 1972.

GIMINGHAM, C.H., *op. cit.* (Chapter 6)

GOLDSMITH, F.B., *et al.*, 'The impact of recreation on the ecology and amenity of semi-natural areas. Methods and investigation in the Isle of Scilly', *Biological Journal of the Linnean Society* 2: 287—306, 1970.

HAGGETT, P., *Geography — a Modern Synthesis*, Harper & Row, London and New York, 1979.

HARDIN, G., 'The tragedy of the commons', *Science* 162: 1243—1248, 1968.

LIDDLE, M.J., 'A selective review of the ecological effects of human trampling on natural ecosystems', *Biological Conservation* 7: 17—35, 1975.

O'HARE, G.P., *Recreation and Conservation in the Peak District National Park: A review of some recent literature*, Internal report for the Peak District National Park Authority, Bakewell, Derbyshire, 1977.

O'HARE, G.P., 'A review of studies of recreational impact in the Peak District National Park', *North Staffordshire Journal of Field Studies* 18: 21–30, 1978.

O'RIORDAN, T., *Perspectives on Resource Management*, Pion Press, London, 1971.

Open University Press, *Resources and Systems*, S26 Block I, OUP, Milton Keynes, 1973.

TIVY, J., *The Concept and Determination of Carrying Capacity of Recreational Land in the USA*, Occasional Paper 3, Countryside Commission for Scotland, Perth, 1973.

TIVY, J., *The Organic Resources of Scotland: their nature and evaluation*, Oliver & Boyd, Edinburgh, 1973.

TIVY, J., 'Changing resource values', *Journal of the Scottish Association of Geography Teachers*, 1975.

TIVY, J. and REES, J., 'Recreational impact on lochshore vegetation', *Journal of the Scottish Association of Geography Teachers*, 1977.

TIVY, J. and REES, J., 'Recreational impact on Scottish lochshore wetlands', *Journal of Biogeography* 5: 93–108, 1978.

SLATTER, R.J., 'Ecological effects of trampling on sand-dune vegetation', *Journal of Biological Education* 12(2): 89—96, 1978.

ZIMMERMANN, E.W., *World Resources and Industries*, Harper & Row, London and New York, 1951.

Chapter 9

ARVILL, R., *Man and Environment*, Penguin, London, 1969.

BOHM, P. and KNEESE, A.V., *Economics of Environment*, Macmillan, London, 1971.

CHISHOLM, M., *Resources for Britain's Future*, Penguin, London, 1972.

CODDINGTON, A., 'The economics of conservation', in WARREN, A. and GOLDSMITH, F.B. (Eds.), *Conservation in Practice*, Wiley, Chichester and New York, 1974.

Countryside Commission for Scotland, *Scotland's Scenic Heritage*, CCS, Perth, 1978.

DUFFEY, E. and WATT, A.S. (Eds.), *The Scientific Management of Animal and Plant Communities for Conservation*, Blackwell Scientific Publications, Oxford, 1971.

DUFFEY, E., *Nature Reserves and Wildlife*, Heinemann, London, 1974.

FISHER, J., *et al.*, *The Red Book: Wildlife in Danger*, Collins, London, 1969.

Geographical Magazine, *Map of Cherished Land*, 1973.

Geographical Magazine, 'Parks under Pressure', a series of monthly articles on each of the National Parks, *Geographical Magazine* XLV(9)—XLVI(7), June 1973—April 1974.

GOLDSMITH, E., 'Can we control pollution?' Part I, the *Ecologist* 9(8/9): 273—290. 'Can we control Pollution?' Part II, the *Ecologist*, 9(10): 316—328, 1979.

HARDY, Sir A., *The Open Sea II: Fish and Fisheries*, The New Naturalist, Collins, London, 1970.

HARRISON, C.M. and WARREN, A., 'Conservation, stability and management', *Area* 2: 26—32, 1970.

HAWKES, J.G., *Conservation and Agriculture*, Duckworth, London, 1978.

HILDYARD N., 'Down in the dumps: the problem of toxic waste disposal in Britain and the US', the *Ecologist* 9(10): 329–332, 1979.

HODGES, R.D., 'A case for biological agriculture', *Ecologist Quarterly* 2: 123—142, 1978.

JAMES, D.B., 'Some aspects of water quality control', in LENIHAN, J. and FLETCHER, W.W. (Eds.), *Measuring and Monitoring the Environment*, Environment and Man 7, Blackie, Glasgow, 1978.

LUMLEY-SMITH, R., 'In double harness', *New Ecologist* 2: 54—58, 1979.

MURDOCH, W.W. (Eds.), *op. cit.* (Chapter 4)

Nature Conservancy Council, *Nature Conservancy Council 4th Report*, HMSO, London, 1978.

ODUM, E.P. *op. cit.* (Chapter 2)

Open University Press, *Changing Environment and Conservation*, S23 Block 4/5, OUP, Milton Keynes, 1972.

PATMORE, J.A., *Land and Leisure*, Penguin, London, 1972.

REES, J.A., 'The economics of environmental management', *Geography* 62(4): 311—324, 1977.

RILEY, P.J. and WARREN, D.S., 'Farming, fuel and horses', *New Ecologist* 2: 46—50, 1979.

SHEAIL, J., *Nature in Trust: The History of Nature Conservation in Britain*, Blackie, Glasgow, 1976.

TIVY, J., *op. cit.* (Chapter 3)

WARREN, A. and GOLDSMITH, F.B., *Conservation in Practice,* Wiley, Chichester and New York, 1974.

Chapter 10

ALLAN, J.A., 'Remote sensing in physical geography', *Progress in Physical Geography* 2(1): 36—54, 1978.

ALLAN, J.A., 'Remote sensing in land and land use studies', *Geography* 65(1): 35–43, 1980.

BECKETT, P.H.T. and WEBSTER, R., 'Soil variability: a review', *Soils and Fertilisers* 34: 1—15, 1971.

BIBBY, J.S., 'Land Capability', in TIVY, J. (Ed.), *The Organic Resources of Scotland*, Oliver & Boyd, Edinburgh, 1973.

BIBBY, J.S. and MACKNEY, D., *Land Use Capability Classification*, Rothamsted Experimental Station, Harpenden, Herts, 1969.

BURNHAM, C.P., 'A new inventory of the land resources of England and Wales', *Area* 11(4): 349—352, 1979.

COOKE, R.U. and HARRIS, D.R., 'Remote sensing of the terrestrial environment — principles and progress', *Transactions of the Institute of British Geographers* 50: 1—25, 1970.

COPPOCK, J.T. and THOMAS, M. (Eds.), *Land Evaluation in Scotland*, Aberdeen University Press, 1980.

CROFTS, R.S., 'The landscape component approach to landscape evaluation', *Transactions of the Institute of British Geographers* 66: 124—129, 1975.

CURTIS, L.F., 'Remote sensing systems for monitoring crops and vegetation', *Progress in Physical Geography* 2(1): 55—79, 1978.

GARDINER, V. and GREGORY, K.J., 'Progress in portraying the physical landscape', *Progress in Physical Geography* 1(3): 1–22, 1977.

HAGGETT, P., *op. cit.* (Chapter 8).

KLINGEBIEL, A.A. and MONTGOMERY, P.H., *Land Capability Classification*, US Department of Agriculture and Soil Conservation Service, Washington DC, 1961.

LINTON, D.L., 'The assessment of scenery as a natural resource', *Scottish Geographical Magazine* 94(3): 219—238, 1968.

MITCHELL, C.W., *Terrain Evaluation*, Longman, London, 1973.

O'HARE, G.P., 'Lichen techniques of pollution assessment', *Area* 5(3): 223—229, 1973.

O'HARE, G.P., 'Lichens and bark acidification as indicators of air pollution in West Central Scotland', *Journal of Biogeography* 1(2): 135—146, 1975.

SMITH, R.M., 'Landsat photography as a resource in secondary school geography', *Geography* 65(1): 44–48, 1980.

STEWART, G.A. (Ed.), *Land Evaluation*, Macmillan, London, 1968.

UNWIN, K.I., 'The relationship of observer and landscape in landscape evaluation', *Transactions of the Institute of British Geographers* 66: 130—134, 1975.

WEDDLE, A.E., 'Techniques in landscape planning: landscape evaluation', *Journal of the Town Planning Institute*, 55: 387–389, 1969.

YOUNG, A., 'Soil survey procedures in land development planning', *Geographical Journal* 139: 53—64, 1973.

YOUNG, A., 'Recent advances in the survey and evaluation of land resources', *Progress in Physical Geography* 2(3): 426–479, 1978.

Glossary

Adsorption   A process whereby a substance is attached by physical or chemical forces to the surface of a solid or liquid.

Adventitious roots   Numerous small fibrous roots emerging from stems and/or leaves.

Anaerobic   In the absence of oxygen.

Anion   Negatively charged ion.

Auricles   Pair of ear-like outgrowths on the side of the grass blade where it joins the sheath.

Bacteria   Unicellular microscopic organisms with a relatively simple cellular organisation fundamentally different from plants and animals.

Benthic   Bottom dwelling.

Cambium   A meristem which, by rapid cell division, increases the girth of a tree. Bark cells are produced on the outside, wood cells on the inside of the meristem.

Cation   A positively charged ion.

Cellulose   Insoluble large molecule of carbohydrate composed of repeating units of glucose. It is the main structural component of plant cell walls.

Diatom   Type of planktonic algae with siliceous skeleton.

Endemism   Quality of being restricted in distribution to one particular area.

Fungi   Simple, largely microscopic, plant-like filamentous or unicellular organisms lacking chlorophyll, which obtain their nutrient supply either by parasitism or saprophytism.

Ion   An atom or molecule which has lost or gained one or more electrons.

Lichen   Dual organism formed from the symbiotic/parasitic association of two plants — a fungus and an alga.

Lignin   Large complex molecule produced by plants as a support and strengthening material which is resistant to biological degradation. Forms between 25–30 per cent of the wood of trees.

Ligule   Membranous outgrowth on the upper surface of grass leaf where the blade joins the sheath.

Lodging   Falling over of grass (cereal) stems.

Meristem   Zone of active cell division in plants.

Parasitic   Metabolically dependent on another organism.

Phytoplankton   Largely microscopic, unicellular algae, found floating in the light zone at or below the surface of lakes, estuaries and seas.

Relict   An ancient species (in evolutionary terms) which normally has a restricted distribution and genetic pool (make-up).

Rhizome   Horizontal stem extending under the ground which gives rise to new shoots.

Saprophytic   Obtaining nutrients and energy from the decomposition of dead organic material.

Soil association   A group of soils, usually soil series, related to one another on the basis of variations in soil drainage.

Soil colloid   Very small electrically charged particles usually less than .001mm diameter which remain in suspension due to electrical repulsion.

Soil series   Basic classification unit defined as a group of soils with similar vertical sections (profiles) developed in lithologically similar parent materials.

Species   A group of organisms able to breed among themselves (if one disregards geographical separation) but not with members of other groups. Also characterised by *generally* similar physical appearance and physiology.

Stolon   Horizontal stem extending along the surface of the ground which gives rise to new shoots.

Stomata   The pores in the leaf and some green stem surfaces through which water is lost to, and gases (CO_2, O_2) are exchanged with, the external environment.

Substrate (substratum)   Ground or other solid medium on which an organism lives and from which it may derive support, attachment or nutrient supply.

Tannin   Organic molecule manufactured by plants to protect against disease.

Tiller   Individual grass shoot.

Transpiration   Physical evaporation of water from stomata when these pores are open to allow gas exchange.

Zooplankton   Small aquatic animals that are nutritionally dependent on and found in close association with phytoplankton in the upper layers of seas, estuaries and lakes; floating, with no or limited means of propulsion.

Table of standard units and conversions

Some useful prefixes and abbreviations

ppm	parts per million			
10^{-2}	centi	c	10^3	kilo k
10^{-3}	milli	m	10^6	mega M
10^{-6}	micro	μ	10^9	giga G
10^{-9}	nano	n	10^{15}	mega $\times$ giga MG

Units of energy and power

Joule (J)   work energy needed to raise 1 kilogram to height of 10 centimetres.

Calorie (cal)   heat energy required to raise 1 cubic centimetre of water 1 degree centigrade (at 15°C).

Watt (unit of power)   1 joule per second.

kW h   kilowatt hour (1000 watts per hour).

Conversions

1 calorie	=	4.18 joules	1 tonne (t)	= 1000 kg
1 Kcal	=	1000 cals = 4184 joules	1 ton	= 1016 kg = 2240 lbs
1 joule	=	0.239 cals	1 metre (m)	= 3.28 feet
1 kJ	=	1000 joules = 239 cals	1 Ångström (Å)	= 10^{-10} = 10^{-1} nm
1 kW h	=	3.6 MJ	1 litre (1)	= 1000 cc = 1.76 pints
1 GW h	=	3.6×10^6 MJ = 3600 GJ	1 hectare (ha)	= 2.5 acres (a)
1 kg	=	1000 grams = 2.2 lbs		

Index